Hitler's
Armed SS

Hitler's Armed SS

The Waffen-SS at War, 1939–45

Anthony Tucker-Jones

Pen & Sword
MILITARY

AN IMPRINT OF PEN & SWORD BOOKS LTD
YORKSHIRE – PHILADELPHIA

First published in Great Britain in 2022 by
PEN & SWORD MILITARY
an imprint of Pen & Sword Books Ltd
Yorkshire – Philadelphia

ISBN 978-1-39900-691-0

Typeset by Concept, Huddersfield, West Yorkshire, HD4 5JL.
Printed and bound in England by CPI Group (UK) Ltd, Croydon CR0 4YY.

MIX
Paper from
responsible sources
FSC® C013604

Pen & Sword Books Ltd incorporates the imprints of Aviation, Atlas, Family
History, Fiction, Maritime, Military, Discovery, Politics, History, Archaeology,
Select, Wharncliffe Local History, Wharncliffe True Crime, Military Classics,
Wharncliffe Transport, Leo Cooper, The Praetorian Press, Remember When,
White Owl, Seaforth Publishing and Frontline Books.

For a complete list of Pen & Sword titles please contact
PEN & SWORD BOOKS LTD
47 Church Street, Barnsley, South Yorkshire, S70 2AS, England
E-mail: enquiries@pen-and-sword.co.uk
Website: www.pen-and-sword.co.uk
or
PEN & SWORD BOOKS
1950 Lawrence Rd, Havertown, PA 19083, USA
E-mail: uspen-and-sword@casematepublishers.com
Website: www.penandswordbooks.com

Contents

List of Plates

(Between pp. 118 and 119)

Léon Degrelle awarding medals to members of his Freiwilligen SS-Sturmbrigade Wallonien in Charleroi, Belgium, who escaped Cherkassy.

Allied bombers targeting the train yards and main roads to impede movement.

Teenage Nazis, such as these, were recruited into the Frundsberg, Hitlerjugend and Hohenstaufen Divisions.

A Hitlerjugend panzergrenadier armed with an MG42.

Young Waffen-SS machine-gunner killed in action.

A Das Reich Sd.Kfz.251 half-track caught on the road in Normandy.

Two Panzer Mk IVs belonging to Das Reich.

A Panther tank belonging to Hitlerjugend knocked out by the Canadian Army.

Wiking Panther in Poland.

Wiking Panzergrenadiers outside Warsaw.

Officers and men of Wiking about to go into action.

Polish fighters in Warsaw with a German Sd.Kfz.251 half-track captured on 14 August 1944.

Assault gun from Sturmgeschütz Brigade 280 supporting troops from Hohenstaufen in Arnhem on 19 September 1944.

Hohenstaufen panzergrenadiers mopping up the streets of Arnhem.

Sepp Dietrich.

A Leibstandarte Hummel self-propelled gun.

A Waffen-SS half-track rolls past a captured American vehicle as Kampfgruppe Peiper advances during the Battle of the Bulge.

Panzergrenadiers belonging to Kampfgruppe Hansen.

Kampfgruppe Hansen panzergrenadiers running past burning American vehicles caught on the open road in the Ardennes.

German propaganda newsreel shot taken on 17 December 1944 showing a Leibstandarte Panzer IV passing American prisoners.

Tiger II of the 501st Heavy SS-Panzer Battalion which supported Kampfgruppe Peiper.

(Between pp. 182 and 183)

Leibstandarte panzergrenadiers in Honsfeld examining equipment abandoned by the US 30th Infantry Division.

A Panther and a PaK 40 anti-tank gun lost in Stavelot on the Amblève river.

Leibstandarte murdered 362 American prisoners and 111 Belgian civilians in the Malmedy area.

The location of a massacre.

Belgian civilians killed in cold blood by the SS.

Exhausted-looking youngsters from Hitlerjugend captured by the Americans.

German assault gun with American insignia from the 150th Panzer Brigade in the Ardennes.

German panzer lost during the Battle of the Bulge crudely disguised to look like an American tank destroyer.

Frundsberg Panthers in Alsace.

Sturmgeschütz III assault guns belonging to the Wiking Division on their way from Warsaw to Budapest.

Leibstandarte half-tracks in Hungary during Hitler's ill-fated Operation Spring Awakening conducted in March 1945.

SS-Obersturmbannführer Otto Skorzeny commanded Himmler's SS commandos.

Members of the tiny ill-fated Britische Freikorps.

A number of Waffen-SS units defending the central government district during the Battle for Berlin.

The final battles for the Waffen-SS were on the streets of Berlin and Prague.

Himmler with Reinhard Heydrich, who was a protégé of his and a key architect of the Holocaust.

Armour belonging to Das Reich lost in Normandy.

Senior members of the Nazi Party and SS on trial for war crimes.

Introduction

Himmler's Private Army

The German Führer Adolf Hitler, after his experiences with the Nazi Party's very powerful pre-war Sturmabteilung (SA – Storm Detachment), was initially not in favour of large private militias run by his supporters. However, once in power he used the rival Schutzstaffel (Protection Squads) to decapitate and take control of the SA, ensuring it could never pose a threat to his political domination of Germany. The very distinct Waffen-SS (Armed SS) grew from the SS-Verfügungstruppen (SS-VT – SS Dispositional Troops), the military wing of the SS and the Leib-standarte SS Adolf Hitler, the Führer's personal guard.

'The SS started with formations of seven or eight men,' recalled Hitler. 'In these we gathered the tough 'uns.' To many people they were just street thugs whose job was to intimidate or beat up political rivals. 'Being convinced that there are always circumstances in which elite troops are called for,' added Hitler, 'in 1922–23 I created the "Adolf Hitler Shock Troops". They were made up of men who were ready for revolution and knew that one day or another things would come to hard knocks.' To differentiate the SS from the brown-shirted SA, they wore black uniforms. Hitler observed in 1926 that 'a small band of the best and most deter-mined is far more valuable than a large mass of camp-followers'. To start with, the SS were led by an old friend, Josef Berchtold, followed by Erhard Heiden, neither of whom proved up to the task.

Former poultry farmer Heinrich Himmler assumed control of the SS in 1929 as Reichsführer and immediately set about building himself an empire. Anti-Nazi Konrad Heiden wrote, 'He looks like the caricature of a sadistic school-teacher, and this caricature conceals the man like a mask.' British intelligence officer and historian Hugh Trevor-Roper called Himmler the 'terrible high-priest of Hitler'. The Führer noted with pride that 'It was with Himmler that the SS became that extraordinary body of men, devoted to an idea, loyal unto death.' Himmler, with Hitler's

1

backing, intended that the SS would become the guardians of German racial purity. 'His racial doctrine was fallacious,' said General Heinz Guderian, 'and led him to commit terrible crimes.'

It is important to highlight that Reichsführer Himmler, despite wearing a uniform, was not a military man but a civilian. Unlike many of his Nazi contemporaries he was not a veteran of the First World War. He had spent the last year of the war as an ensign in a Bavarian regiment but never got to the front. His main ability was choosing skilled subordinates who made the SS look good. In addition, he was a highly efficient organizer, which, tragically for Europe's Jews, included the Final Solution.

Amongst Hitler's other SS acolytes was Josef 'Sepp' Dietrich. 'He's a man who's simultaneously cunning, energetic and brutal ... he is one of my oldest companions in the struggle,' said Hitler. Following the Second World War Dietrich disingenuously moved to try to distance himself from Hitler by blaming military failures on the Führer's constant interference. SA member Gottlob Berger, who was later to head Waffen-SS recruitment, reassured the SA leadership, 'I shall always regard the SA as Number One and shall never be on the side of those who wish to destroy the SA.' Gottlob, though, was a turncoat. SS-Officers were to contemptuously dub him 'The Duke of Swabia' (he was the son of a saw-mill owner) and in a play on his name 'Praise God'. Similarly, Friedrich-Wilhelm Krüger, who became an SS general in Poland, started with the SS, transferred to the SA and then back to the SS.

By the end of 1930 the SA and SS numbered over 100,000 men, almost a greater force than the German army limited by the Treaty of Versailles. Himmler and his SS were supposed to be subordinate to Ernst Röhm, head of the SA, but in reality answered directly to Hitler. The latter largely saw Röhm's organization as a useful manpower reservoir that could provide a new German army with trainable recruits. He had, however, other plans for the SS.

Himmler understood that he needed to instil a distinct fighting spirit in the SS. In 1931 he told his recruits:

The military history of antiquity, the history of the Prussian Army 200 or 300 years ago – again and again we see that wars are waged with men, but that every leader surrounds himself with an organization of men of special quality when things are at their worst and hardest; that is the guard. There has always been a guard; the Persians, the Greeks, Caesar, Old Fritz [Frederick II], Napoleon, all had a guard, and so on up to the World War; and the guard of the new Germany will be the SS.

By the following year, and in time for the German elections, the SA had mobilized 400,000 men. In contrast the SS numbered only 52,000. Both organizations were not armed, at least not officially, and when they were it tended to be with blunt instruments intended for busting heads. Some, though, did carry hand-guns, which were used to assassinate political opponents. An SA unit was openly photographed having their Luger pistols inspected. Hitler, after winning the election, agreed with the army that the SA now posed a threat and agreed to ban it. Fear of a coup was accentuated by the mass columns of SA marching to celebrate the Nazi 'Seizure of Power' on 30 January 1933. This sparked bloody and often fatal street battles with Germany's Communists. Hitler had no further need of the SA and was happy to sacrifice Ernst Röhm's ill-disciplined brownshirts.

In the 'Night of the Long Knives' Röhm was arrested and murdered by members of the SS on 1 July 1934. His killers were SS-Brigadeführer Theodor Eicke, then commandant of Dachau, and his adjutant SS-Sturmbannführer Michael Lippert. Himmler, assisted by Sepp Dietrich, rounded up 150 other SA leaders in Berlin and put them before firing squads. Hitler told the Reichstag on 13 July 1934 that sixty-one people had been shot, including nineteen 'higher SA leaders', and that thirteen more died 'resisting arrest', while three had 'committed suicide' – giving a total of seventy-seven deaths. Later estimates put the number at over a thousand. Although the SA was not completely disbanded, its numbers were drastically reduced. The SS became the instrument with which Hitler liquidated all his political rivals.

To appease the German army, Hitler permitted it to oversee recruitment for the SS-VT, with the result that two-thirds of the volunteers had to join the Wehrmacht, the regular armed forces. Furthermore, in 1935 Hitler secretly agreed that in the event of war, 'The SS-VT will be incorporated into the Army.' Once firmly in power, Hitler saw the SS under Reichsführer Himmler as an elite that should be kept apart from the army. As far as he was concerned it was a police force 'capable of crushing any adversary'. Hitler instructed in August 1938 that the SS-VT was to be treated as 'a standing armed force'. It would be separate from the army and the police, but would serve as part of the Wehrmacht in times of war. Then in April 1940 various SS military units were officially designated the

3

Waffen-SS. Hitler hoped that by creating a separate army, indoctrinated in the Nazi creed, he would be assured of a counterweight to the regular army, which he distrusted to his dying day.

Paul Hausser, a retired army general, took over organizing and training the SS-VT. Two SS officer training schools were established at Bad Tölz and Braunschweig, and Hausser became the head of the SS-VT Inspectorate. 'General Hausser was a first-class officer,' recalled General Guderian, 'a brave and clever soldier and a man of outstandingly upright and honourable character.' He would later prove to be a highly adept SS Corps commander. The training programme came under Felix Steiner, who had served as a junior infantry officer during the First World War. He had more recently commanded SS Standarte Deutschland. Steiner was an advocate of the stormtrooper concept, which had been developed at the end of the conflict. The premier formation Leibstandarte-SS Adolf Hitler evolved from Hitler's bodyguard commanded by Sepp Dietrich. Likewise, Das Reich (formerly the SS-VT Division) evolved from the remainder of the pre-war armed SS. From these units grew Himmler's autonomous army of almost a million men, fully equipped with tanks, assault guns and artillery.

The Hitlerjugend (Hitler Youth) and its junior section, the Jungvolk (Young People), indoctrinated thousands of boys and teenagers who became willing recruits for the ranks of the Waffen-SS. Baldur von Schirach, who headed the Hitler Youth, had an American mother and a great-grandfather who had served as a Union officer at the Battle of Bull Run. Answering directly to Hitler, he took over all of Germany's other youth organizations and made membership obligatory, including for girls. American reporter William Shirer wrote that von Schirach became 'the dictator of youth in the Third Reich'. During the 1930s Nazi propaganda declared, 'Youth serves the Führer. Every ten-year-old into the Hitler Youth.' Youngsters thought they were joining a version of the boy scouts, but instead found themselves being militarized ready for war. Weekend camps involved manoeuvres with rifles and army backpacks. Once the boys reached the age of 18 they were conscripted into the Reichsarbeitsdienst (RAD – Reich Labour Service) or the Army. However, Waffen-SS recruiting posters were soon urging youths to join after they turned 17. By 1939 the Hitler Youth had over 7.7 million members, two-thirds of those available, but that year a law was passed enforcing conscription for everyone on the same basis as adult military service.

Himmler, already in charge of the Nazis' 'political police' in all the German states, now merged his forces, with the help of Reinhard Heydrich, with the regular German police. Previously the police had been run and organized separately by the provincial authorities. Himmler created a unified national German police force firmly controlled by the SS. This single act ensured that Nazi Germany became a police state. Konrad Heiden wrote of this development, 'Staffed by selected SS men, permeated with their silent arrogance and cold indifference towards humanity, this police body gradually became the most frightful organization of its kind in modern history.' This enabled Hitler to imprison trade union leaders, seize their funds and ban strikes. He muzzled the press and took over churches and schools. All opposition parties were banned.

It is very important to clarify that Himmler's SS included a huge variety of organizations with differing functions. The front-line combat troops of the Waffen-SS, with their grey uniforms, should not be confused with the Allgemeine-SS (General SS) in their distinctive ceremonial black uniforms, who were the 'general service' militia of the Nazi Party. The latter over the years have come to epitomize the SS, but in fact were an entirely separate entity from the Waffen-SS. Similarly, the Sicherheitsdienst (SD – Security Service) security police wore grey uniforms, while the Gestapo secret police worked in plain clothes.

In addition, the SS-Totenkopfverbände (Death's Head Units) were responsible for running the concentration camps in Poland and Russia; they also dressed in field-grey uniforms. It was they who oversaw Hitler's Final Solution and the wholesale murder of Europe's Jewish population. The 'Jewish question' had come firmly into focus during the evolution of Germany as a unified state during the mid-nineteenth century. Hitler ordered on 18 September 1939 that the Death's Head units give up their younger recruits for service in SS regiments, which were to be formed into divisions. This meant that there was a direct link between the Waffen-SS and the Holocaust. Then there was a vast range of other brutal auxiliary police and security units raised within occupied Europe and controlled by the SS.

Callously, Himmler felt it was simpler to go to war than to deport helpless Jewish and Polish civilians from the provinces annexed by Germany. In mid-1940 he told members of the Leibstandarte-SS, 'Gentlemen, it is much easier in many cases to go into combat with a company than to suppress an obstructive population of low cultural level, or to carry out executions or to haul away people or to evict crying hysterical women.'

The deployment of armed SS units during the invasions of Poland and the West was designed to allow Himmler's power base to share in Germany's military triumphs. 'It was necessary that the SS should make war,' said Hitler, 'otherwise its prestige would have been lowered.'

Keen to expand the Waffen-SS but blocked by the Wehrmacht, Gottlob Berger decided that his only alternative would be to recruit from outside Germany. On 7 August 1940 he wrote to Himmler stating, 'No objections against a further expansion of the Waffen-SS can be raised by the other armed services if we succeed in recruiting part of the German population not at the disposal of the Wehrmacht. In this I see a task yet to be accomplished by the Reichsführer-SS.' However, Theodor Eicke, commanding the SS-Totenkopf Division, was aghast and refused to accept many of the recruits sent to him: 'Most of the young men you are sending me are criminals and obvious racial inferiors incapable of discipline and unworthy of the SS uniform.' Eventually tiring of Eicke's objections, in April 1941 Himmler instructed that the Totenkopf units be considered an integral part of the Waffen-SS.

Hitler was convinced that he had the absolute devotion of the SS. It was he who gave the SS their notorious motto: 'My Honour is Loyalty.' In mid-December 1941 Hitler told a gathering of Nazi officials, 'I have six divisions of SS composed of men absolutely indifferent in matters of religion. It doesn't prevent them from going to their deaths with serenity in their souls.' Furthermore, he was determined to keep the Waffen-SS an elite. In January 1942 he warned, 'The SS shouldn't extend its recruiting too much ... People must know that troops like the SS have to pay the butcher's bill more heavily than anyone else – so as to keep away the young fellows who only want to show off.' Furthermore, Hitler wanted the SS to be racially pure. 'Thanks to its method of recruiting,' he said, 'the SS will be a nursery of rulers.' This was why he welcomed recruits from the Scandinavian countries, whom he considered suitably Germanic and Aryan.

Bizarrely, Hitler, who had been a fan of wearing shorts when he was younger, said in February 1942, 'I suggested to Himmler that he might dress two or three guard units in leather shorts. Obviously they would have to be handsome chaps, and not necessarily all from the south. I can quite well imagine a soldier with a Hamburg accent displaying his sunburnt knees.' Six months later he returned to this idea, adding, 'In future I shall have an SS Highland Brigade in leather shorts!' Nothing seems to have come of this ridiculous suggestion.

The Waffen-SS raised on paper at least a total of thirty-eight divisions during the Second World War, totalling about 910,000 men. Understandably the German army eyed these forces jealously, although it is important to note that the Waffen-SS never grew to exceed 10 per cent of the army's strength. Field Marshal Erich von Manstein wrote, 'The blame for such unnecessary consumption of manpower must lie with the men who set up these special units for purely political motives, in the face of opposition from all the competent army authorities.' He was not alone in such views. 'The old motto "divide and rule" was carried to its logical absurdity,' grumbled Major General Friedrich von Mellenthin. 'To keep the army in its place the Waffen-SS was created.'

Of these Waffen-SS units seven were panzer divisions and another eight panzergrenadier divisions. The most famous – or perhaps infamous would be a better term – armoured formations are the 1st SS Leibstandarte-SS Adolf Hitler, the 2nd SS Das Reich and the 12th SS Hitlerjugend. The 5th SS Wiking, the 9th SS Hohenstaufen and the 10th SS Frundsberg also gained reputations as fierce and brutal fighters. The least well known is the 3rd SS Totenkopf, initially raised using concentration camp guards.

The panzergrenadier divisions comprised the 4th SS Polizei, the 16th SS Reichsführer-SS, which gained an unsavoury reputation in Italy, the 11th SS Nordland, the 17th SS Götz von Berlichingen, which fought in Normandy, the 18th SS Horst Wessel, the 23rd SS Nederland and the 28th SS Wallonien. The latter only ever reached regimental size. Most of these units included single panzer and assault gun battalions.

The Waffen-SS, though, did not have the monopoly on ardent Nazis. In early 1933 Hermann Göring, then serving as the Nazi Minister of the Interior of Prussia, also formed his own private army. This was an auxiliary police force numbering some 50,000 men, most of whom were drawn from the SA and SS. In his role as Reichsmarschall, Commander-in-Chief of the Luftwaffe, Göring continued a similar policy with the German air force. The Luftwaffe, like the SS, appealed to the more motivated and educated Hitler Youth. As a result, it never experienced problems attracting recruits to its ranks. Once the Battle of Britain was over in 1940, Göring found himself with more ground-crew than he really needed, amounting to some 170,000 surplus personnel. In the summer of 1942 the German army tried unsuccessfully to secure them for retraining as vital infantry replacements.

On the Eastern Front by the close of the winter fighting of 1941–42 German casualties had reached over 1.6 million, not including sick, and

Hitler simply did not have enough replacements. To make matters worse, the numerous components of the Wehrmacht – Heeres (Army), Kriegsmarine (Navy) and Luftwaffe – plus the Waffen-SS and the Labour Service were all competing for increasingly scarce recruits. Göring would not part with any of his personnel, arguing with Hitler that transferring these 'genuinely Nationalist Socialist' young men would expose them 'to an army which still has chaplains and was led by officers steeped in the traditions of the Kaiser'. Göring got his own way and created twenty-two weak Luftwaffe field divisions that were to fight as infantry. These men could have been used as much-needed infantry replacements to replenish Army Groups Centre and North on the Eastern Front; instead, under Luftwaffe control, they added very little to the combat capabilities of the German army, dissipated its already exhausted manpower and further muddled the chain of the command. The Luftwaffe also formed nearly a dozen parachute divisions, which as the war progressed fought as infantry. Half of these appeared late in the war and were woefully understrength.

Over the years the Waffen-SS has been elevated to a largely undeserved elite status. Himmler ensured that its exploits were glorified in the pages of *Das Schwarze Korps* ('The Black Corps'), the official newspaper of the SS. Likewise, the Nazi Party paper *Völkischer Beobachter* ('Völkischer Observer') reported the victories of the Waffen-SS. By 1944 the former had a weekly circulation of 750,000 and the latter 1.7 million daily. The result is that Waffen-SS units are often mentioned in the same breath as Spartan hoplites, Persian immortals, the Roman Praetorian Guard, Viking warriors, Japanese samurai, Delta Force and the SAS, to name but a few elite fighters. This reputation is largely derived from the performance of a handful of tough Reichsdeutsche SS panzer divisions that fought on both the Eastern and Western fronts, with, it has to be said, some distinction.

Many of these divisions consisted of little more than boy soldiers recruited from the Hitler Youth and the Labour Service. While some of the early Waffen-SS field units proved consistently reliable, this was as a result of a selection and training process deeply rooted in Nazi ideology, which included racial superiority. The resulting politically motivated fanaticism spilled over into their conduct and regularly resulted in war crimes and atrocities.

The emergence of Himmler's panzer divisions was not just a political vanity project; there were sound strategic reasons for upgrading them from the early motorized units. The expansion of German strength in 1943 was clearly accelerated after Field Marshal Erwin Rommel's defeat at

El Alamein in November 1942, the Allied landings in French North Africa that same month and by the destruction of the German army trapped at Stalingrad in early 1943. Leibstandarte Adolf Hitler, Das Reich and Totenkopf were transformed into panzergrenadier units for the spring 1943 counter-offensive in the Soviet Union, each with an integral tank battalion. This increase in combat power had been authorized in early 1942 but was not implemented until the second half of the year. Notably the Wiking division was also allocated a tank battalion but, instead of being withdrawn to France to re-equip, it stayed in the line.

Equally important was the appointment of General Guderian as Inspector-General of Armoured Troops in February 1943. Answering directly to Hitler, he was responsible for recruiting, training, organizing and equipping the panzer divisions of both the army and the Waffen-SS. Guderian, working with Armaments Minister Albert Speer, moved to centralize weapons production. This put an end to the private industries that the SS had created in the face of the army's intransigence over sup-plying Himmler with modern equipment. The result of this was that the armoured Waffen-SS divisions began to take priority with new tanks and self-propelled guns. When the fully fledged SS panzer divisions appeared in 1943 and 1944 they had stronger tank establishments than their army counterparts. They also had priority with the new Tiger and Panther tanks when they appeared, despite the fact that these tanks were in short supply.

By 1944 a Waffen-SS panzer division consisted of up to 15,000 fighting men and up to 6,000 support personnel, such as administrative staff, clerks and medics. The basic organization comprised one panzer regiment, two panzergrenadier regiments and a panzer artillery regiment, plus anti-tank, assault gun, flak, pioneer, reconnaissance and signals battalions. An SS panzer regiment had an established strength of up to 2,000 men. It con-sisted of two battalions, each with four companies, with an average of fifteen panzers to a company. The regiment was also issued with about a dozen self-propelled anti-aircraft guns equipped with Möbelwagens, Wirbelwinds or Ostwinds. The latter had become an increasing necessity in light of the waning power of the Luftwaffe. In addition, there was a supporting pioneer company plus up to 400 motorcycles, cars and trucks.

The assault gun battalions in comparison were rather weak, being issued with about twenty Sturmgeschütz III/IVs in three companies total-ling just 300 personnel. The anti-tank or panzerjäger battalions had three companies, two of which had fifteen self-propelled tank-destroyers; these were normally Jagdpanzer IVs. The third company was armed with towed 75mm PaK40 anti-tank guns. The reconnaissance and pioneer battalions were stronger, with almost 1,000 men. Notably the reconnaissance units were equipped with a dozen 75mm self-propelled guns (usually mounted in armoured cars for mobility) and had integral anti-tank and anti-aircraft guns. Such forces proved a scourge to the Allies at Arnhem and Nijmegen.

The mechanized armoured infantry or panzergrenadier regiments were normally organized into three battalions plus support units, and numbered up to 4,000 personnel. Each had five companies equipped with Sd.Kfz.251 armoured half-tracks. For mobile fire support they had six 150mm self-propelled Hummels and twelve 105mm self-propelled Wespes, plus twenty-four flamethrower vehicles and twelve 120mm mortar carriers. The anti-aircraft battalions were formed of five companies, three 20mm light and two 88mm heavy, each with six guns.

An SS panzer artillery regiment comprised twelve batteries in four battalions. One battery in each battalion was equipped with self-propelled guns whilst the rest had towed weapons. From September 1944 Nebelwerfer rocket-launcher battalions were added to SS panzer divisions. Each had four companies, three with 150mm weapons and one with 210mm weapons. These were either on wheeled trailers or mounted on half-tracks.

Although the powerful Tiger I and II tanks fought alongside the SS panzer divisions, they did not form part of the divisional organization and were formed into three independent Heavy (Schwere) Panzer battalions. In 1944 the 1st SS Panzer Corps in the West was allocated Schwere SS Panzer Abteilung 101 as its Tiger I battalion. The Tigers bore crossed keys within a shield with flanking oakleaves insignia to reflect their links with Leibstandarte, although they fought with Hitlerjugend. Schwere SS Panzer Abteilung 102 was assigned to support the 2nd SS Panzer Corps, while 103 was sent to the Eastern Front as part of Felix Steiner's 3rd (Germanische) SS Panzer Corps.

The subsequent Tiger II tank was then allotted to Schwere Panzer Abteilungen 501 (formerly 101), 502 (102) and 503 (103); these were similarly considered corps level assets and deployed at divisional level as and when they were needed. The Tiger IIs of 501 took part in the Ardennes offensive, while those of 502 were destroyed defending Berlin and those of 503, after fighting alongside Nordland, surrendered after being decimated in East Prussia.

What really made the troops of the Waffen-SS visually distinctive and therefore perhaps brought them more notice than they deserved were their disruptive pattern camouflaged smocks and helmet covers. There were four basic patterns that were reversible. The Waffen-SS employed spots, while the army and the Luftwaffe used patterns of angular segments. The Waffen-SS troops were also issued with the M43 and M44 camouflaged uniforms that consisted of jackets and trousers. The tank and self-propelled gun crews wore one-piece non-reversible camouflage overalls during the latter half of the war.

Once manpower became an issue, Himmler was increasingly forced to rely on 'ethnic' Germans and foreign 'volunteers' from the occupied territories. At this point quality and discipline often became an issue. The better known mixed-nationality foreign units such as the Danish and Dutch 5th SS Panzer Division Wiking, the Austrian and Romanian 7th SS Freiwilligen Gebirgs Division Prinz Eugen, the Austrian and Slovenian 16th SS Panzergrenadier Division Reichsführer-SS and the Belgian 28th SS Panzergrenadier Division Wallonien were also equipped with armoured fighting vehicles.

The so-called Waffen-SS foreign Freiwilligen or volunteer cavalry, grenadier, mountain and panzergrenadier divisions were a motley crew, many of whom were of extremely dubious fighting value. Most were employed in security duties and anti-partisan missions that frequently resulted in the deaths of innocent civilians. Confusingly, many units which were under the SS but not part of it were suffixed 'der SS' rather than the more familiar SS prefix. This was political window dressing to hide the inconvenient truth that such units did not meet the Nazis' exacting Aryan racial stereotype.

Considerable elements of the SS were morally bankrupt, representing an organization that had no regard for humanity, and they committed some of the worst atrocities in history. While the SS Einsatzgruppen and concentration camp guards were the main culprits, the Waffen-SS combat divisions were also guilty of such crimes. Although they were tough soldiers, they were responsible for a whole series of massacres carried out across Europe. The worst of these was perpetrated during the Warsaw Rising in 1944, when the SS murdered tens of thousands of civilians.

War crimes and politics aside, Hitler's SS panzer divisions proved particularly adept at conducting rescue and defensive operations and he became increasingly reliant on the Waffen-SS to extricate his armed forces from tricky military situations. Their finest moments during 1944 and 1945 were at Arnhem, Wolomin and in the Ardennes where significant Allied advances were stopped dead by a handful of veteran Waffen-SS divisions. The German army greatly respected the Waffen-SS panzer divisions and fought side by side with them, until they became largely one and the same.

While the Waffen-SS on the whole proved to be a highly competent fighting machine, Himmler on the other hand had no flair for military operations. Towards the end of the Second World War he was appointed to command Army Group Upper Rhine and then Army Group Vistula. Both roles were way above his abilities and both commands were short lived. Indeed, placing him in charge of Army Group Upper Rhine was a political move to keep him away from Hitler's Ardennes offensive, which involved the SS panzer divisions. In the case of Army Group Vistula, he was not only removed but beforehand was prevented from directing Operation Solstice.

As the war came to a close it became apparent that the Waffen-SS's once impressive offensive capability had been all but exhausted, though morale never waned or crumbled. At the very end the Waffen-SS units provided the main strike force for Hitler's final counteroffensives in Belgium and Hungary. When the Waffen-SS failed to secure a victory or come to the rescue of Berlin, Hitler felt personally betrayed. One of his final futile gestures was to order them to remove their once prized SS insignia. 'My Honour is Loyalty' had become meaningless to a deranged madman.

Chapter One

Panzer Elite

The 1st SS Panzer Division Leibstandarte SS Adolf Hitler dates back to the 1920s with the creation of Hitler's SS protection squad, building on the SA's short-lived Stabswache (Headquarters Guard). In March 1933 Sepp Dietrich established the SS-Stabswache Berlin consisting of 120 men; this, along with the SS-Verfügungstruppe, were the forerunners of the Waffen-SS. Initially the unit was based at Berlin's Alexander Barracks but later moved to Berlin-Lichterfelde.

SS-Stabswache Berlin, redesignated SS-Sonderkommando Zossen, merged with the newly raised SS-Sonderkommando Jüterbog in September 1933, to be designated SS-Leibstandarte (Bodyguard) Adolf Hitler (LAH). The following year it was redesignated Leibstandarte SS Adolf Hitler and grew to regimental strength.

Leibstandarte took part in the Austrian Anschluss as a part of the 16th Corps under General Guderian and later in the annexation of Czechoslovakia. During the invasion of Poland it served with Army Group South under the leadership of SS-Oberstgruppenführer Sepp Dietrich and later took part in the invasion of France and the Low Countries, where it was mainly held in reserve, although it was used against the retreating British troops at Dunkirk. Leibstandarte was attached to the 14th Corps during the second and final phase of the invasion of France.

Sister formation the SS-VT-Division Reich, formed in October 1939 from the Deutschland, Germania and Der Führer Regiments, was placed under the command of SS-Oberstgruppenführer Paul Hausser. It was also involved in the campaign in the West in 1940 and, after guarding the border with Vichy France, was transferred to the Netherlands. The division then took part in the campaign in the Balkans, where a small detachment led by SS-Hauptsturmführer Klingenberg managed to persuade the Mayor of Belgrade to surrender the city without a fight.

Still under Hausser's command, SS-VT Division Reich took part in the invasion of the Soviet Union and fought on the front lines until August 1941, when it was withdrawn for refitting. It was sent back to the front in

September and a few months later, commanded by SS-Obergruppen-führer Wilhelm 'Willi' Bittrich, it took part in the failed winter offensive against Moscow.

After the Polish campaign three SS Totenkopfverbände concentration camp guard regiments numbering 6,500 men formed the SS Division Totenkopf (motorized) in October 1939 under the command of SS-Obergruppenführer Theodor Eicke, the Inspekteur der Konzentrationslager un SS-Wachverbände (Inspector of Concentration Camps and SS Guard Formations). The personnel came from the Buchenwald, Dachau, Frankenberg, Mauthausen and Sachsenhausen camps. This created a direct link between the Waffen-SS and the Endlösung (Final Solution), better known as the Holocaust. These men were strengthened by combat-experienced troops from the Totenkopf Standarte Götze, which had been raised for police duties but fought alongside the army in Poland. A cadre of officers and non-commissioned officers was also drawn from the SS-Verfügungs Division. Totenkopf was largely equipped with captured Czech weapons, which gave rise to concerns over its quality.

General Max Weichs, commander of the 2nd Army, inspected Totenkopf in early April 1940 and was pleasantly surprised to discover it was not 'organized and equipped like a Czech foot division' but was a modern motorized infantry division. Totenkopf took part in the invasion of the West and was responsible for the La Paradis massacre, where about a hundred men of the Royal Norfolk Regiment were shot after surrendering. The man who instigated the atrocity, SS-Obersturmführer Fritz Knöchlein, had been a company commander at Dachau after initially enlisting with the Deutschland Regiment of the SS-VT. His men, belonging to the 4th Company, 1st Battalion, Totenkopf 2nd Standarte, lined the prisoners up against a wall and turned their machine guns on them. A survivor later reported Knöchlein's criminal actions. In the meantime the German authorities took no action and Knöchlein was not court-martialled. Instead he was to go on and command an SS-regiment of Norwegian volunteers in Courland.

By mid-1941 the Totenkopf Division and the seventeen Totenkopf Standarten totalled 40,000 men. However, most of the Standarten were deployed on occupation duties in the occupied territories, notably France and Norway. When Hitler launched his invasion of the Soviet Union the division comprised 18,754 men organized into three regiments with full supporting units. Totenkopf and the 4th SS Polizei Division were involved in besieging Leningrad. Subsequently, while recuperating in southern France in November 1942, it became the 3rd SS Panzer-grenadier Division Totenkopf. Then on 22 October 1943 it was redesig-nated a panzer division under the command of SS-Brigadeführer Max Simon. During 1943 it fought at Kharkov, Belgorod and Kursk.

The idea to create a Hitlerjugend (Hitler Youth) division was initially suggested by SS-Gruppenführer Gottlob Berger in early 1943. His plan envisaged the drafting of all 17-year-old Hitler Youth members born in 1926 and assigning them to a combat formation. Hitler liked the proposal and ordered Berger to commence raising such a division, the official order being issued on 10 February 1943.

Berger nominated himself to be the first Hitlerjugend divisional com-mander, but Himmler gave the job to former Hitler Youth member Ober-führer Fritz Witt instead, as he had already commanded one of the 1st SS Panzer Division's panzergrenadier regiments. Witt had won the Iron Cross and Knight's Cross in Poland and France respectively. In the Balkans his men from the 1st SS were instrumental in opening the Klidi pass in the heart of Greece. He then fought in Russia, seeing action at Rostov and Kharkov.

Hitler issued a number of additional decrees in April 1943 regarding the formation of the Hitlerjugend Panzergrenadier Division. On 1 May the first batch of 8,000 volunteers reported for six weeks' training, although they only received four. At the beginning of July the graduating class was released for service, while a second batch of 8,000 was inducted for train-ing. By 1 September 1943 the 16,000 trained recruits were listed on the rosters of the newly formed Hitlerjugend Division and were assembled at an SS training facility located at Beverloo, Belgium.

Under the direction of 'Willi' Bittrich, the 9th SS Panzer Division Hohenstaufen was mainly formed from conscripts, many of them from the Reich Labour Service, also in early February 1943. Bittrich, an able tank commander, controlled the Deutschland Regiment during the fight-ing in Poland and France in 1939–1940; he then assumed control of the 2nd SS Panzer Division Das Reich for just three months in late 1941.

Under the command of SS-Standartenführer Michael Lippert, the 10th SS Panzer Division Frundsberg, like the 9th SS, was raised from conscripts drawn mainly from the Reichsarbeitsdienst in February 1943. Like the recruits in the 12th SS, they were just teenagers: according to Himmler, the average age of the recruits was 18 years. The division was redesignated the 10th SS Panzer Division on 3 October 1943 and named after Georg von Frundsberg (1473–1528), who had fought for the Habsburg monarchy during its many wars.

The Liebstandarte-SS Adolf Hitler (LSSAH) was upgraded to brigade strength in August 1940 for the planned invasion of Britain. When this was called off, the LSSAH was transferred to Romania for the attack in the Balkans. It fought its way through Yugoslavia and Greece, chasing the Allied troops to Kalamata, from where they took flight by sea to Crete. Kurt Meyer, commanding the reconnaissance battalion, attacked the Klussura Pass and captured 11,000 men, and the brigade took the surrender of at least sixteen Greek divisions before Greece capitulated.

In June 1941 the LSSAH expanded into a full motorized infantry division and took part in the invasion of the Soviet Union as part of Army Group South, and was involved in the fighting at Kiev and Rostov. The division was sent to France for refit in 1942 and upgraded to a panzergrenadier division. Sent back to the Eastern Front in 1943 under SS-Brigadeführer Theodor Wisch, it fought at Kharkov and Kursk. After the German defeat at Kursk, the LSSAH was sent to Italy on anti-partisan duties, but was soon deployed back to the Eastern Front as a panzer division.

After heavy losses on the Eastern Front, on 18 April 1944 the remains of the LSSAH under Wisch travelled by train to northwest France and established its headquarters at Turnhout in Belgium, where it became part of the 1st SS Panzer Corps. Over 2,000 men from the 12th SS were transferred to the division and in early May Hitler ordered that it should get new equipment, much of it straight from the factory floor.

A month later the 1st SS was still far from combat ready. In the week before D-Day the division stood at 19,620 strong, though many of the new recruits were untrained and over 1,000 men, mainly drivers and vital technicians, were still in Germany. Wisch was still awaiting replacement Panzer Mk IVs and Vs and these did not arrive until the weeks following D-Day. Motor transport was lacking, the division had less than half of its authorized trucks and over a third of those were undergoing maintenance. None of the panzergrenadiers' armoured half-tracks was operational.

The SS-VT-Division Reich was sent to France in March 1942, with the exception of a small Kampfgruppe, where it was upgraded to become SS-Panzergrenadier Division Das Reich. It was sent back to the Eastern Front in January 1943, where, under the leadership of SS-Obergruppenführer George Keppler, it took part in the capture and recapture of Kharkov, as well as fighting at Kursk.

In April 1944, under SS-Gruppenführer Heinz Lammerding, approximately 2,500 men from Das Reich were transferred back to France to the Bordeaux area, this time to be upgraded to a full panzer division designated the 2nd SS. Lammerding had served as an infantry officer and was involved in anti-partisan operations on the Eastern Front. The subsequent actions of his division during its march north through France may be partly attributed to Lammerding's brutal experiences in the East. In late 1943 he took command of those 2nd SS units on anti-partisan duties and assumed full command of the division on 25 January 1944. There were whisperings that he had been over promoted. It has been argued that he owed his appointment to his relationship with Himmler, indeed it was felt that Lammerding's position had more to do with his political allegiance to the Nazi Party than to any real military aptitude. The 2nd SS was based around Montauban and one of its first priorities was to absorb about 9,000 new recruits, as well as replenishing its vehicle fleet. The division took receipt of fifty-five Panzer IVs and thirty-seven Panthers towards a complement of sixty-two of each, to supplement the existing thirty Sturmgeschütz, on 16 May 1944.

Before the 9th SS had finished its training it was placed under 'Sepp' Dietrich's 1st SS Panzer Corps, along with the remains of the 1st SS and the newly raised 12th SS Panzergrenadier Division. However, in early 1944, along with the 10th SS, the Panzer Lehr and the 349th Infantry Divisions, it became part of the 2nd SS Panzer Corps under Paul Hausser. At the end of March 1944 the Red Army had surrounded the 1st Panzer Army and the 2nd SS Panzer Corps had been despatched to rescue it.

The 9th SS first saw action at Tarnopol in early 1944, where it took part in rescuing German troops from the Kamenets-Podolskiy pocket. Placed into reserve with Army Group North Ukraine, the 9th SS was refitting when the Allies landed in Normandy. Hitler immediately ordered the division to join Panzergruppe West in France. Under Bittrich it was sent to Normandy on 12 June, though it was to have a series of commanders during the Normandy campaign.

Led by SS-Gruppenführer Karl Fischer von Treuenfeld, the 10th SS Panzer Division likewise first saw action at Tarnopol. In mid-June Hitler also ordered the division to be switched to the west to help bolster the situation in Normandy. Under SS-Gruppenführer Heinz Harmel, the 10th SS was sent to France on 12 June, along with the 9th SS, to counter the Allied landings.

On 1 June 1944 on paper the 12th SS Hitlerjugend was an extremely powerful armoured formation with a reported strength of 20,500 men, albeit some 2,400 of these troops were stationed in Arnhem in the Netherlands. It has been estimated that the 12th SS arrived in Normandy with about 17,000 men. SS-Panzer Regiment 12 under SS-Obersturmbannführer Max Wünche had an authorized strength of 101 Panzer IVs and 79 Panthers. A further thirteen Panthers were despatched to the division the day after D-Day.

The SS panzers were poised to take a leading role in the battle for Normandy. It was their presence that helped the Germans hold the Allies at bay for three long months of bitter fighting. There they gained a reputation for tenacity.

Chapter Two

Policemen and Mountaineers

While the Waffen-SS would end up padded out with a plethora of foreign divisions, one of the more unusual early Reichsdeutsche units employed some 15,000 German policemen. Himmler, determined to expand his forces, was thwarted in recruiting amongst the German population thanks to objections by the army. However, as head of Germany's various police forces Himmler was able to call on the manpower of the Ordnungs-polizei, the uniformed civilian police, and Allgemeine-SS reservists.

Turning men whose profession was keeping the peace into war fighters was no easy task. Many of the policemen were middle-aged and had no desire to become soldiers serving away from their families. This also posed potential law and order issues in the cities from which the police were drawn. Some police, though, were already members of the SS. Both Heinz Jürgens and Hans Traupe attended the SS-Junkerschule at Bad Tölz before being posted to the Berlin police. At the outbreak of war they willingly joined the newly forming 4th SS Polizei Division.

The Polizei Division, raised by SS-Gruppenführer Karl Pfeffer-Wildenbruch, was not surprisingly often used for policing duties after the opening stages of the war. Formed in October 1939, it was at first not considered a true Waffen-SS division. Notably its troops wore a combi-nation of SS and police uniforms and remained under the authority of the police's chain of command, answering to Kurt Daluege. The latter was in charge of the Ordnungspolizei and had previously been head of the Berlin SS. Daluege was tasked by Himmler with purging the police of anyone unsympathetic towards the Nazi cause. In doing so, he had driven a large number of experienced police officers out of the force, which left it greatly weakened.

In an effort to rectify the situation Daluege tried to entice officers back if they underwent a re-education programme. He also sought to encour-age members of the Allgemeine-SS to join the Ordnungspolizei. This brought in younger Nazis, but many of the older policemen remained ambivalent about political indoctrination. It was at this point that the term

19

armed-SS was first officially used. An SS order issued on 7 November 1939 directed all Allgemeine-SS members to 'apply to become reserve officers in the Waffen-SS and Police'.

The Polizei Division's status meant that Leibstandarte, Das Reich and Totenkopf were given priority when it came to equipment. It was issued with seized Czech arms, however, Czechoslovakia was a major weapons producer and these were not actually inferior to those used by the Germany army. The division consisted of the 1st and 2nd Polizei Schützen Regiments, which were later converted to grenadier regiments. They were not motorized and had to rely on horses to pull their supply wagons, while the infantry had to get about on bicycles. To try to give the division some firepower it was allocated a horse-drawn army artillery regiment armed with German 105mm howitzers and some captured French guns. It was clear that the Polizei Division lacked punch and mobility, although to be fair this was a fairly standard situation for the bulk of the army's infantry divisions.

This poorly equipped police unit was not considered suitable for front-line combat and initially only undertook occupation duties in Poland. It then briefly saw action during the invasion of France in 1940, fighting against the French rearguard in the Argonne forest. The men of the 4th Polizei Regiment, which was not part of the division, were pleased to find themselves assigned to garrison security duties in Paris. They lined Avenue Foch on 14 June 1940 during the German victory parade beneath the Arc de Triomphe. About thirty Polizei regiments were created between 1940 and 1942, many of which were deployed on anti-partisan duties in the occupied territories. These were not designated SS-Polizei Regiments until February 1943, in order to differentiate them from other German police units and foreign auxiliary police. From outside Germany Volksdeutsche volunteers provided over one hundred Polizei regiments.

The Polizei Division was subsequently sent to East Prussia for further training and in early 1941 control was passed from the police to the SS. Afterwards, under the command of SS-Gruppenführer Arthur Mülverstedt, the division was placed in reserve and committed to the invasion of the Soviet Union as part of Army Group North. Himmler was informed that the front-line strength of the Waffen-SS on 22 June 1941 consisted of 10,796 men in Leibstandarte; 19,021 in Das Reich; 18,754 in Totenkopf; 17,347 in Polizei; 19,377 in Wiking and 10,573 in Nord.

Polizei fought alongside Totenkopf during the fighting around Luga and suffered 2,000 casualties. These losses indicate a level of courage, poor leadership or a combination of both. Its performance was largely considered indifferent, though was superior to that of SS-Kampfgruppe Nord in Finland, which eventually became the 6th SS Gebirgs Division. By August 1941 Polizei had helped to overwhelm the Soviet defence of Luga, though amongst their losses was Mülverstedt, killed in action. Afterwards the division dug in around Leningrad with the rest of the army group to sit out the winter. Polizei regimental commander Alfred Wünnenberg won the Knight's Cross on 15 November 1941.

The following spring Polizei, now commanded by Wünnenberg, was involved in operations against the Red Army along the Volkhov river. He won the Oak Leaves for his division's performance. It was not until February 1942 that Polizei was fully absorbed into the Waffen-SS. At this point its men adopted SS insignia and rank badges. Polizei pattern head-gear was also replaced with standard SS issue. During January and March 1942 Polizei was involved in the fierce fighting that defeated the Soviet 2nd Shock Army. Rudolf Pannier, who commanded the 1st Battalion, 2nd Polizei Schützen Regiment, led the defence of the key strongpoint of Ljubino during the early stages of the fighting for the Volkhov pocket. For his brave actions he won the Knight's Cross on 11 May 1942. Later that month he was presented to Himmler along with Bernhard Griese, another policeman turned soldier. The division remained committed to the Leningrad front for the rest of the year and endured another cold winter.

When the Soviets broke through south of Lake Lagoda in February 1943, Polizei was forced to retreat westwards to new defences at Kolpino. After suffering heavy casualties, elements of the division were withdrawn to Silesia to be reformed. SS-Obersturmbannführer Friedrich-Wilhelm Bock won the Knight's Cross while commanding the 2nd Battalion of the SS-Polizei Artillery Regiment in 1943. That May a Polizei kampf-gruppe was deployed on security duties in Bohemia-Moravia and Poland. The following month Polizei became a panzergrenadier division and was equipped with assault guns thanks to the addition of the 4th SS-Assault Gun Battalion. Shortly afterwards some units were sent to southern Yugoslavia and northern Greece to conduct anti-partisan operations. They soon developed a reputation for brutality, with little regard for upholding the law.

In September 1943 Polizei transferred to Belgrade for training, ready to move into the Balkans should the Allies land there. At the end of the year the division deployed to Salonika in Greece to conduct further anti-partisan operations. However, some units remained on the Eastern Front.

Soviet counterattacks in the Leningrad area in January 1944 broke through the German lines. SS-Hauptsturmführer Hans Traupe, leading a battalion from Polizei, successfully held open the German escape route from the Volkhov for several days against overwhelming odds. He was awarded the Knight's Cross on 23 October 1944 and was subsequently sent to take command of Frundsberg's 22nd SS-Panzergrenadier Regiment. Rudolf Seitz, a veteran gun commander with the Polizei Anti-Tank Battalion, also gained the Knight's Cross.

In Greece, under the command of SS-Hauptsturmführer Fritz Lautenbach, the division committed atrocities at Distomo on 10 June 1944. Some 200 civilians, including women and children, were rounded up and hanged or shot in retaliation for a partisan attack. Other war crimes were committed near Delphi, in Ypati and Spercheida. The division was then redeployed to Romania to try to help stem the advance of the Red Army. Attempts to rescue trapped troops at Timişoara failed, but they were more successful at Drobeta-Turnu Severin. At the end of October 1944 SS-Hauptsturmführer Johannes Scherg, commander of the 1st Company, Polizei armoured reconnaissance battalion, was awarded the Knight's Cross by the divisional commander Fritz Schmedes. This was for continuing to cover the German retreat in the Banat region despite being surrounded. Scherg and his men had then successfully broken out.

Polizei, along with other German forces, was slowly pushed back into Czechoslovakia. The division was subsequently assigned to Army Group Vistula in Pomerania. During the defence of Danzig in 1945 the division was completely fragmented. SS-Hauptsturmführer Heinz Jürgens, commanding Polizei's armoured reconnaissance battalion, which totalled 2,000 men including other attached units, defended the bridgehead at Langenberg. Jürgens and his men held out for four weeks against the onslaught of the Red Army. For his bravery and leadership he gained the Knight's Cross on 8 May 1945 just as the war ended.

Other Polizei units saw action around Hela before being evacuated to Swinemünde. When this port was surrounded some members of Polizei escaped towards Berlin. Few if any, though, made it and the survivors surrendered to the Americans. Those left trapped in Swinemünde were either killed by the Soviets or managed to escape to Denmark, where they were taken by the British. A number were also captured by the British at Lauenberg on the Elbe, including SS-Hauptsturmführer Scherg. The division's final commander was none other than SS-Standartenführer Walter Harzer, the famous Arnhem veteran.

A second police division was belatedly formed in February 1945. This was created using staff and pupils from the Dresden Polizeischule and 120 training personnel from the SS-Junkerschule at Braunschweig. Although called the 35th SS Polizei Grenadier Division and organized into three regiments, it was never more than regimental strength and may have been as weak as a battalion. The only unit with any combat experience was the 14th Polizei Regiment. This had seen some second-line service in Russia and France. Mobilized so late in the war, none of the recruits can have had much enthusiasm for what lay ahead. The 'division' fought on the Niesse front, suffering heavy casualties, and surrendered to the Red Army at Halbe in May 1945.

Another of the more unusual Reichsdeutsche units was the very first SS mountain division. Although the Waffen-SS formed half a dozen such units, the only one of any notable quality was the 6th SS Gebirgs Division Nord. All the others were raised using Volksdeutsche and poor quality foreign volunteers. Once again Himmler turned to Totenkopf and Allgemeine-SS reservists to provide the manpower. The unit started life in Austria in late 1940 and early 1941 when three Totenkopf regiments were brought together to form SS-Kampfgruppe Nord. Foreign volunteers included some Hungarians, Romanians and a few Norwegians who served in the ski battalion. Essentially of brigade strength, this formation was ill-prepared for combat. There was no combined training with the supporting artillery regiment and many of the gunners were unable to practise live firing. Furthermore, infantry training at all levels was inadequate and there was a shortage of infantry support weapons.

Nonetheless, Nord was deployed to Finland ready for the invasion of the Soviet Union. Alongside Finnish troops and other German units it was to push on the Soviet port of Murmansk and secure the Kola Peninsula. When the assault began, the men of Nord found themselves marching through deep forests and wading through mosquito-infested swamps. Anyone who got lost was fair game for the Red Army. None of this did much to boost their morale.

During the fighting around Salla in early July 1941 the inexperienced SS-Kampfgruppe was cut to pieces. The SS launched three attacks to drive the Soviets from their positions and each was repulsed. When the Soviets, supported by armour, counterattacked, the troops of Nord fled. The cry had gone up, 'The Russian tanks are coming!' Five SS battalions were reduced to a shambles. Casualties amounted to 86 dead, 232 wounded and 147 missing. Fortunately for Nord, the Finns and German army units on their flanks threw the Soviets back. Nord's casualties continued to mount and after just over a week had risen to 261 dead and 307 wounded. By the end of August the kampfgruppe had lost 1,085 men in the fighting and to illness.

When Himmler saw the reports on the kampfgruppe's flight he was angry that the men had not fought to the last or taken their own lives rather than be captured. Even more worrying for Himmler, it showed he could not necessarily rely on the Totenkopf regiments. While their ranks undoubtedly contained ardent Nazis, concentration camp guards were little more than policemen who lacked combat experience. SS-Kampf-gruppe Nord suffered the same problem as the Polizei Division in that many of its recruits were middle-aged. In disgrace, it was withdrawn to undergo training as a mountain division. Reinforced by four Gebirgsjäger and three Gebirgsartillerie battalions in September 1941, it was redesig-nated the SS Division Nord. It did not officially become the 6th SS Gebirgs Division Nord until October 1943. A revamped Nord returned to Finland to take part in the renewed push on Murmansk. However, the Soviet defences once again held.

Nord spent much of the summer of 1942 fighting in the Kestenga region as part of the German 20th Gebirgs Army. The following year it was reinforced by Danish, Norwegian and Swedish volunteers who formed the SS-Freiwilligen Schikompanie Norge under the command of Gust Jonassen. This unit, numbering 200 men, soon suffered heavy casu-alties, including Jonassen, and was withdrawn to Norway. Through 1943 the German position in Finland and northern Russia began to worsen.

In the summer of 1944 the Finns, under mounting pressure from the Red Army, sued for peace and the Germans were given two weeks to quit the country. Nord had to safeguard the withdrawal of three German corps from Finland into Norway. This involved them marching almost 1,600km and crossing numerous lakes and rivers. After successfully escaping, the division was then transferred to Denmark for a refit. SS-Obergruppen-führer Friedrich Wilhelm Krüger was awarded the Knight's Cross for his command of the division in October 1944. In early 1945 it was sent to support Himmler's counteroffensive in the Alsace, along with Frundsberg and Götz von Berlichingen. There they fought in the Vosges mountains, but the offensive failed in the face of American and French counterattacks. The survivors eventually surrendered to the Americans at the end of the war.

Chapter Three

Himmler's Foreign Volunteers

Nazi Germany was chronically short of manpower throughout the Second World War, a situation that would eventually cost it dearly. Even at the end of the war German military industry was churning out more armaments than the German armed forces could deploy. Hitler was to recruit in excess of 3 million foreign troops to help prop up the Nazi cause, particularly on the Eastern Front. By 1940 a victorious Germany had already begun raising police and volunteer units all over occupied Europe. Most of these forces' uniforms were indistinguishable from the Germans except for national arms shields.

Collaboration in the Nazi-occupied territories was far more widespread than people generally realize. Hitler received varying support from over fifteen European states, with tens of thousands of foreign nationals volunteering to fight within the ranks of the German Wehrmacht or Waffen-SS. Most volunteers allied themselves with Hitler either out of nationalist self-interest or from a desire to fight Soviet Communism. Some units were to prove more reliable than others and when things started to fare badly for Germany the politically reliable volunteers were absorbed into the Nazi elite Waffen-SS, forming their own weak national divisions. The Cossacks, for example, were to prove some of the Germans' most loyal volunteers.

Many local SS security units were formed that created the basis for many of Himmler's numerous foreign Waffen-SS divisions. Notably, recruits from Scandinavia and the Low Countries formed an SS panzer division. A cadre of willing recruits was initially established when the Waffen-SS set up a number of security units, principally the 3rd SS Guard Battalion Nordwest from Dutch volunteers, the 6th SS Guard Battalion Nord from Norwegians, and the SS Guard Battalion Sjaelland from Danes. The black-clad Allgemeine-SS established foreign branches in the 'Germanische' occupied countries (i.e. non-Slavic) and recruited the most ardent collaborationists in Denmark, Belgium (Flanders), the Netherlands (Holland) and Norway. They likewise provided the volunteers for foreign Waffen-SS units and pro-German security units.

In Denmark the Danish foreign minister Erik Scavenius supported the anti-Komintern Treaty and the recruitment of Danish volunteers for the Waffen-SS to fight the Soviet Union. The Schalburg Korpset was raised as a Danish branch of the Germanic-SS, although it never adopted the SS designation. It also recruited Danish SS Eastern Front veterans for an internal security role. The Schalburg Corps eventually became the SS Training Battalion Schalburg and then the SS Guard Battalion Sjaelland. They helped provide recruits for the 11th SS Freiwilligen Panzergrenadier Division Nordland, which was initially commanded by SS-Brigadeführer Fritz von Scholz.

In February 1942 Hitler appointed Vidkun Quisling 'Minister President' of Norway, although power really rested with the Reichskommissar. Jonas Lie was Quisling's minister of justice and police plus leader of the Norwegian Germanic-SS. In Norway an Allgemeine-SS unit was formed and initially known as the Norges-SS, but later retitled the Germanske-SS Norge – presumably to emphasize its Germanic credentials. This was about 1,300 strong and wore black uniforms. However, most of its members ended up serving in either the Norwegian police or the Waffen-SS.

In Holland the Dutch fascists formed the Nederlandsche-SS militia, which was later renamed the Germansche-SS en Nederland and wore black uniforms. The 11,000-strong Landstorm Nederland militia also came under the SS. Landstorm operated against the Dutch Resistance and the British around Arnhem. It was later amalgamated with other Dutch units, including the SS Guard Battalion Nordwest, to create the so-called 34th Freiwilligen Grenadier Division der SS Landstorm Nederland under SS-Standartenführer Viktor Knapp.

Undoubtedly, the 5th SS Panzer Division Wiking was the first and best of the foreign units raised by the Waffen-SS. Gottlob Berger in October 1940 convinced Himmler of the benefits of raising a European SS, mainly because of the limits placed on ethnic German recruitment by Hitler. Through Berger's efforts, by 1944 of the 910,000 SS troops a staggering 220,000 were foreign volunteers, although in the eyes of their own countries they were collaborators and traitors.

Berger's first foreign recruiting effort began to gather momentum in December 1940. The Germania Regiment of the SS-VT Division was set aside to form the cadre of a new division recruited from Europeans within the occupied territories. Added to this were two foreign regiments already formed that year, the Scandinavian Standarte Nordland using 216 Danish and 294 Norwegian volunteers, and the Standarte Westland with

630 Dutch and Flemish recruits. A Finnish battalion, Nordost, was added in 1941 but later broken up as replacements. These units eventually became the 9th SS Panzergrenadier Regiment Germania and the 10th SS Panzergrenadier Regiment Westland.

This new division, first known as Germania, was placed under SS-Obergruppenführer Felix Steiner, who had his work cut out melding his disparate recruits into an effective unit. Initially discrimination by German officers and instructors proved to be a problem, forcing Steiner to issue an order calling for 'humane' leadership – whatever that meant. To reflect the division's Nordic origins and to make the volunteers feel more welcome, it was renamed Wiking.

Wiking first took part in the invasion of the Soviet Union as a motorized division. The following year it fought in the Caucasus and was redesignated a panzergrenadier division. In the spring of 1943 the 5th SS was involved in the counteroffensive between the Don and the Dneiper. Afterwards the Nordland regiment was detached to create the nucleus of the 11th SS Freiwilligen Panzergrenadier Division of the same name. It was partially replaced in Wiking by an Estonian battalion. Wiking took part in the battles at Kursk in the summer of 1943, and at the end of the year, with the addition of a tank battalion, Wiking became a panzer division.

In early February 1944 the Red Army's 1st and 2nd Ukrainian Fronts linked up near Zvenigorodka, trapping 56,000 troops of the German 11th and 42nd Corps in the Cherkassy or Korsun pocket, around 160km southeast of Kiev. Some thirty-five Soviet divisions surrounded the pocket. The two German corps commanded six divisions including Wiking and what became Leon Dégrelle's 28th SS Freiwilligen Panzergrenadier Division Wallonien.

The latter at the time was only of brigade strength, some 2,000 strong, having been taken over from the army as the Freiwilligen SS-Sturmbrigade Wallonien in June 1943. This was attached to Wiking. Under SS-Obergruppenführer Herbert Otto Gille, who had replaced Felix Steiner in May 1943, the 5th SS, numbering some 11,400 men, had fewer than fifty panzers and self-propelled guns and fewer than fifty pieces of artillery.

The plan was for a two-pronged relief at Cherkassy with the 1st Panzer Army's 3rd Panzer Corps driving from the southwest and the 8th Army's 47th Panzer Corps striking from the south. Despite their losses of transport aircraft at Stalingrad, the Luftwaffe was expected to provide an air bridge to the pocket. As far as Hitler was concerned, the highly successful 1942 Demyansk airlift would be repeated. Weather and road conditions were such that the two relief corps had to be kept supplied by air as well. The Red Air Force shot the Luftwaffe out of the sky as the pilots struggled to keep the trapped troops resupplied. In addition, the 47th Panzer Corps was reduced to just sixty-one panzers and assault guns and could do little more than conduct local attacks.

Hitler told the surrounded corps to stay put while four panzer divisions, including the 1st SS, tried to cut their way through. The 16th and 17th Panzer Divisions of the 3rd Panzer Corps attempted to reach them, pushing northwards on 4 February 1944. In the meantime, Hitler signalled General Stemmermann in the Cherkassy pocket saying, 'You can rely on me like you would on a wall of stone. You will be freed from the ring. For the time being hold on.' Stemmermann had no intention of holding on, and nor was he going to surrender, having rejected an offer to do so on 9 February. Marshal Georgi Zhukov, the Soviet deputy supreme commander, signalled Stalin:

> According to information received from PoWs, during battles in encirclement enemy troops have sustained heavy losses and their officers and men are now in a state of confusion bordering on panic. According to intelligence reports, surrounded enemy forces have concentrated [the] bulk of their troops in [the] Steblev-Korsun-Shevchenkovsky area. The enemy is apparently preparing for [a] last attempt to break out towards [the] Panzer group advancing on Malaya Boyarka.

The German counterattack quickly bogged down, so the 1st SS and 1st Panzer Divisions struck southwards, getting as far as Lysyanka, just 8km from the pocket. Unfortunately for those trapped, the 3rd Panzer Corps just did not have the strength to make the final push. By 10 February the pocket was just 9.5km by 11km. Tanks of the 1st SS-Panzer Regiment cut through four Russian divisions, but the depleted Leibstandarte was left with just three panzers and four assault guns.

Hitler, normally averse to surrendering ground, now agreed to a breakout attempt. The order was finally transmitted to General Stemmermann on 15 February, informing him that he could expect no further help:

> Capabilities of 3rd Panzer Corps reduced by weather and supply difficulties. Task Force Stemmermann must accomplish break-

28

through on its own to line Dzhurzhentsy-Hill 239 where it will link up with 3rd Panzer Corps. The breakout force will be under the command of General Lieb [42nd Corps] and comprise all units still capable of attack.

The 5th SS Panzer Division led the desperate attempt to break out on 16 February, only to be met by the Soviet 4th Guards and 27th Armies. Nonetheless, Wiking successfully punched westwards through a snowstorm, while the men of the Wallonien brigade covered the retreat and held open the corridor. This they did with distinction, with only 632 of their number surviving unscathed. Wiking fought its way to the Gniloi-Tilkitsch river but could find no bridges or fords; in desperation, human chains were formed to help non-swimmers cross to safety.

In the bitter fighting the Germans lost 20,000 killed and 8,000 captured. The Soviets, though, claimed that the battle for Korsun-Shevchenkovsky cost the Germans a total of 55,000 killed or wounded and 18,200 captured. The Germans maintained that 30,000 men managed to escape the pocket, largely thanks to the gallant actions of Wiking and Wallonien. In crossing the Gniloi-Tilkitsch river the 5th SS lost all of its armour and most of its heavy equipment. Although the 11th and 42nd Corps escaped, they were severely depleted and were pulled from the line. This greatly impacted on the defensive effort of Army Group South fending off attacks in the Uman area.

Then in late March 1944 some 200,000 troops of the 1st Panzer Army, including weak battle groups from Leibstandarte with the 3rd Panzer Corps and Das Reich with the 59th Army Corps, were caught in the Kamenets-Podolskiy pocket. The two Waffen-SS divisions had been greatly weakened. By mid-March the 1st SS had fewer than 1,250 men and the 2nd SS around 2,500. The bulk of the latter division had been sent to East Prussia at the end of 1943 to reorganize with a full complement of Panther and Tiger tanks. In early February elements of the division had started arriving at their new training ground in Bordeaux.

A ripple of apprehension went through the German high command, as the loss of 200,000 men would almost match their losses at Stalingrad. Those forces trapped at Kamenets-Podolskiy could not escape the enveloping Red Army so the newly operational 9th SS and 10th SS Panzer Divisions Hohenstaufen and Frundsberg were sent to their rescue. Although the weather was appalling, they managed to break through to the 1st Panzer Army as it fought its way westwards through freezing fog.

Kampfgruppe Lammerding (named after its commander, SS-Oberführer Heinz Lammerding) from the 2nd SS formed the rearguard while the other German units escaped to safety.

While most of the manpower of the 1st Panzer Army was successfully rescued, all the heavy equipment was lost and only forty-five armoured vehicles were saved. The Leibstandarte battle group escaped, although it suffered heavy losses. The remains of the division were then sent to Belgium for rest and refitting in the 15th Army's area of responsibility. Kampfgruppe Lammerding was also sent to Bordeaux, although the small Kampfgruppe Weidinger remained on the Eastern Front and was involved in the fighting retreat through Proskurov and Tarnopol.

It was at Cherkassy that the last of Hitler's offensive strength in Ukraine was lost, creating the conditions for the victorious Red Army advances in the summer and autumn of 1944. SS-Obergruppenführer Gille reported to Hitler that Wiking had ceased to exist as a combat division. The 5th SS survivors were withdrawn to Breslau to refit, although a 4,000-strong battle group remained on the Eastern Front. The division next saw action in July 1944 when it was sent to help bolster the Vistula front in Poland.

Léon Degrelle gained the Knight's Cross of the Iron Cross for his leadership of his Sturmbrigade during the breakout. The survivors, on returning home, held a celebration in Brussels on 1 April 1944, with Sepp Dietrich as the guest of honour. Cherkassy cost SS-Untersturmführer Jaques Leroy his right eye and right arm but he refused to be invalided out of the brigade. The bravery of Degrelle's Walloons convinced the SS of their worth and he was given permission to form a panzergrenadier division, although it never reached full strength.

In Eastern Europe Hungary supplied large number of troops for Hitler's invasion of the Soviet Union in June 1941. Initially the Hungarians supplied the Carpathian Group, then three army corps, bringing their contribution up to 200,000 men. Hungary also provided recruits for three Waffen-SS divisions: the 25th Waffen-Grenadier Division der SS Hunyadi, the 31st SS Freiwilligen Grenadier Division (which included Slovaks) and the 33rd Waffen Kavallerie Division der SS.

It was neighbouring Romania that provided the largest numbers of satellite forces and committed their best troops. In 1941 Romania fielded its 3rd and 4th Armies numbering about 150,000 men, but later, with reinforcements, this figure was to swell to over 300,000. They also contributed men in 1942 to the 7th SS Freiwilligen Gebirgs Division Prinz

Eugen, which consisted of Romanian, Yugoslav and other Balkan volunteers.

Although Hitler had a well-defined racial hatred for Russian Slavs and a determination to crush their nationalism, native Russians were still recruited into the Wehrmacht, including the Waffen-SS. This was done on a rather ad hoc basis, which led to a number of uncentralized armies that included Cossack troops. The brigade-strength Russian National Liberation Army (Russkaia Osvoboditelnania Norodnaia Armiia – RONA) was formed in 1942 and included Ukrainian Cossacks in its ranks. Better known as the infamous Kaminski Brigade, it was later designated the 29th Waffen-Grenadier Division der SS totalling approximately 6,000 men. Kaminski was later court-martialled and executed for his actions in Poland by his commanding officer, while his men were transferred to the Committee for the Liberation of the Peoples of Russia and the 30th Waffen-Grenadier Division der SS Russische Nr 2. SS-Oberführer Oskar Dirlewanger's anti-partisan brigade made up of Soviet deserters formed the basis for the 36th Waffen-Grenadier Division der SS.

Ukraine hoped it would gain independence by helping Hitler's war machine and about 180,000 Ukrainians served in the Wehrmacht. In late 1942 some 70,000 Ukrainians were recruited into the German police units, with 35,000 serving in seventy-one Schuma (police) battalions, which included some Cossack forces, conducting anti-partisan duties. A year later in 1943 Ukraine supplied 30,000 men to form the 14th Waffen-Grenadier Division der SS. The SS had been amazed when 100,000 Ukrainian nationalists had volunteered, but the poorer quality recruits were soon weeded out. This division, in a propaganda sleight of hand, was dubbed Galizien Nr 1. The Galician title was supposed to indicate that the division had been recruited from an area of Poland that had once formed part of the Austro-Hungarian empire and therefore conformed to Himmler's racial stereotyping, rather from racially 'inferior' Slavs.

Likewise, anti-Bolshevik Russians and Ukrainians in brigade strength formed the 30th Waffen-Grenadier Division der SS Russische Nr 2. Initially the volunteers had operated as anti-partisan police battalions, which were grouped into Brigade Siegling. In the summer of 1944 control passed from the police to the Waffen-SS and the brigade was designated a division. The German high command ordered the 30th Waffen-Grenadier Division der SS to France for anti-partisan duties. It arrived in Strasbourg on 18 August with instructions to hold the entrance to the Belfort Gap and counter any French resistance units operating in the area.

The division's 102nd Battalion deployed to the northern end of the gap and reached Vesoul on the 20th, with responsibility for the narrow plateau area between Noidans-les-Vesoul and Echenoz-la-Meline just to the southwest. Men of the 118th Battalion deployed to Besançon at the southern end of the gap on the 19th and then moved to Camp Valdahon, about 32km southeast of Besançon.

The subsequent defection of Ukrainian recruits from the 30th Waffen-Grenadier Division supplied the French with over 1,200 trained men with all their weapons and equipment, who were inducted into the French Forces of the Interior as the 1st Ukrainian Battalion (BUK). On 26 September, attired in French black berets and German uniforms, they marched from Chateau de l'Abbye to take part in the attack on Belfort. In their last action as the 1st BUK on 3 October they assaulted and secured Hill 736 near the town. Afterwards the French took the unorthodox step of recruiting the whole of the 1st BUK into the 13th Demi-Brigade of the French Foreign Legion in order to avoid having to repatriate them. This was the only time in the history of the Legion that an entire foreign unit was embraced in such a manner.

Ironically, just as the 30th Division arrived in France, French volunteers who had enlisted to fight Bolshevism alongside the Germans were engaged in the Carpathians. They had been formed into a regiment in 1943 under the auspices of the SS, but after withdrawing into Bohemia-Moravia this became the SS-Freiwilligen Sturmbrigade Charlemagne. After deploying in the Carpathians, it was decided to expand the unit, creating the 33rd Waffen-Grenadier Division der SS Charlemagne. In early 1945 it was sent to Pomerania, where the division was scattered by the Red Army. Remarkably a battalion of French volunteers died in the closing days of the war defending Berlin. Another group trying to get home were executed by the Free French. Also in the beginning of 1945 five divisions of Latvian, Estonian, Ukrainian and White Russians were established as SS divisions.

Himmler coveted the German army's renegade Cossack divisions. General Helmuth von Pannwitz, a German cavalry officer, began to explore the possibility of raising an independent Cossack division in September 1942. Eventually he was to organize a Cossack Corps of 52,000 men, with a further 18,000 serving as militia. Appointed 'Commander of Cossack Units', Pannwitz resettled the Cossack families first in Poland at Mielau (Mlawa) and then in northern Italy at Tolmezzo in Friuli. By April 1943 Pannwitz had gathered the Von Jungschutz and Lehman Cossack

Regiments from Army Group South, and the Kononow and Wolff Regiments from Army Group Centre. On being moved to Poland they were formed into the 1st Cossack Division, consisting of two brigades. Pannwitz increased his men's morale and esteem by allowing them to wear their traditional clothing. In fact, Pannwitz was so popular he was elected Feldataman, a post traditionally held by the Tsar.

A year later the division was disappointed to find that it was not to fight Stalin's Red Army, but rather Tito's Communist partisans in Yugoslavia. The two brigades then formed the nucleus of the 1st and 2nd Cossack Divisions, which became the 14th Cossack Corps. The Cossacks were involved in Operation Treibjagd against the partisans and probably also in Operation Kugelblitz, launched in December 1943 against eastern Bosnia, western Serbia, Slovenia and the Adriatic islands. It lasted until February 1944 and drove the partisans back towards Bosnia, capturing Dalmatia and all the offshore Adriatic islands except Vis. The new Cossack Corps was then redeployed to relieve the 11th SS Panzergrenadier Division at Sisak in Croatia.

Himmler had his eye on the tough Cossacks and at the end of 1944 the Corps was redesignated the 15th SS Cossack Cavalry Corps. This was a paper transformation and the Cossacks were never looked upon as full members of the Waffen-SS. Although the Corps was renamed it remained unchanged and was not redeployed from Yugoslavia. The SS simply became responsible for resupplying the Corps. All these foreign forces would face uncertain fates at the end of the war.

Chapter Four

Hausser's Junkerschulen

Creating a private army outside the armed forces required considerable training facilities. Initially what the SS needed was officers in abundance. Paul Lettow on 1 October 1934 opened the first of two SS officer training schools with the SS-Junkerschule at Bad Tölz in Bavaria. This started with an intake of just fifty-four cadets. The second one was opened by Paul Hausser in the spring of 1935 at Braunschweig in Brunswick. These two facilities had a total of 759 staff and provided training for all of the SS, not just the Waffen-SS. Later three other officer training schools were set up in Klagenfurt, Posen-Treskau and Prague. Likewise, seven non-commissioned officer schools or SS-Unterführerschulen were created at Arnheim, Braunsberg, Laibach, Lauenberg, Lublinitz, Posen-Treskau and Radolfzell. Specialist training centres were created in Germany, Austria, Czechoslovakia, Poland and in other occupied territories. Once war broke out, experienced combat veterans were rotated back from the front to act as instructors.

Officers signed on for twenty-five years, non-commissioned officers for twelve and privates for four. Basic training was the same for all three categories. Political indoctrination and physical education were important elements at these schools, as much as the military training. The latter consisted of endless parades, weapons training, hand-to-hand combat, assault courses and table-top wargames. Hausser was appointed to oversee the SS-VT Inspectorate on 1 October 1936 with the task of attracting more recruits. For the next four years the inspectorate also acted as the operational command of the SS-VT before it became the Waffen-SS.

Hans Fansalu was Hausser's adjutant at Bad Tölz. He later saw combat with Wiking on the Eastern Front and was accused of being involved in the massacre of Jews at Zborow. Werner Ostendorff was an instructor at Bad Tölz and served on Hausser's staff until 1944, when he took charge of the Götz von Berlichingen Division. Another of the Bad Tölz instructors, Richard Schulze, became Hitler's personal SS adjutant. The forward-thinking Felix Steiner was put in charge of the training programme. After his experiences during the First World War he was an advocate of the kampfgruppe or battle group. This was essentially an ad hoc assault force armed for specific tasks and trained for close-quarter combat. Steiner, while commanding the SS Standarte Deutschland, practised some of his ideas at Dachau, where his men were sharing camp guard duties with the Totenkopf units. He felt that fitness and endurance were key to good soldiering. He wanted his men fitter than the average army recruits and even members of the elite Leibstandarte, who at the time were seen as rivals.

Although the initial recruits sent to Hausser and Steiner only had a basic level of education, their standard of fitness was very high. Himmler was very proud of this, claiming in 1937 that 'we still choose only 15 out of every 100 candidates who present themselves'. The flaw with this was that it slowed the development of the Waffen-SS. Recruits started their day at 0600 hours with an hour's physical training. Sports kit consisted of baggy black shorts and a white vest that was emblazoned with the SS runes. Afterwards they had a breakfast comprising just porridge and water. This was followed by target practice and unarmed combat. Three times a week they had to endure ideological lectures on the merits of Nazism. After lunch they would undergo drill followed by cleaning kit and then capped the day off with circuits of the sports field.

About 85 per cent of SS officers were First World War veterans and about 25 per cent had served in the post-war Reichswehr/Wehrmacht. While it was not permitted to join the Waffen-SS as an existing officer, those who currently held a rank or had previously done so were often commissioned into the SS on passing out at an equivalent rank. Normally potential officers had to serve a minimum of a year in the ranks before being allowed to apply to the SS-Junkerschulen.

Steiner encouraged fraternization between officers, non-commissioned officers and the men to build up trust and encourage team work. He did not like the traditional hierarchal snobbery of the army and encouraged everyone off duty to address each other as 'comrade'. Those who successfully completed basic training, which was failed by a third first time round, enjoyed the traditional passing out parade before being allowed to take the SS oath of loyalty to Adolf Hitler. Once in the SS-VT candidates had to spend 12 months at the SS infantry or cavalry schools before swearing an oath in Munich to obey Himmler's strict marriage laws, which were designed to safeguard racial purity. These quickly proved unworkable.

Afterwards officers who graduated from the SS-Junkerschulen were issued the coveted inscribed SS dagger. Men who received a field promotion were not permitted this unless they subsequently passed the officer's course. Men holding an SS membership number below 10,000 were also permitted to wear the SS signet ring. Eventually this was worn by all SS officers with three years' service. SS officers were then sent on an intensive combat course. This was a test of courage and prepared them for what was to come on the battlefield. The ordeals allegedly included detonating a live grenade balanced on top of their helmet and crouching in a foxhole while a tank drove over it. Live firing exercises were conducted to give officers a taste of real combat. Casualties inevitably resulted for the more unfortunate. Such methods, though, produced men like Fritz Klingenberg, Otto Kumm, Kurt 'Panzer' Meyer, Fritz Witt and many others.

Thanks to the intriguing of Reinhard Heydrich, head of the Sicherheitsdienst, in 1938 Hitler lost faith in Field Marshal Werner von Blomberg, the Minister of War and the German Army's High Command. He proceeded to combine his role as Chancellor with that of War Minister, which gave him direct control of the German armed forces. To allay the army's concerns about the SS, Hitler decreed that SS officers would be seconded to the army for six to twelve months. That same year Gottlob Berger became responsible for SS recruitment and would soon be overseeing the growth of the Waffen-SS.

Training for the Waffen-SS became much less vigorous in 1943 with its massive expansion and the recruitment of growing numbers of foreign volunteers. At that point foreigners began to outnumber the Reichsdeutsche at the cadet schools and the training centres. Himmler was forced to modify his policies on racial purity and political indoctrination. Fritz Klingenberg, in charge at Bad Tölz, began to emphasize that they were all Europeans protecting western civilization from Asiatic Bolshevism. By this stage, though, Germany was losing the war and an appeal for European unity was much too late. Hitler had steadfastly refused to acknowledge the possibility of autonomy within a Greater Reich, which had left the European pro-Nazi political parties struggling for validation with their own people.

Furthermore, the vast majority of Europeans living in the occupied territories had no enthusiasm for Hitler's war. Himmler's police and wartime shortages had seen to that. Nonetheless, some thirty French officers were sent to Bad Tölz in November 1943. Also about a hundred French non-commissioned officers were sent to the SS-Unterführerschulen to be upgraded to Waffen-SS standards. They subsequently served with the French 33rd Waffen-Grenadier Division der SS Charlemagne. Even neutral Sweden saw limited numbers of volunteers serve with the Waffen-SS and about twenty Swedish officers passed out from Bad Tölz.

In Norway at the end of 1943 Himmler aimed to recruit up to 60,000 Norwegians into an SS division and new police units. This was greatly hampered when the SS police chief in Norway proceeded to make a mass arrest of students in Oslo. Later, to try to improve things, SS-Obersturmbannführer Schulze on 28 September 1944 persuaded Hitler to send Norway's puppet ruler Vidkun Quisling the promise of an 'independent national and socialist existence' when the war was won. 'The news,' recalled Hausser, 'of this achievement by one of their staff filled the Bad Tölz school with great rejoicing.' In light of German resistance collapsing on both the Eastern and Western Fronts, there seemed little cause for such rejoicing.

During 1939–45 the SS-Junkerschulen produced at least 15,000 officers, many of them destined for the Waffen-SS. At the end of the war the schools were stripped of their staff and remaining pupils to form various kampfgruppe, which were thrown into the path of the Red Army. Some were sent to the very last divisions raised by the Waffen-SS. Braunschweig formed a cadre for the 35th SS Polizei Waffen-Grenadier Division, while Bad Tölz sent personnel to the 38th SS Waffen-Grenadier Division Nibelungen. Appropriately the latter was initially dubbed Junkerschule in their honour. A few instructors may have been assigned to the seven largely fictitious SS divisions formed in the closing days of 1945.

Other training units also ended up committed to battle, such as the instructors of the Hanover Hitler Youth Cadet School deployed to the defence of Ibbenburen. The 20th SS Training Division saw combat against the British at Bremen. Veteran officers and non-commissioned officers in charge of Hitler Youth with the 18th SS Horst Wessel Training Battalion were also sent to defend Bremen. The 4th SS Field Training and Replacement Battalion ended the war at Neustadt fighting the Soviets.

Chapter Five

Into Battle with an SS Corps

Organized into an SS Panzer Corps, the tanks of the Waffen-SS were to prove themselves in early 1943 on the Eastern Front. Its commander, SS-Obergruppenführer Paul 'Papa' Hausser, had formed the Corps the previous year in France. One of the Red Army's priorities was again to attempt liberating Kharkov, Ukraine's second city. A general Soviet offensive began on 12 January 1943 with the intention of pushing Field Marshal Maximilian Freiherr von Weichs Army Group A and Field Marshal Erich von Manstein's Army Group Don away from the Don and into Ukraine. This offensive started between Orel in the north and Rostov in the south, employing Lieutenant General M.A. Reiter's Bryansk Front, Colonel General F.I. Golikov's Voronezh Front, General N.F. Vatutin's Southwestern Front and General A.I. Eremenko's Southern Front. It was resisted from north to south by the German 2nd, Hungarian 2nd, Italian 8th and Romanian 3rd Armies and the German 4th Panzer Army.

At Kharkov the newly arrived SS Panzer Corps, comprising the 1st SS Leibstandarte, 2nd SS Das Reich and 3rd SS Totenkopf Panzergrenadier Divisions, stood in the Soviets' way but was pushed back. Hausser could see little point in holding the city or committing his tanks to the streets. He signalled the Führer an immediate appraisal of the situation:

> Inside Kharkov mob firing at troops and vehicles. No forces available for mopping-up since everything in front line. City, including railway, stores and ammunition dumps, effectively dynamited at Army orders. City burning. Systematic withdrawal increasingly improbable each day. Assumptions underlying Kharkov's strategic importance no longer valid. Request renewed Führer decision whether Kharkov should be held to the last man.

Hitler signalled back, 'The eastern front of Kharkov must be held. The considerable SS formations now arriving must be employed in freeing Kharkov's communications and defeating the enemy forces pressing against Kharkov from the north-west.' Reluctantly Hausser sent Das Reich into Kharkov but deliberately held back his other two divisions. Das Reich soon found itself engaged in heavy street fighting against superior forces.

Field Marshal von Manstein was concerned that Army Detachment Lanz was expected to hold Kharkov and strike towards Losovaya to relieve the pressure on Army Group South's left flank. It was only in a position to conduct one of the two tasks and von Manstein wanted to avoid another Stalingrad at all costs. His proposal was also to abandon Kharkov, strike south to defeat the Red Army and then reoccupy the city. Hausser, likewise fearing that Kharkov could become another Stalingrad, disobeyed Hitler's orders to stand firm and on 15 February withdrew from the city to Krasnograd.

Hausser, operating outside the German Army's high command, had taken matters into his own hands to avoid being surrounded. By the time Hitler discovered what had happened and issued countermanding orders, it was too late. Das Reich had already withdrawn and, along with Leib-standarte, set up a new defensive line to the south of Kharkov. Fortunately for von Manstein, this forced the army to withdraw as well.

To compound von Manstein's problems, Hitler flew into the factory town of Zaporozhye southwest of Kharkov to be briefed on the situation. Alarmingly, the field marshal was unable to guarantee Hitler's safety as the town was only garrisoned by a defence company and a few anti-aircraft units. When they met on 17 February 1943 Hitler would not discuss von Manstein's plans and refused to admit that the Red Army was posing a very dangerous threat to the junction of the 1st Panzer Army and Army Detachment Lanz. Von Manstein assumed this was because Hitler was keen to see the SS Panzer Corps rumble back into Kharkov, but the reality was that the threat to the Dnieper crossings had to be dealt with first. Also it was now a race against time, for the impending spring thaw would soon put a halt to operations between the Dnieper and Donets rivers.

The mud actually came to von Manstein's rescue because Totenkopf became bogged down between Kiev and Poltava. If Leibstandarte and Das Reich were not comfortable holding the city on their own, they were unlikely to retake it without the assistance of their sister division. In the light of this, Hitler acquiesced to von Manstein's plans but refused to countenance shortening the 750km front held by Army Group South's thirty battered divisions. Despite von Manstein's intelligence, Hitler refused to acknowledge the Red Army's gathering strength in manpower and tanks. Von Manstein observed diplomatically, 'We lived, it seemed, in two entirely different worlds.' Perhaps more importantly, von Manstein noted, 'I had the impression that Hitler's visit to my headquarters had helped to bring home to him the danger of encirclement which immediately threatened the southern wing of the Eastern Front.'

In the meantime, the main Soviet threat was a salient thrusting towards Dnepropetrovsk, containing the 1st Guards and 6th Armies as well as Group Popov. While the Germans held the Red Army west of Kharkov, von Manstein orchestrated a counterattack on 19 February using Hausser's SS Panzer Corps striking south from Krasnograd southwest of Kharkov towards Pavlograd. Three days later Hoth's 4th Panzer Army linked up with the SS at Pavlograd.

General Rybalko's 3rd Tank Army swung south to take on the SS Panzer Corps on 24 February. The SS withdrew to lure the Soviets into a trap. Das Reich and Totenkopf caught the Soviet 1st Guards Tank Corps as well as two rifle divisions. This resulted in the Red Army losing 9,000 dead, as well as 61 tanks, 60 motor vehicles and 225 guns. Totenkopf's commander, SS-Obergruppenführer Theodor Eicke, flew to visit his forward troops on 26 February and inadvertently tried to land by a village still held by the Russians. His plane was shot down and his mutilated body was not retrieved until the following day.

On the southern side of the salient the 1st Panzer Army's 40th Panzer Corps, which included the 5th SS Wiking Division, joined the attack, defeating Group Popov near Krasnoarmeysk. The Wiking and 7th and 11th Panzer Divisions caught four Soviet tank corps and four Soviet infantry divisions at Barvenkovo on 25 February. Fifty Soviet T-34 tanks were captured dug in to the south of the town; these were immobile, having run out of fuel.

The Soviets had interpreted these operations as a means of covering the 1st Panzer Army and Army Group Hollidt's withdrawal from the Mius to the Dnieper. In response, the Southwestern Front was instructed to hold the Germans on the Mius. However, von Manstein's success at Pavlograd had enabled his forces to push forward 240km, thereby threatening the recently liberated Kharkov. Indeed, von Manstein had unhinged the junction of the Soviet Southwestern and Voronezh Fronts. In the fighting the Soviet advances were stopped, having lost 23,000 dead, 9,000 captured, 615 tanks, 354 artillery pieces and 69 anti-aircraft guns.

Having once gained victory between the Donets and Dnieper, the Germans were ready to tackle those Red Army units in the vicinity of

Kharkov. Von Manstein was very clear on what was to happen: 'Our object was not the possession of Kharkov but the defeat – and if possible the destruction – of the enemy units located there.' This principally meant crushing the Soviet 3rd Tank Army using the 4th Panzer Army and Hausser's SS Panzer Corps.

Rybalko's defeat left newly liberated Kharkov open to the Germans once more. His 3rd Tank Army had to fight its way from the Kharkov area and Stalin agreed to a withdrawal to the Donets 65km away. 'In the end it was possible to bring the SS Panzer Corps round to the east. The city fell without difficulty,' recorded von Manstein in his usual no-nonsense manner, 'and we succeeded in cutting off the retreat of considerable numbers of the enemy across the Donets.' He was then able to launch the second phase of his powerful counteroffensive on 6 March 1943. On the left Das Reich, Totenkopf and Leibstandarte spearheaded the attack towards Kharkov. SS-Obersturmbannführer Kurt 'Panzer' Meyer led a kampfgruppe from the Leibstandarte, supported by Tiger tanks, to assault the Soviet defences at Valki to the southwest of Kharkov. Although they successfully overran the Soviet anti-tank defences, they ran into two dozen T-34 tanks.

On his left Totenkopf pushed past Kowjagi along with the army's tough Grossdeutschland Division, while on his right Das Reich moved forward towards the western outskirts of Kharkov. Totenkopf was temporarily held up fighting the Soviet 6th Guards Cavalry Corps.

Within four days they had pushed 16km north of the city, with Totenkopf taking the town of Dergachi. Although Hausser was ordered not to enter Kharkov with his tanks, he was determined to avenge his withdrawal three week earlier and prevent the army grabbing all the glory. He then swung southwards and spent five days clearing resistance from the high-rise housing blocks that lined the approaches to the city centre. Meyer's battle group became trapped in the city cemetery and had to withstand repeated Soviet attacks until help could reach them.

The tenacious defenders now found themselves caught between Leibstandarte and Das Reich. They did not want to give up the city again, and killed or wounded 1,000 Waffen-SS troops fighting to the last. The Germans responded by using artillery, flak guns and tanks to clear the apartment buildings that had been turned into strongpoints. The Luftwaffe was also called upon to pound pockets of resistance. Despite the bitter street fighting, by 14 March Hausser was back in control of Kharkov. After discovering smashed SS graves and mutilated bodies from the January battle, the Waffen-SS mopping up in Kharkov were disinclined to show any mercy. Behind them came the brutal Einsatzgruppen, SS-Sonderkommando units and the Gestapo. In the aftermath, up to 10,000 men, women and children would be murdered.

The day before Totenkopf had swung north of Kharkov. One of its panzergrenadier regiments, led by SS-Obersturmbannführer Otto Baum, supported by a panzer battalion, captured the crossing over the Donets at Chuguyev. This trapped a pocket of Rybalko's troops south of Kharkov. They were liquidated by Totenkopf, Das Reich, the 6th Panzer and 11th Panzer Divisions. Stalin gave Rybalko permission to break out and his 3rd Tank Army managed to fight its way past Chuguyev. Rybalko lived to fight another day. Hausser then sent kampfgruppen north to link up with Grossdeutschland, which was cutting its way towards the city of Belgorod.

The Germans claimed to have killed another 50,000 Soviets and captured 19,594 as well as destroying 1,140 tanks and 3,000 guns. These amounted to fifty-two divisions and brigades, but this did little to compensate for the loss of 250,000 Germans at Stalingrad. The bulk of the German casualties at Kharkov were borne by the three Waffen-SS divisions. In just over two months Hausser's tough SS Panzer Corps sustained over 11,500 casualties, the 1st SS Panzer Division losing 4,500 of these. The 5th SS also suffered thousands of casualties fighting with the 1st Panzer Army.

Von Manstein recorded with some satisfaction his remarkable victory at Kharkov, but also noted a lost opportunity against the Soviets' Kursk salient: 'On 14 March Kharkov fell to the SS Panzer Corps. At the same time, on the northern wing Army Detachment Kempf, the "Gross-Deutschland" Division, moved swiftly to Belgorod. The enemy once again threw in strong armoured forces to oppose it, but these were wiped out at Gaivoron.'

Although Hausser had saved the day, his panzer regiments had less than 50 per cent of the tanks they had started with. Furthermore, his assault on Kharkov had cost thousands of casualties and Rybalko's 3rd Tank Army had escaped. Hitler, though, was delighted when he heard what the Waffen-SS had achieved and bragged that the SS Panzer Corps was 'worth 20 Italian divisions'. Reich Propaganda Minister Goebbels found Hitler in a triumphant mood: 'He was exceptionally happy about the way the SS Leibstandarte was led by "Sepp" Dietrich. This man personally performed deeds of heroism and had proved himself a great strategist in conducting his operations.' Hitler ordered, to the delight of Himmler, that the SS get priority with manpower replacements and with deliveries of the new Panther tank.

Von Manstein assessed the situation:

> The capture of Kharkov and Belgorod marked the conclusion of Army Group's second counterblow, as the increasing muddiness of the ground did not permit any further operations. As a matter of fact the Army Group would have like to wind up by clearing out, with the help of Central Army Group, the enemy salient extending some distance westwards of Kursk in order to shorten the German front. The scheme had to be abandoned, however, as Central Army Group declared itself unable to cooperate. As a result the salient continued to constitute a troublesome dent in our front.

General von Mellenthin was very fulsome in his praise for von Manstein's achievements: 'Having regard to the problems which faced Manstein between December 1942 and February 1943, it may be questioned whether any achievement of generalship in World War II can approach the successful extrication of the Caucasus armies, and the subsequent riposte to Kharkov.'

In a stroke of genius von Manstein had defeated Stalin's Operation Star. He had saved Army Group South and put the Germans back on the Mius/Donets line. While very impressive, such a victory could not offset the disaster at Stalingrad. Although checked by the SS Panzer Corps, the Red Army threatened the whole region from Kharkov via Belgorod to Kursk. The latter would ultimately be Hitler's undoing on the Eastern Front.

Chapter Six

Waffen-SS and the Ghettos

The destruction of the Warsaw Ghetto by the SS was an appalling crime against humanity, and involved training units from the Waffen-SS. Occupied Warsaw was treated as a police state dominated by over twenty military bases and police stations by 1943. The German garrison included some 6,000 military police. German was made the official language and the Germans controlled the media. Many buildings and streets were given German names. Apartheid became a way of life with 'Germans Only' signs springing up throughout Warsaw. Any resistance was punishable by firing squad or hanging. Governor Frank authorized the Gestapo to shoot on suspicion in the autumn of 1943.

That year Warsaw was the scene of a horrific tragedy. It occurred because of the Nazis' abhorrent anti-Semitic policies. The previous year the Communist underground was becoming active and the Germans escalated the arrests, especially in the Polish capital. Mass shootings also occurred outside Warsaw. The Germans then decided to liquidate the Jewish Warsaw ghetto. This had not existed before the war but the Germans had started segregating the population on the basis of Jewish and non-Jewish in November 1939, barely two months after the invasion.

All non-Jews in the designated ghetto area were expelled and the city's Jews were herded in and surrounded by a wall, 20ft high and topped with barbed-wire. It was patrolled by armed guards who shot any Jews who were caught outside the ghetto without permission. There were two areas west of the Vistula, joined by a footbridge, that were known as the 'Large' and 'Small' ghettos. The former was some three times the size of its southern neighbour. The 'Little Ghetto' was filled with affluent residents and was considered the better place to be.

Himmler's Gestapo supervised the Jewish population with the assistance of the Ghetto Police and the Jewish Council. The two prisons taken over by the Gestapo, the Pawiak and the Serbia, were inside the ghetto perimeter. This meant that all those non-Jews who were arrested in

Warsaw were sent there for interrogation, torture, execution or shipment to the concentration camps.

In October 1940 Hitler's henchmen had decided that Warsaw would be a good place to gather all the Jews rounded up from the occupied territories. At first, those living in the ghetto were free to pass through the gates during the daytime as long as they were wearing a yellow star of David. Then, from 15 October 1941, the gates were sealed and the ghetto effectively became a concentration camp. The following year the forced deportations to the death camps started. By then children living on the streets had begun to die of starvation despite the presence of some well-stocked food shops.

Around 380,000 people from Poland and across Europe were crammed in the ghetto under the administration of the SS-appointed Council of Jewish Elders. Inside, communication was a problem, as the Poles spoke Polish or Yiddish and could not easily understand the German, French and Greek Jews. Every day 5,000 Jews were sent to the gas chambers at the Treblinka concentration camp. A Jewish policeman called Szmerling, known as 'the Jewish Torturer', oversaw this process at the Umschlagplatz (Collection Point) rail siding. This was located at the northern edge of the 'Large Ghetto' and was concealed from the rest of the area. The entrance was near the junction of Zamenhoff and Low Streets and led via a maze of pathways to an open square. From there the people were herded into an old hospital forecourt, where they spent the night before being put into cattle trucks in the morning. Around 150,000 Jews had been murdered in this way by early August 1942.

In October 1942 Himmler set up a little-known concentration camp within the city limits known as KZ Warschau. It consisted of five sub-camps linked by railway lines. Two were located in the area of the ghetto and two were near Warsaw's Western station. The fifth had served as a transit camp for prisoners of war. The KZ Warschau complex had space for over 41,000 inmates. It included gas chambers. The camps operated until August 1944, by which time up to 200,000 people had died there.

Although conditions in the ghetto were increasingly intolerable, the Jews remained compliant. By 10 September 1942 there were just 30,000 left, with another 40,000 in hiding across the city. The Polish Home Army offered to conduct diversionary attacks if there was a Jewish rising. However, the ghetto's leaders felt it best to cooperate with the Nazis, for fear of the consequences. Few were convinced by such a feeble argument. The younger Jews decided to fight back and created the underground Jewish

Combat Organization. The Home Army did what it could to assist, smuggling in small quantities of arms and ammunition.

Reichsführer Himmler made a surprise visit to Warsaw in January 1943 to see how the liquidation of the Jews was progressing. When SS-General Friedrich-Wilhelm Krüger, the police chief for Cracow, enquired why they had not been notified, he was swiftly put in his place: 'I did not know I was going to Warsaw and I did not inform you!' snapped Himmler in response. By now the remaining Jews were confined to an area just over 2.5 square kilometres. It was evident that at this rate the Jewish presence in the city could not last much longer.

Himmler, convinced his work was almost done, ordered the complete destruction of the Warsaw ghetto by 16 February 1943. In light of commitments elsewhere, especially at Stalingrad, there were too few resources to carry this out. SS-Oberführer von Sammern-Frankenegg was initially in charge but was relieved by SS-Brigadeführer Jürgen Stroop, who commenced the operation on 19 April.

Those units involved conspicuously included two reserve SS training battalions from the Totenkopf Division and the 8th SS Cavalry Division Florian Geyer. Members of training units from Leibstandarte, Das Reich, Polizei and Wiking were also present. There were two battalions of SS police and the army provided troops from several combat engineer battalions. In all, they numbered just over 2,000 men. These forces were backed by Lithuanian militia and some Polish police and firemen.

Himmler did not oversee things personally and scurried back to Berlin. Instead he sent Krüger to act as his observer. It was anticipated that this 'special action' would last just three days – in the event it took four weeks. Earlier in the month a Jewish revolt had brought the deportations to a halt. The resistance killed some of the Jewish collaborators and built barricades. These fighters belonged to either the Jewish Military Union or the Jewish Combat Organization. They then waited for the inevitable German assault. About 600 armed Jews stopped the initial attack but the Germans quickly brought up artillery with which to bombard their positions.

'Hardly had [the] operation begun,' reported Stroop, 'than we ran into strong concerted fire by the Jews and bandits.' A panzer and two armoured cars leading the advance were attacked with Molotov cocktails and forced to retreat. 'At about 1730 hours we encountered very strong resistance from one block of buildings, including machine gun fire,' said Stroop. A German assault party stormed the buildings but the Jews slipped away.

Stroop's first attack cost him twelve men. On the second night the Red Air Force bombed the city but it did little to help the uprising.

Slowly but surely the defenders were driven back by Stroop's artillery, flame-throwers and tanks. Stroop was baffled why the Jews did not simply give up. During the first phase of his operation it was possible to round up large numbers of Jews, but by the second phase it had become much more difficult. As soon as resistance was overcome, his forces would encounter another Jewish battle group of twenty to thirty men supported by a similar number of women. The latter fought with pistols and hand grenades.

By the fifth day Himmler was increasingly impatient for results. 'I therefore decided,' said Stroop, 'to destroy the entire Jewish area by setting every block on fire.' He hoped this would drive out the Jews but many preferred to perish. His flame-throwers rapidly helped set the ghetto ablaze. The flames were soon threatening the factories that made spare parts and uniforms for the Germans. However, when the Polish fire brigade turned up to try to prevent the fire from spreading, they were stopped by the SS. The Jewish fighters trapped in the burning buildings were forced to jump from the upper storeys. Those who survived tried to reach the neighbouring blocks, but most were too badly injured or were shot. According to Stroop, the defenders were 'going insane from the heat, the smoke and the explosions'.

Himmler was informed on 25 April that 27,464 Jews had been captured. Many were sent to Treblinka. The following day Stroop signalled Himmler to report that his forces had killed 362 Jews in battle and shot another 1,330. Just thirty prisoners were taken. In early May the SS rounded up all the members of the Jewish Council and executed them. Community Chairman Chernyakov took his own life. In London Shmul Zigelbaum, a member of the National Council of the Polish Government in Exile, also committed suicide to draw attention to the terrible plight of the ghetto. The fighting continued. Stroop even resorted to flooding the sewers in an effort to flush out the remaining Jews. His men also dropped smoke bombs down the manholes.

Jewish resistance was finally stamped out on 16 May 1943. '108 Jews, bandits and subhumans were destroyed,' reported Stroop that day. 'The former Jewish quarter of Warsaw is no longer in existence.' At 2015 hours his men blew up the Warsaw synagogue. According to Stroop, some 56,065 Jews were killed or captured. This included 7,000 killed in the ghetto and 6,929 sent to Treblinka. A further 6,000 perished in the flames of the burning ghetto. This left around 36,000 unaccounted for but it was assumed they had gone to the gas chambers. Stroop claimed he had lost sixteen dead and ninety wounded, but these figures seemed suspiciously low. In light of the involvement of the SS training units, the Waffen-SS clearly had innocent blood on their hands.

Stroop, who had been serving as the higher SS police leader in Greece, treated the destruction of the ghetto as if it were a military campaign rather than a police operation. His 75-page report and photographs were bound as an album called 'The Warsaw Ghetto is No More!' and presented to Himmler. The latter used this to convince Hitler that the Jews had built strongpoints in the ghetto and that the SS had fought a real battle. Stroop said the conduct of his men had been 'exemplary'. Warsaw's agony, though, was far from over.

In the wake of the destruction of the ghetto the Home Army stepped up its attacks on the occupiers. A casino frequented by German officers was blown up. The Gestapo and German police were attacked on the streets. Five insurgents gunned down SS-Oberscharführer Franz Bürkl, the deputy commander of Pawiak prison, on 7 September 1943. He and several colleagues were killed near the Gestapo headquarters in Szucha Avenue. His Alsatian dog, which had been trained to attack prisoners, was also shot. In the western Praga district fuel supplies for the German armed forces were set alight. Then on 8 October the Home Army blew up all the railway lines leading out of the city. This paralysed supplies being sent to the Eastern Front.

The ghetto in Warsaw was not the only one, as the Germans established them elsewhere, most notably at Lodz, where up to 250,000 Jews were gathered. In September 1942, 17,000 people were removed and killed. In December of that year another 25,000 suffered the same fate. There were just 74,000 left by 1 January 1944. Himmler gave the order to liquidate the Lodz ghetto on 10 June 1944. By the time the Red Army arrived there were just 850 people left. Himmler, thanks to the Waffen-SS, saw himself as a heroic warlord defending the Third Reich. In reality he was a murderous psychopath, who along with Hitler consigned millions of innocent people to their deaths.

Chapter Seven

Fought to a Standstill

In the summer of 1943 Hitler vainly hoped that the premier armoured divisions of the Waffen-SS would help him gain victory on the Eastern Front at a place called Kursk. General Hausser's command was now known as the 2nd SS Panzer Corps, comprising Leibstandarte, Das Reich and Totenkopf. A new 1st SS Panzer Corps was in the process of being formed in Belgium under Sepp Dietrich. Hausser's men were still with the 4th Panzer Army, which formed part of von Manstein's Army Group South. The latter also had the Wiking Division in reserve.

Stalin's operations had left him in possession of a vast salient around Kursk, flanked by enemy forces centred in the south on Kharkov and in the north on Orel. Belatedly Hitler's intention was to snip off the salient, employing all available means. Capitalizing on his spring victory on the German right, von Manstein's forces, spearheaded by Hoth's 4th Panzer Army and General Werner Kempf's Armeegruppe Kempf, were to attack northwards from Belgorod and Kharkov. At the same time General Model's 9th Army, belonging to Field Marshal von Kluge's Army Group Centre, was to strike south from Orel with the aim of meeting von Manstein at Kursk. This, Hitler hoped, would trap the Red Army inside the salient, but did not allow for all the Soviet reserves massed just outside it.

For the battle of Kursk Hitler gathered the greatest force ever assembled on such a small front. Barbarossa had flung 3,300 panzers at the Soviet Union along a 1,500km front, but for Operation Citadel Hitler squeezed 2,700 tanks along just 95km. Some 63 per cent of all battleworthy armour on the Eastern Front was assigned to von Manstein and von Kluge. While this sounded impressive, with 1,850 front-line panzers, 200 obsolete panzers and 533 assault guns divided amongst sixteen panzer and panzergrenadier divisions and three assault gun brigades, in reality the units were under-strength. By 1943 a panzer division had a theoretical strength of up to 200 panzers and 15,600 men. In reality the average strength was just seventy-three tanks. However, the 2nd SS Panzer Corps' divisions averaged 166 panzers and assault guns.

Hitler's generals were hoping that their newly deployed armour would help to counter the Red Army's growing strength. These new tanks offered the opportunity to destroy Soviet tanks at arm's length and stop them closing, which would prevent the panzers from being overwhelmed by superior numbers. Indeed, for the first time since Barbarossa, Hitler was fielding tanks and self-propelled guns that had a distinctive qualitative edge. He was placing great faith in his menagerie of tanks and fighting vehicles named after wild beasts, notably the Tiger, Panther, Rhinoceros, Bison and Grizzly Bear, plus the Ferdinand. It was anticipated that these would tear great holes in the ranks of the Soviet tank corps.

Crucially, none of these vehicles was available in decisive numbers. There were fewer than 90 Ferdinands, about 200 Panthers and about 100 Tigers; over 1,000 older Panzer IIIs and IVs remained the backbone of the panzer forces. Also making their debut were the Hummel, the Nashorn or Hornisse and the Marder III or Wespe. Again numbers available were a problem, as all three had only gone into production in early 1943, with about a hundred of each type ready for the summer. To help smash the Soviet fortifications were sixty-six newly built Grizzly Bear tanks comprising a short 150mm howitzer mounted on a Panzer IV chassis.

Stalin was not only well prepared for Hitler's massed panzers but also ready to switch over to his own offensive once they had been stopped. The Soviet defences around Kursk were formidable: by June 300,000 civilians had dug a series of eight in-depth defence lines stretching back almost 175km. Using brute strength, picks and shovels, they carved out approximately 5,000km of trenches. Just to be on the safe side, the reserve Steppe Front had dug its own defences to protect the eastern bank of the Don.

The fields of wheat and corn ripening in the summer sun concealed another deadly secret that would tear machines and men apart with ease. Soviet sappers toiled to sow over 40,000 mines across the length and breadth of the salient. In the killing grounds between the strongpoints they meticulously concealed about 2,400 anti-tank mines and a further 2,700 anti-personnel mines per 1.5km. Initially, as the panzers and supporting infantry blundered through these minefields they would be deluged by fire from howitzers and heavy mortars supported by anti-aircraft guns.

Once through the minefields the panzers would encounter 'pakfronts' consisting of batches of anti-tank guns supported by anti-tank rifles, machine guns and mortars. The plan was that along the expected axis of attack the panzers would meet clusters of guns whose job it was to funnel them into yet more minefields. There was little doubting the quite extraordinary volume of fire that the Central and Voronezh Fronts could call upon – at their disposal were 6,000 anti-tank guns, 20,000 guns and mortars and 920 Katyusha rocket batteries.

Operation Citadel commenced on 5 July 1943 but made little headway before it was checked. Hausser's 2nd SS Panzer Corps struck towards Bykovka with 365 tanks and 195 assault guns. The SS took the town, while other units cut the Oboyan-Belgorod road, only to be obstructed by the Soviet 96th Tank Brigade. Similarly, a penetration was made on the right flank but the panzers could get no further. The strength of the Soviet defensive positions stopped the Germans breaking through north of Belgorod, which was to cause Hoth problems.

On 6 July Leibstandarte and Das Reich with 120 tanks fought their way to the northwest up the Belgorod-Oboyan road. Around Yakovlevo Liebstandarte encountered forty-two tanks of the Soviet 1st Armoured Guards Tank Brigade. At 1,000 metres distance they engaged each other and after 60 minutes twelve T-34s had been destroyed. Rolf Erhardt, serving with Leibstandarte, did not get off to a good start. 'My experience as a panzer driver in the few days since 5 July consisted of a gigantic bang,' he said, 'when I ran over a mine on 6 July, and a few meaningless missions.'

By 1100 hours the Soviet 155th Guards Rifle Regiment had been forced out of the way and Das Reich had taken Luchki to the east of Yakovlevo. This cut a sizeable hole in the defences between generals Chistyakov and Kryuchenkin and put Hausser firmly amidst the Soviet second defence line. The slowness of Breith's forces exposed Hausser's flank to Soviet infantry counterattacks. This was a setback for von Manstein because it meant a third of his armour was being used as flank guards rather than as the cutting edge of the assault. The Soviet high command was not slow to react and during the night of 8/9 July they hastened to get Lieutenant General Rotmistrov's 5th Guards Tank Army, with 630 tanks and self-propelled guns, and the 5th Guards Army to the Prokhorovka region.

Leibstandarte suffered considerable attrition to its armour. Rudolf von Ribbentrop, the adjutant of the 1st SS Panzer Regiment, reported:

> The losses of my 6th Company so far had been heavy. Of the twenty-two tanks which we had started on 5 July, only seven were still operational on the evening of 11 July. Fortunately, not all of these had been

total losses, and a steady stream of repaired Panzer IVs was returning to the company.

At 0830 hours on 12 July Preiss's Totenkopf was to sweep to the west from the Psel as Wisch's Leibstandarte and Kruger's Das Reich cut through to the south of the town across the area between the Psel and the Prokhorovka railway. This was good rolling tank country covered in wheat and rye. Opposing them were the freshly arrived Soviet 2nd, 18th and 29th Tank Corps.

On the morning of the 12th, under cover of the Luftwaffe and artillery bombardment, the SS panzers sped forward in tight wedge formations to be met by Soviet rockets and shells. Von Ribbentrop with the 1st SS Panzer Regiment was caught by surprise and his men soon found enemy tanks amongst them:

> We had no time to take up defensive positions. All we could do was fire. From this range every round was a hit, but when would a direct hit end it for us? Somewhere in my subconscious I realized that there was no chance of escape. As always in such hopeless situations, all we could do was take care of what was at hand. So we knocked out a third, then a fourth T-34, from distances of less than 30 metres.

The fighting at Prokhorovka was confused and chaotic. Elements of Leibstandarte were dug in on Hill 252.2 when their positions were overrun by the Soviets' great tank charge. 'It all happened within such a short space of time that one hardly knew what to make of it,' said SS-Rottenführer Johannes Bräuer with Leibstandarte. 'In a flash we were wedged in by T-34s, firing in all directions, ramming each other because so many of them were exploding and burning.' He watched as the tanks charged through their advanced positions and came to grief in an anti-tank ditch.

Werner Kindler was serving with a platoon of self-propelled guns belonging to Leibstandarte near Prokhorovka. Under fire from two stationary Soviet T-34 tanks parked near a farm building, Kindler could not target them accurately because his gunsight and range finder were not working. 'I had to fire two straddling rounds, one long and one short and the third might hit,' he recalled. 'I tried it, was lucky in my estimation of distance and destroyed both tanks at a range of between 1,100 and 1,200m.'

Jochen Peiper and his Leibstandarte panzergrenadiers found enemy tanks right in their midst. He waited until a T-34 had rumbled by then ran

Adolf Hitler in Nuremberg in 1935 with the brown-shirted SA to the left and black-clad SS to the right.

(*Above left*) Hitler and Reichsführer Heinrich Himmler watching military exercises. Once in power, Hitler supported the expansion of the Waffen-SS as a way of countering the regular army. (*Above right*) Himmler created the Waffen-SS from Hitler's personal protection squad and it grew to thirty-eight divisions. (*Below left*) Josef 'Sepp' Dietrich seen here as an SS-Obergruppenführer. He is wearing the Knight's Cross with Oak Leaves and Swords. Dietrich was one of the Waffen-SS's most highly decorated soldiers and was one of only two to gain the Oak Leaves with Swords and Diamonds. (*Below right*) SS-Obergruppenführer Paul 'Papa' Hausser was also one of the most successful generals in the Waffen-SS.

Waffen-SS soldiers acting as a ceremonial guard for one of their fallen comrades during the invasion of Poland in the summer of 1939.

Waffen-SS troops from Leibstandarte-SS Adolf Hitler being awarded Iron Crosses by Sepp Dietrich in the summer of 1940. Hitler allowed Himmler's forces to share in Germany's early military victories.

Men of Leibstandarte during the invasion of the Balkans in early 1941. As a motorized infantry division, it took part in the attack on the Soviet Union that summer.

Reichsführer Himmler inspecting Red Army prisoners of war in Russia. The SS and Waffen-SS carried out numerous horrific atrocities on the Eastern Front throughout the war.

Panzer Mk III serving with the 2nd SS Panzergrenadier Division Das Reich.

Crew of a Panzer Mk III also belonging to Das Reich prior to the decisive Battle of Kursk in the summer of 1943.

Members of the 5th SS waiting to go into action in the Belgorod Salient. The Waffen-SS slowed the Red Army but could not save the day nor prevent the liberation of Belgorod and Kharkov following the Battle of Kursk.

Soviet troops with a captured Totenkopf Panzer Mk IV.

Leibstandarte and its supporting Tigers struggling through the mud on the Eastern Front at the end of 1943. The winter of 1943/44 proved a particularly challenging time for the Waffen-SS.

On the Eastern Front the Waffen-SS were reliant on the assault gun battalions for armoured support. The Sturmgeschütz III was a highly versatile weapon and was deployed throughout the Waffen-SS.

Hohenstaufen's Hummel self-propelled guns and ammunition carriers on their way to the Russian front.

Their dark base colour paint, presumably panzer grey, with patches of lighter camouflage in either olive green or reddish brown, made them stand out on the winter landscape.

This is what greeted the Waffen-SS panzer divisions as they deployed to Normandy. Allied bombers targeted the train yards and main roads to impede their movement.

after it, clambered onto the hull and up onto the turret. Yanking open the hatch, he dropped a bundle of hand grenades inside and jumped off just as the interior of the tank exploded. Peiper was impressed by his adjutant SS-Untersturmführer Werner Wolff and SS-Hauptsturmführer Paul Guhl, who rallied their men to ward off the enemy tanks and organized counterattacks.

Much of the action was at close quarters, with Leibstandarte's men engaging the T-34s with limpet mines and bundled charges. 'I watched as individual armoured personnel carrier drivers with their lightly armoured vehicles attempted to ram Russian tanks with their heavy armour broadside-on,' recalled SS-Obersturmbannführer Frey. 'It seemed to me to be a form of expression of the unshakeable will of our men to survive and win.' Company commander SS-Untersturmführer Erhard Gührs was horrified by the intensity of the fighting and the number of casualties inflicted on his command.

During shelling by Soviet artillery, Kindler's platoon commander SS-Untersturmführer Otto Bölk was struck by a large piece of shrapnel just beneath his collar bone. Although Kindler drove him to the main dressing station, Bölk was to die three days later. 'The mental pressure threatened to tear me apart,' lamented Gührs. 'One can tolerate the most terrible things ... no Russian tank survived. 148 of them lay mangled and crushed on the battlefield ... but it was a victory bought at a price.' Leibstandarte claimed 192 Soviet tanks on 12 July 1943. The following day Gührs was rendered temporarily deaf after his left ear-drum was ruptured.

Leading the 1st Panzer Company of Totenkopf's 3rd SS Panzer Regiment, Martin Steiger was involved in the horrors of this enormous swirling tank mêlée:

> None of us would forget that assault. The 'gully of death', so named by us because of the heavy losses, was to become everyone's terrible memory ... We had barely crossed the Psel river and conquered its steep banks, ... when the counterattacks by the Soviets began.

Just before noon Totenkopf's forces were attacked by the 29th Tank Corps and the 33rd Guards Rifle Corps. It was vital that they hold their ground or they would open the flank of their sister divisions. 'They came in battalion and regiment strength,' recalled Steiger. 'They came with whole brigades and divisions ... Tanks charged our lines in numbers that we had not experienced in such a small area during the Eastern Campaign.' Soviet artillery also took a punishing toll on Totenkopf. 'They moved their guns in battery strength in front of the bridgehead,' observed Steiger, 'and sent salvo after salvo into the riverbank and the occupied high ground.'

On both sides the tank crews ran out of armour-piercing ammunition and had to resort to high explosive until they could break off and take on reloads. Again von Ribbentrop experienced this: 'Just then I heard my loader report: "No more armour-piercing available!" We had expended our entire supply of armour-piercing ammunition. All we had left on board at that point were high-explosive rounds, which were ineffective against the heavily armoured T-34s.'

Although Leibstandarte and Das Reich attempted to defeat the 18th Tank Corps, the latter was reinforced and Hausser could not break Rotmistrov's second echelon of reserves. There was no escaping the fact that Hausser had been fought to a standstill by the end of the day and his divisions forced over to the defensive. To achieve this feat Rotmistrov sacrificed over half of his tank force and initially Stalin was furious until he learned the extent of the victory. 'The losses suffered by both sides were considerable and practically equal,' noted Rotmistrov. 'But the German advance was halted and the counterblow by our army's major forces was successful.'

Hausser lost hundreds of panzers; those that could have been repaired were beyond help because Rotmistrov remained master of the battlefield. The countryside surrounding Prokhorovka was a massive tank grave-yard. Almost everything had been incinerated. Rotmistrov said that 'more than 700 tanks were put out of action on both sides in the battle. Dead bodies, destroyed tanks, crushed guns and numerous shell craters dotted the battlefield.' After touring the destruction, he remarked 'There was not a single blade of grass to be seen; only burnt, black and smouldering earth throughout the entire depth of our attack – up to 8 miles [12km].'

Within six days Citadel had run out of steam. Decisively, it was the first occasion on which a German panzer offensive had been stopped before achieving a breakthrough. Von Manstein's forces managed 40km, losing 10,000 men and 350 panzers. Leibstandarte alone suffered 2,753 casualties, including 474 dead, and nineteen panzers were knocked out. In the north Model covered just 10km before being halted in front of Olkhovatka and Ponyri, losing 25,000 men, 200 panzers and 200 aircraft in the process. By 13 July von Manstein claimed that the forces facing him had lost 24,000 men captured as well as 1,800 tanks. Also that day von Manstein and Kluge were summoned to East Prussia, where Hitler informed them that Citadel must be called off as the Allies had landed in Sicily, thereby threatening Italy.

On 17 July 1943 Leibstandarte redeployed its armoured group west of Teterevino. 'When we were relieved,' noted Gührs, 'I had fifteen dead and more than thirty-five wounded.' Peiper awarded him the Iron Cross First Class. Werner Kindler was hospitalized in Kharkov after the wound in his right arm developed into blood poisoning. Later an officer turned up and told Kindler and a number of other men that they should discharge themselves as the division was heading for Italy. It seemed a much more promising posting than the Eastern Front.

Meanwhile Zhukov unleashed his massive counteroffensive, sweeping back the panzers' hard-won gains and pushing them out of their Orel and Kharkov salients to the north and south of the Kursk bulge. Operation Kutuzov ran from 12 July–18 August working to destroy the Germans' Orel bulge, which overlapped Operation Polkovodets from 3–23 August against the southern sector of the bulge. This pushed the Germans back, liberating both Belgorod and Kharkov. The success of this operation meant that Hitler's forces in Ukraine were obliged to withdraw behind the Dnieper and paved the way for the liberation of Kiev.

The battle for Kursk lasted fifty days and according to Soviet sources cost Hitler thirty divisions, including seven panzer divisions. Zhukov recorded their casualties as half a million men and 1,500 tanks. Both were undoubtedly grossly inflated figures. The Soviet victory came at a terrible price, however. Casualties for the three Soviet Fronts totalled 177,847 men and 1,614 tanks and self-propelled guns, five times greater than the Wehrmacht's losses. However, from this point on Hitler was on the defensive on the Eastern Front.

To Himmler's embarrassment, his elite 2nd SS Panzer Corps had been unable to give Hitler victory at Kursk, nor could it stop the Red Army from liberating Belgorod or Kharkov. Fortunately for him, Hitler was preoccupied by the Allied invasion of Sicily and the crisis it had triggered in Italy. It would be up to the Waffen-SS to retrieve the situation there and prevent the Italians from defecting to the Allies wholesale. Leibstandarte was about to pull off a most audacious coup.

Chapter Eight

Leibstandarte's Italian Coup

The Leibstandarte Division not only played a key role in preventing Italy from defecting to the Allies in 1943 but also deterred the Italian army from changing sides. After the surrender of the Axis forces in Tunisia, the writing was on the wall for Italian dictator Benito Mussolini. His fate was sealed when Operation Husky assaulted Italian soil with the invasion of Sicily. The fighting on the island triggered a political crisis in metropolitan Italy. Fifteen days after the invasion Mussolini was arrested in Rome and the new government under General Badoglio began secretly to negotiate with the Allies. Hitler was furious and did not trust Badoglio's claims that Italy would remain loyal to the German cause. General Jodl, Hitler's Chief of Operations urged caution, but the Führer knew the situation called for decisive action by his panzers before his southern flank became unhinged.

Just two days after Mussolini's fall, Hitler convened an emergency conference and presented four military options for dealing with Italy if she should abandon the Axis. The first envisaged a maritime or airborne rescue mission to secure Mussolini's release; the second was more ambitious and called for the seizure of Rome in order to reinstate Mussolini; the third proposed the total occupation of Italy; and the fourth planned for the capture or destruction of the Italian fleet. The last two were to be combined under the codename Axis. Hitler gambled that this would force Italy to carry on fighting in support of his war effort.

By late July Hitler, fearing the worst, drafted War Directive 49 outlining the occupation of Italy and all her overseas possessions. The directive was never issued, but on 31 July a series of separate orders were sent out informing commanders of what they should do if the Italians dropped out of the war. Although Hitler was dissuaded from putting the 3rd Panzergrenadiers onto the streets of Rome, he swiftly secured the Alpine passes between Germany and Italy and between Italy and France. Eight German divisions were assembled from France and southern Germany as Army Group B, ready to rescue those German forces in Italy.

Had the Italians acted decisively, they could have sealed the Alpine bridges and tunnels and cut off the Wehrmacht units already in Italy. The Italians had prepared the Brenner Pass for demolition and if they had blown this vital rail link it would have been out of action for at least six months. However, changing sides took time and Badoglio had to establish contact with the Allies and agree terms for an armistice before he could act against his former comrades in arms. Six weeks were to be wasted, leaving Italy vulnerable to Hitler's counterstroke.

According to the German Intelligence Bureau established to monitor Italian troop movements, the Italian army was suffering a severe ammunition shortage. Field Marshal Erwin Rommel, placed in command of securing Italy, was not surprised; he already had a low opinion of Italian industry after his experience with the ill-resourced Italian army in North Africa. Rather than defend the whole of Italy, the Germans drew up plans for a defensive line through the Apennines well to the north of Rome. During August the 1st SS and 25th Panzer Divisions and five infantry divisions crossed the frontier.

'General Feuerstein reports that a critical situation developed on the Brenner about midday yesterday [1/8/43],' recorded Rommel in his diary, 'when the Italians tried to hold up the advance of 44th Infantry Division. General Gloria had given orders for fire to be opened if 44th Division attempted to continue their march.' Fortunately, the local Italian troops did not obey the order and instead withdrew. The Italians concentrated 60,000 men in the Verona-Bolzano area, but in the face of the tanks of Leibstandarte, which crossed the Brenner pass on 3 August, chose not to deploy them. The panzers rolled over the frontier alert to possible resistance, but in the event the only casualties were two Tiger tanks that did not like the concrete roads: one overturned and another caught fire. In truth the 1st SS was a bit disorganized as most of its armour had been left in Russia for Das Reich and Totenkopf, and it had to re-equip en route. 'For the exhausted troops of the Leibstandarte,' observed SS-Oberscharführer Werner Kindler, 'the move to Italy was pleasant and interesting after the harsh months of privation in Russia.'

Belatedly, the Italians moved their Alpine, Julia and Trentina Divisions towards the Brenner. The road to the Italian naval base at La Spezia was also blocked. An SS patrol sent towards the base was unable to get any further than Aulla. On 9 August Rommel wrote to his wife, 'The situation with these unreliable Italians is extremely unpleasant. To our faces they protest their truest loyalty to the common cause, and yet they create all kinds of difficulties for us and at the back of it all seem to be negotiating.' The Germans also became alarmed by the Italians withdrawing their occupation forces from southern France and the movement of two Italian divisions from southern Italy to the north.

Rommel seemed concerned that the Waffen-SS was about to start aggressively confronting the Italians. That day he noted 'Oberführer Ostendorf, Chief of Staff of the 2nd SS Panzer Corps (Commander Gruppenführer Hausser) reported. I instructed him on the situation and drew his attention to the fact that it was the Führer's wish that we should take up our position in Italy on the basis of good understanding.' Leibstandarte first occupied Bolzano south of the Brenner and then moved west to Milan, where it was issued with new armoured vehicles and oversaw the disarming of Italian troops in the Po valley. Field Marshal Kesselring, commanding the German forces defending Sicily and southern Italy, was later to remark, 'Rommel ... would have been better advised if he had demobilized the Italians in the north, instead of letting them desert *en masse* to form the nucleus of the partisan guerrilla bands.'

SS-Oberscharführer Werner Kindler recalled, 'The APC [armoured personnel carrier] battalion arrived at Trento on 13 August and received orders to move the next day to the west side of Verona. In case of need, the Leibstandarte was to support the 44th Infantry Division in the Brenner sector from the south.' In central Italy Kesselring's 10th Army was activated, able to call on five divisions and another two near Rome. Up until the end of the Sicilian campaign and the successful escape of four German divisions from the island, Kesselring only had two covering the whole of southern Italy. The Italians were not pleased about the presence of these German troops and Kesselring's chief of staff, General Siegfried Westphal, spent a great deal of time trying to smooth ruffled feathers.

On 15 August Rommel travelled to Bologna to discuss the situation with General Roatta, chief of staff of the Italian army. To his alarm, German intelligence indicated that the Italians intended to either poison him or have him arrested; in response he took German panzergrenadiers to secure the conference building beforehand. Roatta claimed that the withdrawal of Italian troops from southern France was to help fight the British and that the Alpine Division had moved north to resume garrison duties. He confirmed that a second division had moved north to secure the railways from sabotage. Roatta dismissed any ideas that these refitting formations were in any way a threat to German interests.

Roatta reiterated that the defence of Italian soil against the Allies must be left to the Italian army, although the Germans could take over air defence. He also tried to get rid of the powerful 1st SS Panzer Division by suggesting it be sent to Sardinia; he also suggested that other German forces should be moved into southern Italy. The meeting broke up without agreement and the following day Italian representatives offering Italy's unconditional surrender approached the British Ambassador in Madrid.

After securing Sicily by mid-August, the Allies then invaded mainland Italy at Reggio, Salerno and Taranto at the beginning of the following month. To defend southern Italy, Kesselring had the 10th Army, by now consisting of two panzer corps and one flak corps. By September the Italian army had twenty-one divisions in mainland Italy, although half of these were of poor quality, plus four in Sardinia and another thirty-six overseas. To fend off a German takeover of northern and central Italy the Italian army had eight infantry divisions and two motorized/armoured divisions, supported by another eight weak infantry divisions. Against these forces the Germans could field about sixteen highly experienced divisions. Rommel's Army Group B in the north consisted of three corps, with the Leibstandarte assigned to the 51st Mountain Corps.

If the Allied invasion fleet gathered off Naples on 8 September had sailed north and put its forces ashore near the Italian capital, the Italian army would probably have used its remaining tanks against the Germans and Hitler would have abandoned Kesselring and his eight divisions. Instead fate played a cruel hand and the American 5th Army landed not near Rome but at Salerno south of Naples. Kesselring's headquarters at Frascati, near Rome, lost all communication with the outside world on the 8th after an American air raid killed nearly a hundred of his staff.

'It was made known to the Leibstandarte divisional staff towards 1800 hours on 8 September that Italy had capitulated,' said Werner Kindler. 'II Panzer Corps was ordered to the highest state of alert.' After the Italian armistice with the Allies, Hitler issued the code word Achse (Axis). When the Germans learned of the armistice through a BBC broadcast, Kesselring was alerted.

To the north Werner noted:

In Verona the 1st SS-Panzergrenadier Regiment and the SP-group disarmed the Italian garrisons, and 650 officers and 16,599 other ranks at Cremona were made prisoner of war by the 1st and 3rd

Battalions. Once the disarmament process was almost complete, it was announced that after handing over their weapons the Italians would be allowed to return to civilian life or could enlist in the Wehrmacht as auxiliaries. Martial law came into force throughout the corps area.

For a day or two the fate of those German forces in central and southern Italy hung in the balance. A tense stand-off took place between two German divisions and five Italian divisions equipped with tanks near the Italian capital. General Westphal, trying to reach General Roatta at Monte Rotondo, found himself obstructed by troops from the Italian Grenadier Division. Fearing that something was wrong, Westphal insisted on seeing Roatta, and upon his arrival the Italian general informed him that Italy had signed an armistice with the Allies. Returning to Frascati, Westphal acted quickly and with more aggression than Kesselring would have liked. He called a conference with the general staff of General Carboni's Italian Corps, which was responsible for Rome.

Once the Italian officers were gathered, Westphal expressed his regret that they were no longer comrades in arms, having served alongside them in North Africa. He said they had one of two options: they could lay down their arms or suffer Stuka dive-bomber attack. To support his threat Field Marshal von Richthofen had eighty fighter aircraft at his disposal in Italy. The next day an Italian officer arrived and signed the surrender order for the Carboni Corps. Kesselring and Westphal heaved a sigh of relief – their coup would be bloodless.

Elements of Leibstandarte moved into Turin and Milan. Once it became known that the Italians in the south had sided with the Allies, all disarmed Italian soldiers were treated as prisoners of war and shipped to Germany. By 11 September Leibstandarte had rounded up 106,046 Italian troops. However, many had escaped into the mountains southwest of Turin. Werner noted with some satisfaction that 'The men of the Leibstandarte profited much by equipment and vehicles from Italian stocks.'

Hitler's next move was to 'rescue' Mussolini. For this job he called on SS-Sturmbannführer Otto Skorzeny. On 12 September Mussolini was snatched from the Hotel Albergo-Rifugo 160km from Rome. A German glider was landed right in the hotel grounds, delivering Waffen-SS commandos and an Italian general. The men guarding Mussolini were unsure what to do; some simply fled, while the others faced the quandary of whether to open fire on an Italian general, or indeed their former leader.

At the behest of Skorzeny and Mussolini, they decided to lay down their arms. Skorzeny hurried the former dictator to a small plane and he was flown to Vienna via Rome. A few days later he arrived at Rastenburg to meet his saviour. Sepp Dietrich was far from happy when he was instructed to act as escort for Mussolini's mistress.

While the men of the Leibstandarte found the Italian sun a relief from the rains and snow of the Eastern Front, their occupation duties in Italy were not without incident. Understandably they were frustrated that they were not employed in throwing back the Anglo-American invaders, but instead were acting as Mussolini's private security force. Kesselring was likewise disappointed that Rommel's eight divisions, including Leibstandarte, were left in the north. 'Two of them', he said, 'would have sufficed to repel the Allied landing at Salerno.'

When SS-Standartenführer Joachim 'Jochen' Peiper, commander of the 3rd SS Panzergrenadier Battalion, received reports that pro-Allied Italian troops had taken two of his NCOs prisoner at Boves, he took matters into his own hands. He sent a company to rescue them but this was attacked. In retaliation he employed 150mm self-propelled guns to shell Boves and in the process killed thirty-four men, women and children. Peiper claimed: 'I am of the opinion that our action to free our encircled comrades in Boves nipped in the bud the Italian army's attack, for the army fell apart and no attack ever took place on Cueno [province] or Turin.' He also reasoned that 'our one-time intervention prevented further immeasurable casualties which would have resulted from continual Italian attacks'. Troops from Leibstandarte were also reportedly involved in rounding up Italian Jews in the Lake Maggiore area to be shipped to the concentration camps. The 1st SS was not the only Waffen-SS division to commit atrocities in Italy.

In November the division was sent back to the Eastern Front. Shipped to Tarnopol via Lvov, it took up positions on the southern flank of the Kiev salient for a counterattack towards Zhitomir. This was launched on 19 November 1943 and although Zhitomir was taken, it subsequently had to be relinquished. Leibstandarte was then sent to Brusilov where it fought the 5th and 8th Guards Armoured Corps and the 1st Guards Cavalry Corps. Although it and the 1st and 7th Panzer Divisions trapped the Soviet armies at Meleni, a lack of manpower forced the Germans to retreat. In the meantime Peiper had been appointed commander of Leibstandarte's 1st SS Panzer Regiment.

Meanwhile, in northern Italy loyalist pro-Fascist Italian troops under German officers and non-commissioned officers were formed into an SS-brigade. Sent to southern Germany for training, they were then ordered back to Italy to conduct anti-partisan duties. The SS-Freiwilligen Legion Italia was commanded by SS-Brigadeführer Peter Hansen. In April 1944 some of these troops, notably the 29th SS Fusilier Battalion, fought against the Allies at Anzio, where they suffered heavy casualties. They were supported by the Vendetta Battalion from the Italian Fascist Black Brigades. The latter suffered 340 casualties from a force of 650. These units fought alongside the 36th SS Panzergrenadier Regiment from the newly formed 16th SS Panzergrenadier Division Reichsführer-SS.

Such was the Italians' performance that Himmler ordered: 'Because of the demonstration of courage and devotion to duty displayed by the volunteers of the Italian SS, they are designated as units of the Waffen-SS, with all the rights and duties which that implies.' In September 1944 they became the 9th Waffen-Grenadier Brigade der SS Italienische Nr 1. Although still only at brigade strength, in April 1945 the unit was renamed the 29th Waffen-Grenadier Division der SS Italienische Nr 1, which briefly fought Italian partisans and the US Army just as the war came to a close. Some were fortunate enough to surrender to the Americans, but others were massacred by the partisans.

Italians from South Tyrol also served in the 24th Waffen Gebirgs Division der SS Karstjäger, although these were mainly Volksdeutsche. The division included Yugoslav recruits from Croatia and Serbia in its ranks. Paul Hausser was far from impressed with Karstjäger, concluding, 'The more or less volunteer mixture of nations, Germans, Italians, Slovenes, Croats, Serbs and Ukrainians, formed no true combat unit. It befell that somewhere in March or April 1945 they offered an armistice to Tito's partisans.' This was a little unfair as a kampfgruppe consisting of the German-speaking part of the division, under SS-Brigadeführer Heinz Harmel, surrendered on 9 May 1945, a day after the official end of the war in Europe.

Chapter Nine

Das Reich and the Maquis

Throughout late June and early July 1944 both the American and British armies had found themselves up against Hitler's battle-hardened Waffen-SS divisions. Just four weeks earlier, on 7 June 1944, the very day after the start of the Allied landings in Normandy, General Heinz Lammerding, commander of Das Reich, received the order to be ready to march north. In the run-up to D-Day, while Lammerding grappled with getting his division up to strength and carrying out its training, the French Maquis or Resistance began to make their presence increasingly felt. Frustratingly for Lammerding and his men, the actions of the Maquis ensured that what should have been a three-day journey took Das Reich a fortnight. Lammerding signalled General Walter Krüger's 58th Reserve Panzer Corps in Toulouse with his catalogue of woes; he was understandably annoyed that his panzer division was wasting its valuable time fighting the Maquis, which was a role that should be handled by the local security divisions. Large areas were under the Resistance's control, leaving local German forces surrounded and cut off.

By June Colonel René Vaujour claimed to have 5,000 Resistance fighters under his command. Three months earlier he had ordered his men in the event of an Allied invasion to cover the bridges over the Dordogne in south Corrèze and northern Lot. Vaujour correctly assessed that Das Reich would move north to reinforce a German counteroffensive and it would fall to him and his men to obstruct any such move. The SAS was also to conduct Operation Bulbasket with the same goal.

Lammerding's response to the Resistance was to treat them as a partisan army, with predictably brutal results. Throughout May his command undertook anti-Resistance operations with units raiding Montpezat-de-Quercy, St Céré and Bagnac, Cardaillac Lauze. This culminated on 2 June 1944 when, following a Maquis attack, the village of Terrou was burned along with twenty-nine surrounding farms. When the SS discovered a Resistance arms dump at Ggeac, a thousand townspeople were arrested and deported.

On top of the Maquis attacks, only 40 per cent of Lammerding's panzers were serviceable and 70 per cent of his half-tracks and prime movers. Prior to the march north following D-Day, repeated calls for spare parts had fallen on deaf ears, which meant broken-down vehicles could not be moved and therefore required infantry to guard them. Six depots had to be set up for the waifs and strays and efforts to commandeer local civilian vehicles produced few results.

The Resistance first really made themselves known at Groléjac after Lammerding moved into the Dordogne region. As Das Reich approached the river crossing, the French, although unprepared, opened fire. Aged 14, Maurice Jadel recalled, 'The Maquis had driven unexpectedly into the German column and Marcel Malatray, leader of the group, was wounded and later died. The driver was killed outright. I was nearby and [the] Das Reich officer in command, using impeccable French, ordered me to push the stalled vehicle out of the way.'

Jadel had a narrow escape, for the troops of Das Reich, upon being shot at, immediately returned fire on the Maquis positions in a nearby hotel. 'I deliberately took my time in pushing the vehicle out of the way,' said Jadel. 'The troop carriers were lined up with their engines running and steel-helmeted German soldiers were glaring down at me ... Once I had completed the task, I walked very slowly away until I turned the corner then ran and joined the Maquis on the railway line. The tanks and troop-carriers stretched back for at least 2km ... an overwhelming sight.'

At Tulle railway station Lammerding's column was yet again ambushed and the resulting firefight left dead on both sides. His patience was running out and on 9 June a proclamation was posted throughout the city: 'Forty German soldiers have been murdered in the most abominable fashion ... policemen and gendarmes have made common cause with the communist gangs ... forty German soldiers have been murdered ... 120 Maquis will be hanged ... for the future, three Maquis will be hanged for every soldier wounded, ten for every soldier killed ...'

Lammerding's progress had not been good. By the 10th his command was scattered across the Lot, Corrèze and Haute-Vienne, with broken-down panzers and Sturmgeschütz assault guns stretching from Tulle to Montauban. He was also furious that Das Reich continued to waste its time fighting the Resistance and signalled General Krüger saying:

> The task of eliminating this danger must be transferred to the local divisions. Panzer divisions in the fifth year of the war are too good for

this. In the division's opinion, the local forces are quite capable of maintaining order if they are pulled together sharply, given transport and led energetically. Their present isolation is a standing invitation to the terrorists.

In his heart Lammerding must have known there was not much that could be done about the lamentable condition of the local second-rate infantry divisions.

In response, General Johannes Blaskowitz's Army Group G, head-quartered in Toulouse, requested Hitler's High Command provide troops to replace Das Reich once it had left Corrèze and Dordogne. A battle group from the 11th Panzer Division (comprising two infantry battalions, an artillery battalion and an anti-tank company) was assembled with instructions to contact the 2nd SS in Tulle. These forces arrived on the 11th and Lammerding rolled north to Limoges.

In the meantime, the situation boiled over at Oradour-sur-Glane, 20km northwest of Limoges. Male villagers were herded into the church and the village torched on 10 June 1944. In the bloody mayhem 646 people were murdered by members of SS-Panzergrenadier Regiment Der Führer under SS-Sturmbannführer Otto Diekmann (who was subsequently killed in action on 30 June). The actions of Das Reich at Oradour-sur-Glane and elsewhere during the march north have been hotly debated ever since. What is clear is that Lammerding's men over-reacted and the distraction of fighting the Resistance was time-consuming and clearly frustrating to the point of killing unarmed civilians.

Das Reich had now suffered seventeen dead and thirty wounded; the Maquis, fighting an uneven battle, lost 500 killed and 1,500 taken prisoner. The French figures included civilian executions. On 12 June Blaskowitz finally took personal control of the anti-partisan operations and requested that the German High Command formally declare the southwest a battle zone. The Resistance then found itself at war with Army Group G.

Major Stuckler, issuing Das Reich's order of the day on the 10th, was much more optimistic, noting:

In the course of its advance, the division has already dealt with several Resistance groups. The armoured regiment has succeeded, thanks to a neatly executed surprise attack, in carrying out a knife stroke – a coup de filet – against a band organized in company strength [at Bretenoux].

The division is now proceeding to a rapid and lasting clean-up of these bands from the region, with a view to becoming speedily available to reinforce the fighting men and join the line on the invasion front.

The Der Führer regiment and the reconnaissance battalion crossed the Loire at Saumur and Tours, where the bridges remained standing, on 13 June. However, due to the lack of transport, by the end of June some units remained stranded in the south of France and it was not until late July that the last elements began heading north. Only 11,195 of Lammerding's total strength of 17,283 men had reached Normandy by 1 July. Nonetheless the Allies in Normandy faced a very tough and experienced force.

SS-Obersturmbannführer Christian Tychsen commanded Das Reich's 2nd SS-Panzer Regiment. By the beginning of June he had fifty-four Panzer IVs (of which ten were in the workshops), thirty-nine Panthers and forty-one Sturmgeschütz III assault guns. Further deliveries of armour meant that the 2nd SS was to field a total of eighty-three Panzer IVs, eighty Panthers and forty-five Sturmgeschütz IIIs during the fighting in Normandy. Divisional self-propelled artillery consisted of five Hummels and six Wespe, along with the usual towed artillery batteries.

The SS-Panzergrenadier regiments also had 249 armoured personnel carriers. Despite this impressive inventory, resupply with spares and ammunition was a major problem for Lammerding, especially parts for the motor transport. The division had less than half the required number of trucks and out of the 1,821 it did have, only 617 were operational. It was obvious that the division would have problems getting anywhere in a hurry. In May Lieutenant Fritz Langanke was ordered to survey the local railways to assess their suitability for moving the panzer regiment.

Arriving in Normandy, SS-Sturmbannführer Otto Weidinger, who had replaced Sylvester Stadler as commander of Der Führer, expected to take part in a major counterattack to drive the Allies back into the channel. Instead his men were directed to plug a gap in the line besides Panzer Lehr, whose commander, General Fritz Bayerlein, was amused when he heard they wanted to take the offensive, remarking, 'It will be a miracle if we can stand where we are.'

During June, Battlegroup Weidinger, consisting of elements of Panzergrenadier Regiments 3 and 4 along with the 9th SS, resisted the British Epsom offensive. Then, during July, elements fought in the American sector. Battlegroup Weidinger came under General von Choltitz's 84th Corps on 5 July, when it was tactically attached to the 353rd Infantry Division for the defence of La Haye Du Puits and Monte Castre. They launched a counterattack against the Americans on the afternoon of the 7th, striking the American 79th Infantry Division on the recently won Montgardon ridge south of La Haye Du Puits. The Germans inflicted 2,000 casualties, but American tanks, tank destroyers and artillery claimed three panzers and the attack died out. Such was the 79th's mauling that it had to withdraw to be refitted.

Holding a line between Les Landes and Lemonderie, two companies from Das Reich were attacked by the US 83rd Infantry Division on 7–8 July. The US 9th and 30th Infantry Divisions pushed on Lé Desert after crossing the Vire-Taute canal. In the meantime, the US 3rd Armored Division attacked northwest of St Lô. Commanding Panthers from the Das Reich 2nd SS Panzer Division, SS-Unterscharführer Ernst Barkmann knocked out his very first Sherman tank on 8 July 1944, claiming two more on the 12th. The next day his luck nearly ran out when American armour hidden amongst the Normandy hedgerows almost killed him. He recalled:

First came a clattering noise; then, from behind the hedge, the rounded hull of a Sherman heaved into view ... and behind it, five more. The first armour-piercing rounds hit the leading tank in the hull. Smoke appeared from its open turret hatch. The other Shermans had come to a halt. A second round from the Panther knocked off one of the leading tank's tracks. The hedge behind which it had sought shelter had a hole in it as large as a man. The damaged Sherman was returning fire ... a third round hit its turret. The four tanks that were left opened fire with their machine guns, which merely tore jagged holes in the Panther's anti-mine coating. One of them was unwise enough to show its side. A fourth round went right through it. Three of the crew got out ...

Although the Americans moved their anti-tank guns behind Barkmann's panzers, he surprised them using high explosive shells and his bow machine gun. In response, a shell skidded off his turret and he hit the gun with his second shot. The American gunners struck his turret again and a fire broke out. Although he and his crew were forced to bail out, they later got the tank back to their repair company.

On the 9th elements from Das Reich then ran into the 30th Infantry Division's right flank near Lé Desert. The SS, though, were driven back by American artillery fire. However, also on the 9th Das Reich caught a company of the US 743rd Tank Battalion pursing two Panzer IVs near Lé Desert. The surprised American tanks reeled back with the loss of twelve Shermans. By the close of the 10th the division had claimed ninety-eight enemy tanks destroyed in the space of just eight days. On the 13th Das Reich knocked out another thirty American tanks.

The SS Panzertruppen's morale was high, but the Americans' limitless resources dismayed them. Das Reich, like all the other panzer divisions in Normandy, was plagued by ammunition and fuel shortages. Due to the lack of supplies, by 11 July they had lost twenty-two tanks, seven guns and seven lorries. By the end of the month the 2nd SS was the only significant formation rated suitable for offensive operations within the 7th Army. It had thirty-seven Panzer IVs, forty-one Panthers and twenty-five Sturmgeschütz assault guns available for combat. It was tasked with stopping the Americans seizing the main coastal road that led to Avranches, the best north–south route in the Cotentin peninsula. Das Reich at the time of Cobra was supported by two 105mm artillery companies from Artillery Regiment 275, formally part of the infantry division of the same number.

On 26 July Das Reich rushed to fill the gap left by Bayerlein's decimated Panzer Lehr, having deployed its panzer regiment to the St Aubin-du-Perron area south of the Périers-St Lô road the previous day. Some of those tanks south of Périers were sent southeast to Marigny. Two companies from Das Reich counterattacked elements of the US 3rd Armored Division on the outskirts of the town that afternoon.

It was now that Ernst Barkmann's Panther was caught in the open; attacked by four fighter-bombers, it burst into flames. Working through the night, his men had the tank up and running again by the morning. At the village of le Lorey, north of the St Lô-Coutances road, they were confronted by comrades fleeing American Shermans driving from St Lô, where Das Reich's panzers were supposed to be deployed. Barkmann decided to try to halt elements of the US 3rd Armored Division trundling down the Coutances road on the 27th, at the junction of the Lorey road and the N172 between Coutances and St Lô.

When the Americans drove into view, Barkmann's gun-layer Poggendorf opened fire at 200 metres. The Americans tried desperately to back off but soon the road was a twisted mess of smashed jeeps and half-tracks.

Although the roar of the gun, the clang of the spent shell cases and the hum of the ventilator sucking out the noxious cordite fumes deafened his crew, Barkmann kept a constant look out. Two Sherman tanks advancing to the left of the road were dealt with, though not before his Panther took two shuddering hits to its armour. The Americans then called in fighter-bombers to shift the stubborn Barkmann, which damaged his tank's running wheels. Again two more Shermans trying to outflank him found their guns had no effect and paid a deadly price.

Barkmann's efforts to halt the 3rd Armored destroyed up to nine Sherman tanks, but his tank was damaged and had lost a track. Miraculously, although his driver was wounded, they managed to withdraw to Neufborg. Despite holding up the Americans, the end result was still the same. Left behind by the rest of Das Reich, Barkmann's Panther, with two others in tow, reached Coutances on 28 July only to find the Americans already in the city. Two days later Barkmann had lost all three panzers and he and the crews made their way back to their own lines on foot.

Meanwhile panzers of SS-Obersturmführer Schlomka's 2nd Company, previously deployed east of Carentan, were ordered to hold the Americans west of Périers. Following a briefing by Tychsen, Fritz Langanke and his platoon moved into position to be greeted by heavy artillery fire. Langanke's tank then got stuck in a ditch and had to be towed out. The American advance, though, was brought to a brief halt and at nightfall the panzers withdrew. The 2nd Company was then ordered to block the St Lô-Coutances road.

The ever-present fighter-bombers did all they could to hamper the 2nd SS. Langanke witnessed:

> As soon as we turned onto it, in the direction of St Lô, we were engulfed in the heaviest fighter-bomber activity I experienced during the war. The only thing similar occurred during the breakout from the encirclement at Falaise/Trun. The light coloured ribbon of concrete of this road was littered, as far as we could see towards Coutances, by wrecks of vehicles and other military equipment. Some of it was burning, smoking, entangled, or just abandoned. Here and there we saw dead or wounded soldiers. Once our small unit had been spotted driving on the road, fighter-bombers dived on us from all sides, dropping bombs and firing onboard weapons. To catch our breath, we pulled off the road to the right for a while into an orchard. That did not help very much as that area was being hammered as badly.

Like all German tank crews, they faced the dilemma of bailing out or staying inside their tanks: either option could be equally fatal. In this instance Langanke's panzer drove on, passing a knocked-out Panther. He observed:

> As far as we could see along the road, there were German and American vehicles of various types, cars, trucks, half-tracks, tanks, some of them burning and entangled. In between, German and American ambulances were driving back and forth, flying Red Cross flags, recovering dead and wounded who were strewn on the road or still in their vehicles.

There was a pause before the American armour opened fire amidst the chaos and Langanke's panzer beat a hasty retreat and took up an ambush position. That evening Schlomka appeared and guided the panzer crew back to the regiment in the Coutances area. On the night of 29/30 July elements of Das Reich, including Langanke, battered their way out of the Coutances pocket, allowing troops from a number of divisions to escape.

SS-Obersturmführer Otto Baum, assuming command of both Das Reich and the 17th SS Panzergrenadier Division, with his corps commander's permission withdrew his troops towards Brehal southwest of Coutances to avoid the westward-moving American army. This, though, was countermanded by General Hausser, 7th Army's commander, who ordered them towards Percy to the southeast.

A major battle ensued at the crossroads southwest of Notre-Dame-de-Cenilly as Das Reich attempted to force a passage towards Percy on 28 July. One column of thirty panzers and 2,500 men, led by a Hummel 150mm self-propelled gun named 'Clausewitz', became trapped after the lead vehicle was knocked out. In the subsequent fire-fight the American 2nd Armored Division devastated most of this column. At La Pompe about fifteen Panzer IVs from Das Reich and 200 paratroops successfully forced the Americans to fall back, but they could get no further.

Unable to get through, the bulk of Das Reich and the 17th SS were trapped around Roncey west of La Pompe. American fighter-bombers caught 122 tanks, 259 other vehicles and eleven pieces of artillery in the Roncey pocket on the 29th, reaping a cruel harvest of tangled metal. The 2nd SS Panzer's Panzerjäger battalion lost some of its self-propelled guns, most notably several Panzerjäger 38(t) were abandoned in the shattered streets of Roncey.

About 1,000 dazed survivors with almost 100 vehicles, including several dozen armoured vehicles, escaped the Roncey pocket and broke through at St Denis-le-Gast to the south. By dawn the town was back in American hands and the Germans had suffered 754 casualties and lost a further seven panzers and eighteen other vehicles. Only a battalion of panzers from Das Reich and elements of the 17th SS managed to escape the chaos. Near La Baleine, to the southeast of St Denis, RAF Typhoons again caught those trying to flee, knocking out nine panzers, eight armoured vehicles and another twenty vehicles, leaving dead Germans strewn everywhere.

Christian Tychsen, Das Reich's panzer commander, was killed at the crossroads near Cambry southwest of Roncey on 28 July when the vehicle he was travelling in bumped into an American patrol. Rudolf Enseling, commander of the 1st Battalion, succeeded him. Two days later the Americans reached Granville, about 17km northwest of Avranches, where Barkmann's Panther had retreated to; he and his crew abandoned their tank the following day.

In order to close the gaping gap between the Vire and Avranches, Hitler foolhardily decided to counterattack, a move that would force his remaining panzers further into the noose. For the attack on Avranches on 6 August Das Reich with just twenty to twenty-five tanks was to take Mortain and the hills to the west. Elements of Panzer Lehr's reconnaissance battalion were assigned to Das Reich to screen their southern flank. It proved highly successful in its mission, though groups of Americans remained cut off in their rear.

Lammerding's men swept into Mortain, brushing aside elements of the American 30th Infantry Division by 0230 hours, and attacked the high ground to the west. However, an American infantry battalion holding Hill 317 blocked any further progress by the 2nd SS towards Avranches. The obstruction could have been bypassed but this would have exposed the panzers to American fire from the hill. General Hausser visited Das Reich's command post at 1000 on the 8th and told them the attack would be renewed after the 47th Panzer Corps had received additional tanks promised by Hitler. The 9th Panzer Division was to be diverted to Mayenne to seal up a breakthrough in the 81st Corps' front line. At 1400 hours Das Reich counterattacked the northern flank of the American 35th Infantry Division, which had moved south of Mortain between the 30th Infantry and the 2nd Armored at Barenton.

Then the Americans broke through north of Mortain in the 1st SS Panzer Division's area, threatening Das Reich's northern flank, and the division came under heavy artillery fire. American Shermans were also soon pushing up from Barenton. The failure of Hitler's ill-advised Avranches/Mortain counterattack sealed the fate of the 5th Panzer Army, Panzergruppe Eberbach and Hausser's 7th Army.

At 1800 hours on 10 August Das Reich came under the control of General Krüger's 58th Reserve Panzer Corps, having previously been under the operational direction of General von Funck's 47th Panzer Corps. The division was then pulled back to the main line of resistance just to the east of Mortain. Elements of Das Reich were involved in heavy fighting and on the 11th alone destroyed nineteen American tanks. Despite all this fierce action, the division still had well over 13,000 men and was far from destroyed. Successfully withdrawing eastwards, Das Reich did not end up in the Falaise pocket and counterattacked against the advancing Allies to help some of those who were trapped to escape.

To the south of Vimoutiers two battlegroups from the 2nd SS struck towards Neauphe-sur-Dive and St Lambert. Under pressure from German paratroops within the pocket, the Polish 1st Armoured Division was forced to relinquish control of some of the roads and up to 4,000 paratroops escaped, supported by three tanks from Das Reich. When it was clear that all was lost, Das Reich made for the Seine. During the campaign the division claimed over 200 enemy tanks for a combat loss of seventy-five panzers, with another thirty abandoned around Falaise for want of fuel and spare parts.

Chapter Ten

Hitlerjugend at Ardenne Abbey

After all the bloodletting on the Eastern Front, many of the premier divisions of the Waffen-SS were next to find themselves resisting the opening of the Allies' Second Front in Normandy. Dietrich's 1st SS Panzer Corps came under the control of Panzergruppe West, which was part of Rommel's Army Group B tasked with defending northern France and the Low Countries. Dietrich's command comprised the Leibstandarte and Hitlerjugend Panzer Divisions, plus the 17th SS Panzergrenadier Division Götz von Berlichingen. Das Reich was also in France, but under the control of the 47th Panzer Corps. These divisions would be reinforced by Hausser's 2nd SS Panzer Corps.

Hitler dithered on D-Day, 6 June 1944, in the face of the Allied land-ings. After midday he passed control of the 12th SS Panzer Division Hitlerjugend over to General Friedrich Dollman's 7th Army. Hitler-jugend, under the command of SS-Brigadeführer Fritz Witt, prepared to send its panzer regiment, supported by two regiments of panzergrena-diers, into action. Later that day Hitlerjugend's 25th SS-Panzergrenadier Regiment, under the command of 33–year-old SS-Standartenführer Kurt Meyer, came under air attack, as he graphically related:

> A chain of Spitfires attacks the last section of the 15th Company. Missiles and cannon reap a devilish harvest. An elderly French woman is coming towards us screaming, 'Murder, Murder!' An infantry-man lies in the street. A stream of blood comes out of his throat – his artery has been shot through. He dies in our arms. The munitions of an amphibious vehicle explodes into the air – high tongues of flame shoot up. The vehicle explodes into pieces.

The divisional reconnaissance battalion under SS-Sturmbannführer and Ritterkreuzträger Gerd Bremer was among the first units to reach the front on 7 June. Upon arrival, it manoeuvred through 12km of no man's land to the division's far left flank to establish a security line. The battalion beat off numerous heavy attacks during 7–11 June, during which Bremer's command vehicle was knocked out and he was hit by shrapnel. Twice wounded, he nevertheless remained with his unit until the situation was secure.

Shortly after Kurt Meyer arrived and appraised the situation, he proposed a counterattack on the left flank of 21st Panzer Division. He established his headquarters at Ardenne Abbey, outside Caen. His panzergrenadier regiment, part of Kampfgruppe Meyer/Wünsche, went into action against the Canadians north of the city on 7 June, supported by fifty Panzer IVs of the 2nd Battalion, 12th SS-Panzer Regiment, commanded by SS-Sturmbannführer Prinz. The counterattack was set for 1600 hours, but four Panzer IVs of the 5th Company under SS-Untersturmführer Porsh ran into Sherman tanks along the Franqueville-Authie road. Three of the panzers were knocked out and it became impossible to wait. Wünsche gave the order and the 5th and 6th Companies advanced to the left of Ardenne Abbey, with the latter claiming ten enemy tanks for the loss of five Panzer IVs.

SS-Sturmmann Hans Fenn was almost killed in this battle:

> Ours, the fifth panzer, took a direct hit between the side of the hull and the turret ... The shell ripped a leg off my commander, Oberscharführer Esser. As I heard later, he managed to get out of the turret. The incendiary shell immediately set fire to all parts of the panzer. I lost consciousness ... Somehow, I managed, without being fully conscious, to crawl over the hatch of the loader.

The attack was broken up by Canadian artillery, naval gunfire and air strikes, followed by a counterattack. That evening the kampfgruppe of panzergrenadiers and panzers held defensive positions stretching from the railway line Caen-Luc sur Mer to Rue Nationale 13 from Caen to Bayeux. Although the Canadians had pushed through the Carpiquet airfield, the Hitlerjugend had stopped them in their tracks, destroying a total of twenty-seven tanks for the loss of fourteen Panzer IVs. Over the next few days the Canadian 3rd Infantry Division, striking from the Caen-Bayeux railway near Bretteville, fought Hitlerjugend.

Hitlerjugend found Carpiquet airfield deserted by the Luftwaffe and unoccupied by the Canadians. Its forces now turned on the Canadian 7th Brigade, also part of the Canadian 3rd Division. The 25th SS-Panzergrenadier Regiment supported by Panthers struck towards Bretteville from three directions. The attack from the south resulted in the platoon commander's tank being immobilized in the town and surrounded. The attack from the southwest was ordered to rescue him, but the lead tank was knocked out and driven off. In the attack from the west three Panthers were hit simultaneously by concealed Canadian anti-tank guns; two managed to withdraw, but the other burned like a torch although its crew escaped. The following morning the attack was broken off.

On 9 June Panthers of the 3rd Company, 12th SS-Panzer Regiment, under SS-Obersturmführer Rudolf von Ribbentrop, having missed the attack on Bretteville, moved on Norrey with the Caen-Cherbourg railway embankment protecting its right flank. However, Von Ribbentrop had been wounded so SS-Hauptsturmführer Lüdman led his twelve Panthers instead. Once they moved beyond the cover of the railway bank, well concealed anti-tank guns knocked out seven of the Panthers and the advance was halted. Crew losses were also heavy, with eighteen of the thirty-five men involved killed.

The company moved to Fontenay-les-Pesnel to the west but, with all the remaining tanks suffering mechanical problems, withdrew to Harcourt. Two days later the division's tanks claimed thirty-seven Shermans for the loss of three panzers in the fighting south of Le Mesnil.

The stark reality of war soon came home to Emil Werner, who was serving with Meyer's panzergrenadiers:

> Until Cambes everything went well. So far as we were concerned, the village looked fine. But on the outskirts we came under infantry fire and then all hell broke loose. We stormed a church where snipers had taken up positions. Here I saw the first dead man from our company; it was Grenadier Ruehl from the headquarters platoon.

On 11 June the Canadian 6th Armoured Regiment lost thirty-seven of its seventy-six tanks in the fighting around Le Mensil-Patry against Hitlerjugend. By now the 12th SS had lost about 25 per cent of its manpower, 20 per cent of its tanks and 10 per cent of its guns. In total, about sixty Panzer IV and V tanks remained serviceable. SS-Brigadeführer Fritz Witt was killed at Venoix on the morning of 14 June when his headquarters was caught in an Allied naval bombardment and shrapnel struck him in the face. Kurt 'Panzer' Meyer took command, making him the youngest divisional commander on either side.

It seemed that General Montgomery's Operation Epsom, designed to punch west of Caen on 25 June, could not fail; however, directly in its path lay Hitlerjugend units holding the line from Fontenay-le-Pesnil through St Marvieu and Cheux eastwards to Carpiquet airfield. The British

30th Corps was to jump off first, followed by the 8th Corps the following day. It fell to the 12th SS-Panzer Regiment and 25th SS-Panzergrenadier Regiment to resist the 8th Corps, while just to the west of Caen the 26th SS-Panzergrenadier Regiment was facing the Canadian 3rd Division.

The plan was for the British 8th Corps to break through between the 47th Panzer Corps and 1st SS Panzer Corps, force a bridgehead over the Odon river and take the strategic height of Hill 112. For the British it was a race against time as the 2nd SS Panzer Corps and 2nd SS Panzer Division were known to be heading for the sector, and even if the Allied attack pierced the in-depth defences of the 12th SS, the intervention of German armoured reinforcements could kill Epsom. On 25 June the 30th Corps conducted Operation Dauntless, a subsidiary attack to secure 8th Corps' western flank before the main offensive carried out by the 49th (West Riding) Infantry Division supported by the 8th Armoured Brigade. The 49th also conducted Operation Martlet, intended to capture Fontenay-le-Pesnil.

Second Lieutenant Stuart Hills, with the 8th Armoured Brigade, remembered a stiff reception from the 12th SS:

> The fighting in Fontenay was fierce and confused, with enemy tanks of 12th SS Panzer dug in defensively east of the town, and we did not have enough infantry to take the village. At about four o'clock in the afternoon the attack had clearly run out of steam, infantry losses had been heavy and we withdrew to the heights of Point 102 above Fontenay to replenish our stocks of ammunition, refuel and have something to eat.

The attack, though, was renewed and Fontenay captured and the road to Caen cut. A Squadron moved forwards to attack Rauray, but as Lieutenant Hills relates, it was in for a nasty surprise:

> As they cleared Fontenay, they were suddenly confronted by an enormous tank coming round the bend in front. It was hard to know who was the more surprised, but John [Semken, the Squadron Leader] shrieked, 'Fire, it's a Hun,' and they loosed off about ten rounds into the smoke. As this cleared away, it was observed that the crew were baling out as small flames came from inside the tank. It was a Tiger of 12th SS Panzer, the first Tiger to be captured in Normandy, and made an impressive sight at close quarters as both its size and the thickness of its armour became apparent.

Some of Semken's tanks included Sherman Fireflies armed with the powerful 17-pounder anti-tank gun and by the end of the day these had accounted for thirteen Panzer IVs, a Tiger and a Panther tank.

Between Tessel Wood and Rauray ten Tiger tanks were dug in and the 26th SS-Panzergrenadier Regiment repulsed the British attack through Le Manoir from Tessel towards Rauray and established positions near Le Haut du Bosc facing towards Cheux. Assembling across the line Fontenay-Tessel-Bretteville to attack towards Juvigny, the Tiger Company's actions left the 26th SS-Panzergrenadier Regiment, which lay directly in the path of the British attack, unsupported. The latter regiment was thrown into a counterattack at 0500 hours on 26 June. Hubert Meyer, the operations staff officer of the 12th SS, expecting an armoured attack, tried to get the order to counterattack rescinded, but the 1st SS Panzer Corps would not comply. The results were predictable:

> At 0700 on 26 June this great British attack of about 500–600 tanks on a breadth of about 3 miles [5km] rolled over the Pioneers and the Panzergrenadiers. Eventually it came to a halt only because our artillery fire separated the enemy infantry from their tanks ... As late as 28 June, our operators picked up radio messages from British tanks attacking the remnants of the 3rd Pioneer Company which still held several strongpoints in the old front line between St Mauvieu and Fontenay. We tried to convince the 1st SS Panzer Corps that a well-planned counterattack by tank units from the southwest might restore the original front, or at least, relieve the surrounded units, but fresh forces were not available.

The British 15th (Scottish) Division, with the 11th Armoured Division and 31st Tank Brigade, also broke through the 12th SS's defences. Likewise, the 43rd (Wessex) Division, supported by the 4th Armoured Brigade, reached Mouen. On 27 June the 15th (Scottish) Division captured a bridge over the Odon and the 11th Armoured Division moved to take Hill 112.

The following day British tanks and air attacks drove Hitlerjugend from the hill. The British 20th Armoured Brigade withdrew from Hill 112 on the night of 29/30 June, not because of the dogged resistance by the 12th SS but in the face of the arrival of the 2nd SS Panzer Corps with the 9th SS and 10th SS Panzer Divisions, which came into the line between the 47th Panzer Corps and the 1st SS Panzer Corps. The Germans had succeeded in containing Epsom but at a cost of over 2,600 casualties sustained by the 12th SS.

On 6 July panzergrenadiers of the 12th SS deployed to the northern suburbs of Caen. Within two days they and a regiment from the 16th Luftwaffe Field Division were ejected by General Montgomery's frontal assault on the city known as Operation Charnwood that commenced on the 7th. The Canadians sought to exploit their gains at Carpiquet, striking Caen from the west. To the east the 3rd Infantry was to secure Lebisey and Herouville, their original D-Day objectives. Aerial bombing by the Allies, while impeding the progress of the attackers, did not completely neutralize the defenders, and the advancing tanks met 75mm and 88mm anti-tank guns. At La Bijude the 12th SS was well entrenched and it took two attempts before the village was firmly in the 59th Division's hands.

The British 3rd Division reached Lebisey and Herouville within an hour and brushed aside the 16th Luftwaffe Field Division, only to find Caen an impassable sea of craters and rubble. In the meantime, the 1st SS tried to mass its armour for a counterattack, but air strikes and naval gunfire drove back the thirty-five panzers, which suffered some losses.

At the village of Buron northwest of Caen elements of the 3rd Battalion, 25th SS-Panzergrenadier Regiment, were surrounded and on the verge of being overrun by Canadian tanks. Kurt Meyer and General Eberbach, Panzergruppe West's commander, were at Ardenne Abbey. Meyer recalled the dramatically unfolding events:

> All available tanks were sent towards Buron. The attack failed to get through. From the [Ardenne] monastery church tower I watched the tank fight as it surged back and forth. Both sides suffered heavy losses. Then, suddenly, enemy tanks appeared from Authi [to the north], heading straight for Ardenne.

Von Ribbentrop's panzer company, with its fifteen Panthers, deployed against this mass of enemy tanks and successfully shot up the enemy armour, halting its advance. The last enemy tank was destroyed only 100 metres west of Ardenne but von Ribbentrop had saved the command post. His initial instructions had been to relieve the panzergrenadiers and clear the Canadians from Buron, but he was distracted by the Canadian armour to the left of the village and sent a platoon of Panthers to deal with them. Reaching Buron, von Ribbentrop's Panthers knocked out several Canadian tanks.

SS-Unterscharführer Freiberg, serving with von Ribbentrop, found himself in one of the three Panthers knocked out: 'I saw some movement there and then a flash from the muzzle of an anti-tank gun. The round struck our gun mantlet and the solid projectile ended up in the fighting compartment. Our sight was smashed, and the gunner was wounded in the face. I received several fragments in my left arm.'

Although Hitlerjugend could not retain Caen, it had, along with the Panzer Lehr Division, denied it to the Allies for just over a month. By 9 July the 12th SS had lost fifty-one Panzer IVs and thirty-two Panthers. Three days later it received a welcome respite from the bloodletting when it was relieved by an infantry division and sent to Potigny 32km north of Falaise to recuperate. After the liberation of Ardenne Abbey it was discovered that the 12th SS had slaughtered twenty Canadian prisoners in the grounds in early June 1944. Kurt Meyer was put on trial for this war crime after the war.

By the end of 10 August Meyer had just thirty-five panzers facing 700 enemy tanks. However, in the area defended by the 12th SS alone, over a hundred were destroyed in the fierce and brutal close combat. By now the American breakout from Avranches was well under way and the US 1st and 3rd Armies were charging westwards. Officer-cadet Kurt Misch and his comrades in Hitlerjugend soon realized that after all their tough resistance against the Canadians and Poles, they were now surrounded. Misch remembered the sense of apprehension:

> On the night of 15 August we were marching in an unknown direction. During the night we suddenly saw Verey lights [flares] on three sides; we looked at each other knowingly – surrounded? Next day, we were sure. We tried to keep it from the men as long as possible. But they realized it as soon as the field kitchen did not turn up and the rations got smaller. Something new, unknown, takes possession of us. All the usual joking is silence. We are all inwardly preoccupied, wondering how to meet the situation, as individuals. If it does not mean death, being taken prisoner will mean a long separation from home. We 'old' ones stick together. Our Chief leaves no doubts in our minds about the gravity of the situation, and I come back from the conference deep in thought. The Verey lights hang like great signs in the heavens. The front lies beneath them in a breathless silence. Low-flying German planes drop rations, and a large container of chocolate lands near me. A nice surprise, and a greeting from the outside world. We have not yet been abandoned.

Although the Canadians reached Falaise on 16 August 1944, Hitlerjugend held out in the town for a further two days. By now the battle for

Normandy was all but over. Between 6 June and 22 August 1944 Hitler's fanatical and resolutely fearless teenage Nazis lost around 8,000 killed in action, wounded and missing. This seemed a deathblow from which no unit could hope to recover. Nonetheless, most of the division's combat arms and rear services were not encircled at Falaise. Also many of the missing who were not captured managed to make their way back to the division. It would soon rise from the ashes of Normandy ready to fight again in the Ardennes.

Chapter Eleven

Hohenstaufen's Normandy Hills

As part of Hausser's 2nd SS Panzer Corps, the 9th SS Hohenstaufen under SS-Obergruppenführer Wilhelm Bittrich moved to Normandy in the summer of 1944 with its sister division, the 10th SS Frundsberg. It took them longer to reach Caen from the French border than it had taken to make the journey from Poland to France. All German reinforcements from the east were delayed by virtue of having to pass through the Chartres gap between the Seine and the Loire, which was vulnerable to Allied air attack and French sabotage.

Hohenstaufen reached the French border on 16 June 1944, but it was another four days before the lead elements were unloaded from their railway carriages between Paris and Nancy. It then deployed south of Aunay-sur-Odon with a total of 18,000 men, 170 panzers, 21 self-propelled guns, 287 armoured half-tracks, 16 armoured cars and 3,670 trucks. Initially the 9th SS was deployed south of a line that ran from Falaise to Condé-sur-Noireau, but then moved north between Caen and Villers-Bocage on a line between Tournay-sur-Odon and Neuilly-le-Malherbe.

Operation Epsom, launched on 25/26 June, was a preventative strike by the Allies to help tie down the newly arrived 2nd SS Panzer Corps west of Caen and prevent it moving to the American sector. General Montgomery's intention was to push south over the Caen-Bayeux road and on to the Fosse de l'Odon before turning southeast to Bretteville-sur-Laize, 16km south of Caen. During the fighting against the Epsom salient Hohenstaufen suffered 1,145 casualties and lost sixteen Panzer IVs, six Panthers and ten assault guns. Over the next few days the division's assault guns accounted for forty-nine enemy tanks, while its Panzer IVs and Panthers claimed another thirteen. On 29 June Hohenstaufen, now formally assigned to the 2nd SS Panzer Corps, deployed facing Hill 112 along the Odon river between General von Funck's 37th Panzer Corps and Sepp Dietrich's 1st SS Panzer Corps.

At a critical moment before their counterattack the Germans were forced to conduct one of their habitual command reshuffles. Willi Bittrich suddenly found himself commanding the 2nd SS Panzer Corps after Hausser succeeded General Dollmann as commander of the 7th Army. Dollmann had dropped dead on 28 June of a suspected heart attack, though his chief of staff General Max Pemsel suspected he may have poisoned himself. SS-Oberführer Thomas Müller took control of Hohenstaufen. The division was destined to have three more commanders before the end of the war.

Hausser with the 2nd SS Panzer Corps organized the counterattack employing Hohenstaufen. This was scheduled for 29 June at 0700 hours with the 9th SS on the left of the Odon, but attacks by the RAF delayed the preparations until 1430 hours. In addition, in a stroke of bad luck, an officer from the 9th SS, carrying the plans for the coming attack, was out early reconnoitring the routes to Cheux when he was captured. The first group of Hohenstaufen forces took Grainville-sur-Odon and the second group also reached Cheux, but everywhere else the British and Canadians held fast. Several flame-throwing tanks assisted with the assault on Le Valtru, but although the panzers overran the British infantry, the latter still held firm.

SS-Brigadeführer Sylvester Stadler then took command of the 9th SS, having previously commanded the SS-Panzergrenadier Regiment Der Führer of the 2nd SS Panzer Division. It was units of this regiment under SS-Sturmbannführer Otto Diekmann that had conducted the massacre at Oradour-sur-Glane during the division's march northwards to Normandy. Stadler was a hardened Eastern Front veteran, having gained the Knight's Cross for his part in the capture of Kharkov in 1943. He had then gained the Oak Leaves for the latter after his involvement in the massive Battle of Kursk. Thomas Müller assumed command of the 17th SS Panzergrenadier Division for a brief period in September, after SS-Oberführer Eduard Deisenhofer was wounded.

Stadler soon found his division being thrown into action and recalled the bitter fighting:

> Within one hour after the Division had been taken over, orders for a counterattack on Maltot, Eterville and on Baron by way of Hill 112 were received from the Corps by telephone, and a short time later confirmed in writing. So the attack on Baron was to be launched at 2000 and that on Eterville at 1200. Although the time was very short, the execution of this task was still possible thanks to the fact that the 20th SS-Panzergrenadier Regiment was not too far away and that a

tank battalion, together with the artillery, could support the operation from the positions they were in at the time.

Things did not run smoothly, however, as the Allies did all they could to impede the massing of the 9th SS; in addition, its position was compromised by the loss of Hill 112. The latter was to become the scene of heavy casualties for both sides. Stadler discovered flexibility was an increasing prerequisite of such operations:

> Concentration of the Division was greatly impeded and delayed by serious traffic jams on roads, harassing fire from the enemy artillery directed on villages along the routes of advance, and on road junctions, as well as by the strong enemy air activity. In addition to that, the enemy managed at about 1800 to capture height 112, which dominated the entire Corps sector. Thereupon the mission assigned to the Division was altered by the Corps, to the effect that only height 112, and later Eterville, had to be recaptured.

The British quickly contested Hohenstaufen's successes at Eterville and Hill 112 on 4 July. The panzers managed to knock out a number of British tanks for little loss, but the panzergrenadiers suffered from the enemy's artillery. Stadler recalled perhaps with some pride:

> In the course of the forenoon the enemy, in turn, resumed his attacks and managed to take Eterville once again, whereas his attacks on height 112 were repelled with considerable losses. A counterattack launched immediately on Eterville succeeded and, by noon, the village was again in our hands. An extremely heavy and fluctuating battle ensued afterwards for the ruins of Eterville, which place changed hands repeatedly until, finally, it was firmly in our possession late in the evening of 4 July 1944 ... Nevertheless, the panzer battalion operating near Eterville managed to destroy twelve to fourteen enemy vehicles, whereas they lost only two tanks. Thus, it could be figured out that the enemy losses were at least as high as ours.

During the night of 4/5 July Hohenstaufen was relieved on the eastern sector by elements of Hitlerjugend and on the west by Frundsberg. The British renewed their attacks on 6 July, this time along the road from Caen to Noyers. To help the 277th Infantry Division recapture Noyers, the 9th SS despatched its armoured reconnaissance battalion. The latter successfully retook the town and remained to support the 277th Infantry.

The panzers' regimental HQ was established at Bully about 4km east of Hill 112 between Caen and Evrecy on 12 July. When the British attacked between Gavrus and Noyers-Bocage four days later, the division's tanks were undergoing maintenance. However, the 277th Infantry was ordered to counterattack supported by the 9th SS. About twenty panzers were mustered to the right of Hill 113 north of Evrecy, but the British put down smoke and they were forced to withdraw. While Hill 113 remained unoccupied, the panzers took Bougy and reached Gavrus, moving up the Orne valley. During the various engagements they knocked out a total of forty tanks, including eighteen around Bougy and eight at Hill 113 for the loss of just five panzers.

Sylvester Stadler recalled the battle:

> A serious crisis occurred only once on the occasion of a concentrated attack carried out by British armoured troops with some forty to fifty tanks late in the evening of 16 or 17 July 1944, on Height 113. All day, the enemy had pounded the hill with undiminished intensity and covered it with a smokescreen. Sometimes, the smoke was so dense that the majority of the troops felt sick and therefore believed that the enemy was using gas.

Stadler remembered the sudden British armed assault that came late in the day and threatened to overwhelm his men. The troops of Hohenstaufen, though, were quick-witted and soon turned the tables on their attackers, as their commander noted:

> Our own tanks, a battalion of about fifteen to twenty tanks, were located on the rear slope of the hill and noticed the enemy only at the very last moment, either on account of the dense smoke, or perhaps owing to the swift and surprising advance of his forces. During the ensuing tank battle, fifteen enemy tanks were destroyed with no losses at all on our side.

By 17 July the exhausted Hohenstaufen could muster thirty-three panzers and fifteen assault guns, while the infantry amounted to little more than a regiment. The 9th SS was called back from the left flank of the 10th SS at the height of the Goodwood battle and positioned in the Orne valley, guarding the southern suburbs of Caen. Over the next few days Hohenstaufen helped Leibstandarte defeat Montgomery's Goodwood armoured offensive. Notably, on 18 July the division captured sixty-seven tanks, fifty-six of which were destroyed, the rest still running.

Frundsberg and the 277th Infantry Division were instructed to retake St Martin, St André and May-sur-Orne east of the river and south of Caen on 22 July with support from Hohenstaufen. However, the Panthers of the 9th SS were still engaged around Bougy and could only be freed up slowly. Some were assigned to two companies of the 10th SS while the rest were to attack south of May. Few of the Panthers materialized except for those directed to take the high ground northeast of May.

On 30 July Montgomery launched Operation Bluecoat southwards towards Vire and Mount Pincon. Within two days the 9th SS had lost most of its armour. It remained southwest of Caen until early August, when it moved northeast of Vire. British tanks got to within 8km of the town, the very heart of the 7th Army's resistance against the Americans. Wanting to counterattack against the Americans, who were considered inferior fighters, the Germans first had to secure Mont Pinçon against the British to control the network of roads westwards.

The division was relieved by Leibstandarte on 1 August and that night a kampfgruppe under Otto Meyer, including seventeen panzers and assault guns, moved west to take up positions on a line from Arclais to Mont-chauvet and Montchamp, to the west of Mont Pinçon and between Villers-Bocage and Vire. RAF Typhoons soon located the SS tank columns in the afternoon of 2 August and launched 923 sorties, destroying thirteen tanks and seventy-six trucks and holding up the deployment of the German panzers for most of the day. The kampfgruppe then held the 15th (Scottish) Division with dug-in tanks, 88mm guns and Nebelwerfer rocket launchers. Those troops at Montchauvet were embroiled in heavy fighting around Hill 170 and, although surrounded, managed to escape.

On 4 August 1944 Hohenstaufen attempted to cut off the British break-through at Chênedollé, knocking out thirty-nine Allied tanks in the process. Otto Meyer, near Estry with thirty-two panzers and assault guns, had to block the road northwest of Chênedollé and went over to the defensive. Between 11 and 12 August the division claimed another twenty-two enemy tanks in the unrelenting fighting, before escaping Normandy and withdrawing across the Seine. At the end of the month SS-Standarten-führer Walter Harzer took command of Hohenstafen. He would lead it at Arnhem in the Netherlands and afterwards Stadler resumed control until the end of the war.

Chapter Twelve

Frundsberg at Hill 112

Under the command of SS-Standartenführer Michael Lippert, Frundsberg, like Hohenstaufen, was raised from conscripts drawn mainly from the Reich Labour Service in February 1943. Like the boys of Hitlerjugend, they were just teenagers. According to Himmler, the average age of the recruits was 18 years. The division was redesignated the 10th SS Panzer Division on 3 October 1943 and named after Georg von Frundsberg, who had served the Hapsburg monarchy during its many wars.

Subsequently led by SS-Gruppenführer Karl Fischer von Treuenfeld, Frundsberg first saw action at Tarnopol in April 1944, where it took part in rescuing German troops trapped in the Kamenets-Podolskiy pocket. In mid-June Hitler cancelled a proposed offensive near Kowel and from his Rastenburg headquarters ordered the division to be switched to the west to help bolster the situation in Normandy. Under SS-Gruppenführer Heinz Harmel, it was sent to France on 12 June alongside the 9th SS to fight the Allied landings.

The 10th SS-Panzer Regiment's 2nd Battalion was loaded onto six trains in Russia and headed west from Sokol and Krystinowpol. It took five days to reach the assembly point at Saarbrücken. The first train reached Houdan southwest of Paris on 18 June and the tanks took to the road, rumbling through Dreux, Châteauneuf, Digny and le Magne to Longy, where they dallied until 25 June.

SS-Obergruppenführer Hausser, commander of the 2nd SS Panzer Corps, presented himself to Field Marshal Rommel on 23 June to inform him that the 10th SS had arrived in northern France. By the following day most of the division, with an official strength of about 14,800 men, had reached the assembly area in Normandy, although fuel was a problem. These units consisted of the 10th SS-Reconnaissance Battalion, 10th SS-Panzer Regiment, 10th SS-Panzerjäger Battalion, 21st and 22nd SS-Panzergrenadier Regiments, 10th SS-Artillery Regiment, 10th SS-Flak Battalion, 10th SS-Pioneer Battalion and 10th SS-Training Battalion.

Harmel's command had the dubious accolade of being the weakest panzer division in Normandy. The 10th SS-Panzer Regiment, under SS-Obersturmbannführer Otto Paetsch, was only able to field a single tank battalion. The latter, under SS-Sturmbannführer Reinhold, consisted of thirty-nine Panzer IVs, thirty-eight StuG IIIs and three Panzer III command vehicles, providing a tank force of just eighty panzers. Other divisional armoured fighting vehicles consisted of the 10th SS-Artillery Regiment's six Hummel and eleven Wespe self-propelled guns. It may have also had a few Grille self-propelled guns.

Frundsberg suffered the same problem as Hohenstaufen, whose Panther battalion was still being worked up at Mailly-le-Camp. Both divisions experienced problems with tank deliveries. This meant they were really only panzergrenadier divisions. Although the 10th SS-Panzer Regiment's 1st Battalion was already at Mailly-le-Camp, it only had training vehicles available and was unable to join its parent unit until 1945. Therefore this battalion was not destined to see action in Normandy. The ten Panthers it did receive had to be handed over to the Panzer Lehr Division and by 1 August the 1st Battalion had been assigned to the 10th Panzer Brigade, which had only seven Panthers out of an authorized strength of seventy-three. Similarly, the division's panzerjäger battalion was still forming and did not receive any Jagdpanzer IV tank destroyers until the end of August.

On the night of 25/26 June, just as the British were renewing their efforts, the 2nd SS Panzer Corps' headquarters and Frundsberg were instructed to move to the St Remy-Rousamps-La Bgne-St Symphorien-Les Buttes-Campeaux-Vire-Tinchebray area. The 10th SS was soon thrown into action against the British 2nd Army's Operation Epsom, enduring heavy fighting around the strategic Hill 112. The British 30th Corps by 30 June had reached Rauray and Tessel, but in the face of determined resistance from 2nd SS could not maintain its momentum and failed to reach the Odon. In contrast the 8th Corps forced its way over the river, creating a narrow bridgehead between Gavrus to the west and Baron to the east.

In countering Epsom, Frundsberg attacked the Gavrus bridgehead on the flank of the British 11th Armoured Division on Hill 112. Problems with shortages of fuel greatly limited the number of panzers the division could initially throw at the British. Paetsch and Reinhold's tanks and assault guns were committed to the fighting on 29 June along with the 9th SS when they attacked along the Odon. The two assault gun companies supporting the 22nd SS-Panzergrenadier Regiment retook Gavrus but could not reach Baron-sur-Odon. Near Evrecy the panzers took Hill 113 and the division claimed twenty-eight enemy tanks for the loss of just two Panzer IVs.

Flanking fire from Avenay and St Martin hampered the push to Hill 112 and Esquay-Notre-Dame, but that night the panzers and panzergrenadiers crossed the Guigne river between Avenay and Vieux, which enabled them to climb the southern slopes of Hill 112. Hitlerjugend attacked Hill 112 from the east and by midday on 30 June its forces were on the summit. Hill 113 was attacked at the same time. During 30 June–1 July elements of the 10th SS lost 571 casualties in resisting Epsom and the division suffered badly from air strikes on 1 July 5km south of Villers-Bocage.

On 3 July the British counterattacked and Frundsberg's tanks were moved up the hill. On 10 July the British, under the guise of Operation Jupiter, tried to wrest back control of the high ground around Hill 112. Major General G.I. Thomas' 43rd (Wessex) Division, consisting of the 129th, 130th and 214th brigades, was to attack positions held by the 10th SS supported by Tiger tanks from the 101st SS Heavy Panzer Battalion, in what was to prove an extremely fierce battle.

The German defenders survived naval bombardment, air attack and artillery fire. The British then launched frontal attacks on Hill 112 and the village of Maltot on its northern slope, against the SS panzer troops supported by dug-in and concealed Tiger tanks holding an almost impregnable position. The British made some initial progress before being driven back by Tigers from the 102nd SS Heavy Panzer Battalion.

Just at the moment when it appeared that twenty-five British Churchill tanks were going to take the summit of Hill 112, the 1st Battalion arrived from its reserve position and knocked out almost all of them. In particular, the concealed Panzer IVs of the 5th Company were confronted by twenty-five British tanks and were forced to attack a section at a time to avoid the Allied fighter-bombers. The British advance came to a halt to return fire, knocking out two panzers and killing two platoon leaders, SS-Hauptscharführer Borrekott and SS-Oberscharführer Leven. In the meantime, the remaining Panzer IVs and the Sturmgeschützs advanced between Hills 112 and 113, catching the Allied spearhead in the flank, but the British had already reached the top.

The British attack on Maltot did not go well either, as the Tigers on Hill 112 opened up on the British left flank, while Hitlerjugend's Panzer IVs and Panthers were to the attackers' front, and elements of the 1st SS Kampfgruppe were on the right. The British threw in a further attack and took the summit once again, but at nightfall the British tanks withdrew, leaving the infantry unsupported, to be thrown back yet again by a German counterattack under cover of darkness.

The 43rd Division alone lost more than 2,000 men in the first 36 hours of Operation Jupiter and it was reported that the Odon river was dammed with corpses. On 15 July the British launched Operation Greenline, tying down the Frundsberg west of Caen. When Hohenstaufen was withdrawn into reserve on that day, the 10th SS was left to cover the entire sector, and its forces were driven off part of Hill 113, just north of Evrecy, by Major General G.H.A. MacMillan's 15th (Scottish) Division.

Despite the commitment of Tiger tanks and the return of the 9th SS, the Scots held on to their gains, although the SS remained in possession of the lunar surface of Hill 112 until finally relieved by the 271st Infantry Division. Frundsberg, having lost well over 2,200 men since the beginning of July, was withdrawn for a brief period of rest. The division had also lost a quantity of self-propelled guns and anti-tank weapons, including four Grille self-propelled guns, eight 75mm light infantry assault guns, six 75mm anti-tank guns and eighteen 80mm mortars, as well as nearly a hundred machine guns.

In the face of such determined SS resistance, British casualties during the period 10–22 July amounted to approximately 25,000 men and 500 tanks. In particular, the 43rd (Wessex) Division suffered a total of 7,000 casualties. By the end of the month Frundsberg had lost seven Panzer IVs, three Sturmgeschütz IIIs and 168 other vehicles. They continued to fight southwest of Caen. In early August the 10th SS halted the British 43rd Division, which, attacking from Dois du Homme, had driven the 21st Panzer Division from Jurques and seized Hill 301. They also drove the British 7th Armoured Division almost back to Breuil.

On 1 August a Kampfgruppe under Otto Paetsch headed for Aunay-sur-Odon, about 29km southwest of Caen. The next day the Kampfgruppe – with seven Panzer IVs and eighteen Panthers – entered the fray and successfully held most of Hill 188, claiming responsibility for destroying twenty British tanks. The remainder of the division arrived on 3 August, threw back the British units that had established a foothold on Hill 188, and took nearby Hill 301 to form a defence line between the two high points.

This and other SS attacks brought British tank losses since the start of Operation Bluecoat on 30 July to a massive 200 vehicles. Bittrich's tired troops kept pressing forwards until the battle reached a climax on 6 August. Frundsberg was switched from Aunay-sur-Odon to attack the British positions on the Périers ridge. It was then ordered to disengage, and on 6 August was committed to an attack on British units north of Chênedollé. They seized two prominent high points, Hills 242 and 224, only to be driven back by shellfire and air attacks. Having brought Bluecoat to a halt, Bittrich established a strong defensive line around Vire.

For the German counterattack on Avranches on the American front, Field Marshal von Kluge had instructed that the 10th SS be available by 5 August in the Vassy area. However, the 5th Panzer Army could not comply due to the tactical situation with the 2nd SS Panzer Corps. Army Group B informed the 7th Army that the 10th SS and 12th SS were to be brought up on 8 August under the direction of General Walter Krüger's 58th Panzer Corps. The latter had only just assumed control of the sector southwest of Caen from Bittrich's 2nd SS Panzer Corps.

Moving towards Mortain, Heinz Harmel's Frundsberg became the reserve for General von Funck's 47th Panzer Corps. The division was deployed to the Beauchene area east of Mortain to relieve elements of the 275th Infantry Division. During the night of 8/9 August the 10th SS found its extended front line compromised when the enemy penetrated both sides of Barenton. The SS launched a counterattack on 9 August along the road from Barenton to Ger, reaching the hill 4km northeast of Barenton. The 10th SS was then committed to recapture Barenton, although they could only muster twelve panzers. Elements had to be committed to action near Barenton almost immediately, however, to block the constantly probing American attacks.

Frundsberg launched its counterattack against the American penetration north of Barenton on 10 August and made some ground, although they could not reach the town. Heavy losses soon forced the division over to the defensive. Instead of being committed to the renewed Avranches/Mortain counteroffensive, Frundsberg was pushed eastwards via Domfront and Fromentel as the Germans pulled back to defend Argentan.

By 14 August the division was in danger of being encircled and Domfront had fallen to the Americans. Its fighting strength stood at just 4,136 men. In stark contrast to all the British tanks it had accounted for, the division had lost only twelve Panzer IVs and eight Sturmgeschütz since arriving in Normandy. SS-Brigadeführer Harmel mustered eight

Panzer IVs and some panzergrenadiers in the hills to the north of Dom-front and with the assistance of the 2nd SS and 17th SS prepared to attack the American forces.

They drove the Americans back, but this localized victory meant nothing. During the night the remains of the division withdrew eastwards on St-Bomer-les-Forges and then north of Argentan. Harmel and his men now faced the gauntlet of the Trun-Chambois bottleneck. Elements of the 10th SS along with the 1st SS and 2nd Panzer were trapped in the Falaise pocket. The survivors, though, were eventually withdrawn to Arnhem in the Netherlands.

Chapter Thirteen

The Iron Fist

The grand-sounding 17th SS Panzergrenadier Division Götz von Berlichingen was authorized by Hitler on 3 October 1943. However, it did not start coming together until six weeks later in France within General Kurt von der Chevallerie's 1st Army area of responsibility. Created from replacement units and conscripts under SS-Gruppenführer Werner Ostendorff, the formation found itself relying on Volksdeutsche from Romania and captured French vehicles and assault guns. Under the circumstances it needed a man of some character to meld the fledgeling division.

Werner Ostendorff's background was as a qualified Luftwaffe pilot and he had served in Russia on a technical exchange. In the mid-1930s he joined the SS and served in Poland during the invasion. In 1942 Ostendorff became chief of staff with Paul Hausser's SS General Kommando (later the 2nd SS Panzer Corps), seeing action at Kharkov and Kursk, during which time he gained a reputation as a highly respected staff officer. The division was to have ten different commanders before the end of the war, with Ostendorff and SS-Standartenführer Otto Binge serving with Götz von Berlichingen twice.

The division's title derived from Götz von Berlichingen, a knight who lost a hand in battle near Landshut in 1504 during the Bavarian War of Succession. His hand was replaced with an iron fist and this was adopted as the 17th SS's symbol. Himmler travelled from Berlin on 10 April 1944 to attend the division's formal activation, with Panzergruppe West's commander Geyr von Schweppenburg and the 1st SS Panzer Corps' commander Sepp Dietrich at Thouars, northwest of Poitiers. Divisional cuff titles were also bestowed on the unit.

The only other German divisions in the region were the 158th Infantry Division way to the west, deployed between Nantes and Fontenay-le-Comte, and the 708th Infantry Division to the southwest near Royan, guarding the Bay of Biscay against possible Allied invasion. Elements of the latter division were also to end up fighting the Americans in Normandy.

Even further south lay the 11th Panzer Division, the only armoured unit not to be eventually drawn north to Normandy.

By the time of D-Day, Götz von Berlichingen was not fully combat ready and although some 157,321 men strong, it lacked 40 per cent of its officers and non-commissioned officers. The division also lacked transport and by mid-May had just 257 trucks and towing vehicles. The 17th SS-Panzerjäger Battalion had received none of its Jagdpanzer IV tank destroyers.

By mid June the situation was little better, with its armoured forces consisting of just forty-two Sturmgeschütz III assault guns equipping the 17th SS-Panzer Battalion and twelve Marder self-propelled guns with the 17th SS-Panzerjäger Battalion. Three Panzer IV command vehicles did not arrive until 12 August. The panzer battalion, though, was in capable hands. SS-Sturmbannführer Ludwig Kepplinger was a Waffen-SS veteran who had fought in Russia with the 5th SS Panzer Division Wiking.

On 8 June 1944, two days after the Allies landed, the independent 902nd Sturmgeschütz battalion stationed at Tours on the Loire, northeast of Thouars, with thirty-one assault guns was placed under Ostendorff's control. These guns were a welcome supplement to the division's meagre armoured forces. En route, though, the battalion was side-tracked, for while the 17th SS was attached to General der Fallschirmtruppen Eugen Meindl's 2nd Parachute Corps, the 902nd Battalion ended up with von Choltitz's 84th Corps. By 24 June it was with the 91st Airlanding Division and, escaping encirclement, it eventually ended up with Wiese's 19th Army in southern France.

On 6 June the 17th SS's divisional HQ was still at Thouars and it would take a week for Ostendorff to get the division to the front. The day after D-Day the division received orders to depart its marshalling area and head for Normandy. Götz von Berlichingen redeployed from the area of General Chevallerie's 1st Army south of the Loire to the sector of General Dollmann's 7th Army facing Lieutenant General Omar N. Bradley's US 1st Army at the base of the Cotentin peninsula.

The complete lack of transport meant that the division could only be moved piecemeal, and the most readily available unit was the 17th SS-Panzeraufklärungs Abteilung, the armoured reconnaissance battalion. A kampfgruppe had to be formed from three battalions. Nonetheless, the division moved off in good spirits, the men were happy at last that the uncertainty was over and they would be seeing action. The Allies, though, were determined that this unit would not have an easy time of it.

Only four of the division's six infantry battalions moved on 7 June; the other two battalions had to rely on bicycles. Similarly, a flak battery and the artillery units began to move on the evening of the 7th while the assault guns and self-propelled guns were loaded onto trains. Allied fighter-bombers quickly pounced on the freight cars, claiming one StuG III for the loss of two aircraft. Three days later the guns had been unloaded between Montreuil and la Feche and were rumbling towards Mayenne.

Some units, including the 17th SS-Flak Battalion and the SS-Pioneer Battalion, had to be left behind to protect the crossings over the Loire at Saumur, located between Angers and Tours. The flak battalion did not deploy to Normandy until the end of June and then the 1st Battery and its 88mm guns were left to guard the bridges for the want of prime movers or tow trucks. Similarly, the pioneer battalion, some 726 men, did not reach Normandy until mid-July.

A divisional staff officer recalled how moving in daylight soon drew the unwanted attentions of the Allied fighter-bombers:

> Our motorized columns were coiling along the road towards the invasion beaches. Then something happened that left us in a daze. Spurts of fire flicked along the column and splashes of dust staccatoed the road. Everyone was piling out of the vehicles and scuttling for the neighbouring fields. Several vehicles were already in flames. This attack ceased as suddenly as it had crashed upon us fifteen minutes before.

An hour later the fighter-bombers were back, inflicting even more damage, wrecking the division's anti-tank guns and even more vehicles. Ostendorff's men gave up the advance and abandoned the road, trying to camouflage their vehicles and equipment in the nearby farms and farm-land. From now on the 17th SS would move towards the battle only at night: the cost of doing otherwise was simply too great.

By 8 June the armoured reconnaissance battalion, although under fighter-bomber attack, reached Balleroy, halfway between St Lô and Bayeux. Two days later it went into action for the first time when it was committed to the 352nd Infantry Division's sector north of St Lô; the latter had suffered 1,200 casualties on D-Day. At the same time the 37th SS-Panzergrenadier Regiment arrived at La Chapelle southeast of the city.

While the reconnaissance battalion was sent to help the 352nd Infantry near Caen, Ostendorff went forwards to make contact with the 6th Fallschirmjäger Regiment defending Carentan, which had been advised by the 7th Army via the 84th Corps that the SS were on the way. The German paratroopers were so short of ammunition that they requested an air drop by the Luftwaffe, but late in the afternoon of 11 June they abandoned Carentan to the Americans just as the 17th SS was preparing to relieve them.

The US 101st Airborne Division captured Carentan on 12 June and Götz von Berlichingen adopted defensive positions to the south. The first real test of strength occurred the following day when the Panzergrenadiers, supported by the Sturmgeschütz IIIs, set about the 101st Airborne southwest of the town. The bulk of the 17th SS began to arrive in its assembly areas prior to a counterattack to recapture Bayeux on 11 June and was subordinated to the 2nd Parachute Corps. After D-Day, General Meindl's 2nd Parachute Corps with the 3rd Parachute Division were redeployed from Brittany to counter the Americans in the St Lô area.

Formed from the 13th Flieger Corps, Meindl's command came into being in February 1944 and deployed in reserve near Paris under Field Marshal von Rundstedt, CinC West. In May it was placed under Dollmann's 7th Army. Unusually for a command and control staff, Meindl's corps had its own dedicated armoured unit in the shape of the 12th Fallschirm-Sturmgeschütz-Brigade with eleven combat-ready assault guns. Numerous units including the 17th SS would pass through the 2nd Parachute Corps' hands.

Ostendorff and his operations officer SS-Obersturmbannführer Konrad set up their command post at St-Sébastien-de-Raids, southwest of Carentan, to direct the attack. At 0700 hours on 13 June Sturmgeschütz of their panzer battalion got to within 550m of Carentan before being stopped by elements of the US 2nd Armored and 101st Airborne Divisions. Similarly, the 37th SS-Panzergrenadier Regiment made no progress and by midday it was clear the attack on Carentan had failed. By the 15th the division had suffered 456 casualties in its struggle with the Americans.

In the meantime, the 7th Army's reserve – the 100th Panzer Battalion, attached to the 91st Airlanding Division – fared poorly at Baupte, meaning that the Americans were soon threatening the flank and rear of Götz von Berlichingen. The battalion was in fact a training unit equipped with obsolete French tanks, stationed west of Carentan and covering Baupte and Ste Mère-Eglise. Panicked by the American airborne landings that had claimed a number of officers and men, within two weeks the unit ceased to exist. Ostendorff and Konrad were furious at the commander of the 6th Fallschirmjäger Regiment for withdrawing southeast from Baupte, and arrested the man. Only the intervention of the 2nd Parachute Corps secured his release.

General Max Pemsel, chief of staff of 7th Army, noted:

> The failure of the attack launched by the 17th SS Panzergrenadier Division in the direction of Carentan was due not so much to the lack of air support as to the inadequate training of the young division, which ran into the simultaneously launched counter-attack. The 100th Panzer Training Battalion had only a few obsolete and hardly manoeuvrable French tanks. It was intended to deceive the enemy by the name of this unit.

By mid-June nearly all of Götz von Berlichingen's units had arrived, although the flak and pioneer battalions were still held back at Saumur to assist with the crossings over the Loire river. In total the 17th SS Panzergrenadier Division fielded about 15,500 men. On 16 June SS-Brigadeführer Ostendorff was wounded and was relieved by SS-Oberführer Eduard Diesenhoffer.

The division was bolstered with a number of units of dubious quality. The disgraced 6th Fallschirmjäger Regiment, which had previously been part of von Choltitz's 84th Corps based south of Carentan, was tactically attached to the 17th SS on 20 June. Two units of Soviet deserters known as the 439th and 635th East Battalions also came under its direction, along with the remains of the 7th Army's Storm-Battalion Armeeoberkommando and Pioneer-Battalion Angers. The division was also assigned the 5th Fallschirm Pioneer Battalion from the wholly inadequate 5th Parachute Division in mid-July. This battalion was of little value as it lacked small arms: in late May it had just twenty-eight rifles.

The presence of Götz von Berlichingen in the Carentan area helped persuade the Americans that they should first clear the Cotentin peninsula and capture Cherbourg before making further efforts to strike southwards. In the face of the US 4th, 9th and 79th Divisions, the German garrison did not surrender until 26 June.

At the end of June the division's six infantry battalions were still combat ready, but the armoured reconnaissance battalion had been considerably weakened. By this stage the 17th SS had lost nearly 900 casualties. Similarly, the panzer regiment only had 18 combat-ready assault guns, supported by thirty-two 75mm anti-tank guns, including the self-propelled weapons, and four powerful 88mm Pak 43s. During early July the 5th and 7th Companies from the 2nd SS-Panzer Regiment were attached to the 17th SS along the Périers-Carentan road. However, by the middle of the month it had lost another eight Sturmgeschütz and Kampfgruppe Fick was formed using the 37th SS-Panzergrenadier Regiment and the 17th SS-Pioneer Battalion under SS-Obersturmbannführer Jacob Fick.

Other units facing the Americans were suffering much higher rates of attrition. Deployed to the east of St Lô, the 3rd Parachute Division, consisting of three regiments with little heavy equipment of note apart from nine 75mm Pak 40 anti-tank guns and twelve 105mm field guns, by 12 July had suffered 4,064 casualties. Likewise, the 352nd Infantry had been through the grinder and lost 7,886 casualties. All the infantry formations west of St Lô fighting alongside the 17th SS were in similar dire straits.

This meant that the principal forces that would have to withstand and deflect the Americans' breakout offensive, Operation Cobra, were the 17th SS Panzergrenadier Division and Panzer Lehr Division. West of the Vire, the sector facing the American 19th Corps, was part of the 32km front held by Götz von Berlichingen. Its right wing consisted of Kampfgruppe Heintz, employing units from the battered 275th and 352nd Infantry Divisions.

Just before the Americans attacked with overwhelming force, using four infantry and two armoured divisions, the 17th SS reported to the 84th Corps that it could field just two weak infantry battalions with another five combat ineffective, ten assault guns, ten heavy anti-tank guns and five light artillery batteries. Mobility was poor and its heavy artillery was assigned to Panzer Lehr.

When the American blow fell, SS-Unterscharführer Günther, of the 17th SS reconnaissance battalion, was caught up in the chaos following Cobra. He heard the neighbouring paratroop unit under attack on 23/24 July. Although not in the path of the assault, he and his men were ordered to withdraw as the front collapsed. Günther recalls:

We were marching, marching back all the time. One morning we were ordered to keep a road open, but we found that the Americans had already blocked it. The roads were crowded with American vehicles, and all we could do was take to the fields on foot. On the fourth day, by sheer coincidence we ran into some of our own unit's vehicles, and kept going by road. But we were losing stragglers all the time – some of us later had letters from them from America. Once when we were moving to take up position an army staff car stopped beside us. I saluted. The officer in it asked me where we were going. 'Have you gone crazy?' he said. 'The Americans are there already.'

With the American armour hot on their heels, Günther discovered that there was not even time to eat:

We found a pig in a farm, killed it and cooked it. We took sheets from the farmhouse and laid them out on the table and prepared to eat. Suddenly a Luftwaffe man burst in shouting: 'The Americans are right behind me.' We grabbed the corners of the sheet with everything inside it, threw it in the back of a field car, and pulled out just as the first Sherman came in sight ... I had seen the first retreat from Moscow, which was terrible enough, but at least units were still intact. Here, we had become a cluster of individuals.

The 17th SS, driven south, was partly caught in the Coutances pocket. The division then fought closely with the 2nd SS, forming a joint battle-group to break out from the Roncey pocket to the southeast. At Roncey the survivors joined a huge stationary three abreast column of vehicles on 29 July. To the south lay the American 2nd Armored Division barring their way; American fighter-bombers swooped in and wrecked a 3km stretch of vehicles. The strafing and the bombing continued for 6 hours. Eleven vehicles from the 17th SS assault gun battalion, escaping westwards from St Denis-le-Gast, bumped into American artillery and tank destroyers near La Chapelle during the night. All the vehicles were lost, along with ninety men killed and 200 captured.

Survivors from Götz von Berlichingen, Das Reich and the 6th Parachute Regiment continued to flee southwards along with the 91st Airlanding Division. By the end of July the 84th and 2nd Parachute Corps and their divisions facing the Americans had been destroyed and 20,000 German troops captured. Although many of the 17th SS escaped, they left much of their equipment littering the Normandy countryside.

The division's condition was such that by August it was withdrawn for a refit, although elements served with Das Reich during the Mortain counterattack and later with Frundsberg. Kampfgruppe Fick was expanded to include all the remaining battle-worthy elements of the division, but on

6 August von Rundstedt ordered that Götz von Berlichingen was to be subordinated to the 2nd SS.

The 17th SS-Panzerjäger Battalion finally received some of its thirty-one Jagdpanzer IVs from Germany in early August. Only the 3rd Company of the battalion (with the self-propelled guns) had originally moved to the front with the assault guns. Now equipped with the Jagdpanzers and twelve Flakpanzers it headed north, reaching Château Gontier with instructions to move westwards between Laval and Rennes.

The battalion finally went into action against the Americans on 5 August in the Laval area, where there were also elements of the 708th Infantry Division. On 6/7 August SS-Sturmbannführer Kepplinger, the 17th SS-Panzer Battalion commander, was killed near Laval by the French resistance. The fighting did not last long and the battalion retreated towards Sablé-sur-Sarthe. American forces had already bypassed Laval and by 9 August elements of the US 5th Armored Division were south of Le Mans. The battalion was forced to fight its way eastwards, suffering heavy casualties as it went.

Kampfgruppe Fick, joined a week later by Kampfgruppen Braune and Günther, drawing on men from the armoured reconnaissance battalion and a Reich Labour Service flak battalion, headed for the Saar and Metz. It was felt that these separate units would be less vulnerable than if the division tried to withdraw as a coherent whole. Therefore, because large parts of the division had already been withdrawn, it avoided the Falaise pocket and escaped to fight another day. It would end up taking part in Himmler's ill-fated counteroffensive in the Alsace.

Chapter Fourteen

Loyal Catholic Ukrainians

In Nazi-occupied Ukraine SS-Brigadeführer Wächter, one of the area commandants, began to detect a high level of anti-Communist feeling and indeed Ukrainian nationalism amongst the population. When Hitler had invaded Ukraine in the summer of 1941, some locals had welcomed the Wehrmacht as liberators rather than conquerors. Wächter discovered that many Ukrainians had no love for Stalin or Soviet rule. He suggested to Himmler that the SS capitalize on this and that anti-Communist Ukrainians be recruited to form a volunteer division. A precedent for this had already been established.

In the Balkans Himmler had recently approved the recruiting of Croatian and Bosnian Muslims to help fight the Christian Serbs, who formed the bulk of Tito's partisans in German-occupied Yugoslavia. The pro-Nazi Croatian dictator Ante Pavlic was not happy about this as he saw it as a move to destabilize his state. Himmler simply chose to ignore his concerns. Feeding off historic hatreds, Muslim volunteers were issued with an anti-Semitic propaganda pamphlet called 'Islam and Judaism'. The resulting 13th Waffen-Gebirgs Division der SS Handschar Kroatische Nr 1, under the command of SS-Brigadeführer Sauberzweig, was to prove a complete disaster.

Nazi propaganda minister Joseph Goebbels always capitalized on the media opportunities provided by the premier divisions of the Waffen-SS. Therefore, he was aghast when Himmler informed him that he was recruiting Islam to the Nazi cause. Responding to Goebbels' concerns, the Reichsführer said he had 'nothing against Islam because it educates the men in this division for me and promises them heaven if they fight and are killed in action; a very practical and attractive religion for soldiers!' All this was wishful thinking on the part of Himmler. In March 1943 he granted permission for the creation of a Catholic Ukrainian division, which seemed a much better prospect.

The Ukrainians proved eager recruits for Wächter's proposed SS division. They were, though, largely Galician Ukrainians. Himmler insisted they must come from western Ukraine, formerly Polish Galicia, and be Greek Catholic rather than Russian Orthodox, thereby barring Soviet Ukrainians. The idea was that anti-Communist volunteers would be drawn from the area of Poland that had once been part of the Austro-Hungarian Empire and therefore former loyal servants of the Habsburg Emperor. This area had been cynically ceded to the Soviet Union under the terms of the Nazi-Soviet non-aggression pact of August 1939, under which the Red Army had occupied eastern Poland. Himmler, a Catholic himself, permitted his Ukrainian volunteers to have their own chaplains, which was a rare concession and unheard of in other SS units.

When recruitment commenced in April 1943 there were a staggering 100,000 applicants for 30,000 places. Typically, a Waffen-SS division numbered about 15,000 fighting men and 5,000 support troops. Many of the others were not turned away but were recruited to form five Galician police regiments. Imprisoned Ukrainian nationalists were released from Sachsenhausen, but most chose not to join the SS and some were promptly sent back again.

Initially the new division was under SS-Brigadeführer Schimana. Then in November 1943 Himmler placed an Austrian major-general, the elderly and professorial-looking Fritz Freitag, in charge. The infantry was organized into three grenadier regiments, while about 350 Galician volunteer officers and 2,000 non-commissioned officers were despatched to Germany. After their training was complete in May 1944 the 14th Waffen-Grenadier Division der SS Galizien was shipped to the Eastern Front just in time to face the onslaught of the Red Army's Lvov-Sandomierz offensive. Himmler took it upon himself to personally inspect his Galician Nazis that June, an event that was photographed for prosperity.

Lvov was a key military communications hub, acting as an important road and rail junction. Indeed, after Hitler was driven from much of Ukraine during the first half of 1944, Lvov became of great importance to him as a focal point between his forces in Poland and those in Romania. It provided the shortest route to the upper Vistula, particularly the Nazis' vital Silesian industrial region. It also protected the Polish oilfields in the region of Berislaw and Drohobycz.

Stalin had occupied Lvov in September 1939, in accordance with the secret provisions of the Nazi-Soviet pact. After Hitler's invasion of the Soviet Union, it was discovered that Stalin's secret police had massacred thousands of prisoners, many of them Ukrainian nationalists. The Jews of

Lvov also suffered at the hands of the Nazis and Ukrainian nationalists, who felt the region should belong to Ukraine not Poland. The Germans claimed that the city's Jewish population had helped with the massacres, and in the pogroms that followed Ukrainian partisans, supported by the German authorities, killed about 4,000 Jews.

Hitler's defences in 1944 were considerably stronger than the Austro-Hungarian fieldworks of 1914 when the Russians failed to achieve a decisive breakthrough. His troops were firmly entrenched east of the Western Bug and everywhere between Brody and Vladimir Volynsk. Marshal Konev planned to cut his way through Hitler's lines in the region of Zolochev, which would provide a tactical breach, while the strategic line of attack would be to the north towards Kamenka and Rava Russkaya.

Stalin's Lvov-Sandomierz offensive was an unusual operation in that it was the only time during the war that a single Soviet Front was tasked with destroying a whole German Army Group largely unassisted. Nonetheless, Konev's forces were greatly strengthened: he mustered seven tank corps, three mechanized corps, six cavalry divisions and seventy-two rifle divisions. These units numbered well over a million men, equipped with 1,600 tanks and assault guns, 14,000 guns and mortars and 2,806 combat aircraft from General S.A. Krasovsky's 2nd Air Army.

North of Lvov the 3rd Guards and 13th Armies, 1st Guards Tank Army and General V.K. Baranov's mechanized cavalry corps were to strike in the direction of Rava-Russkaya and the 4th Panzer Army. In the south the 60th and 38th Armies, plus the 3rd Guards and 4th Tank Armies and General S.V. Sokolov's mechanized cavalry group, were to push on Lvov, cutting their way through the 1st Panzer Army. Even further south the 1st Guards and 18th Armies, with the 5th Guards Army following up, were to attack the weak Hungarian 1st Army guarding the approaches to Stanislav. Further north, beyond Konev's Front, lay elements of General Konstantin Rokossovsky's 1st Byelorussian Front, which had not been committed to Operation Bagration in June 1944 and would attack 56th Panzer Corps.

According to Stalin's intelligence, Army Group North Ukraine consisted of thirty-four infantry divisions, one motorized and five panzer divisions, and two infantry brigades. This totalled 600,000 men plus another 300,000 in logistical units, with 900 panzers and assault guns and 6,300 field guns and mortars. Other assets included 700 aircraft of Luftflotte 4, in particular the veteran 8th Fliegerkorps, although the Group did not have direct control of them. The Soviets assessed that at the approaches to the Vistula and the Carpathians German defences had been constructed to a depth of almost 48km.

Major General F.W. von Mellenthin, chief of staff for the 48th Panzer Corps, recalled:

> By 13 July the Russians had taken Vilnius and Pinsk, and had reached the outskirts of Kovno and Grodno. They were within 100 miles [160km] of the German frontier, and there was "a very real danger" of their "breaking through into East Prussia as a result of their victory and our absence of reserves". This was the moment chosen by Marshal Konev to launch the new offensive in Galicia.

General Josef Harpe's Army Group North Ukraine had created three main defensive belts that were only 30km deep. In addition, the towns of Valdimir Volynskiy, Brody, Zolochev, Rava Russkaya and Stanislav had been turned into fortified strongpoints. The 3rd Panzer Corps was deployed from Lvov to Brody to the northeast, which was expected to be the main Soviet line of attack. The area east of Lvov, the sector where the main attack thrust was expected, was mined with 160,000 anti-personnel and 200,000 anti-tank mines.

Konev tried to convince Harpe that his main attack would fall far to the south of the city rather than on it, and indeed Harpe's intelligence did not notice the Soviet 1st Guards Tank Army moving north. Konev's deception plans made it appear that he had a major strike group on his left flank poised to thrust towards Stanislav rather than towards Lvov and Rava Russkaya. Opposite Stanislav, he simulated the concentration of a tank army and a tank corps behind the 1st Guards Army and a tank army behind the 18th Army. These efforts included 453 fake tanks and 568 fake guns, thirty mock-up field kitchens and six dummy fuel points.

Konev's attack opened with General V.N. Gordov's 3rd Guards Army and General N.P. Pukhov's 13th Army launching their troops towards Soka, Radekhov, Rava Russkaya and Lublin respectively. The main assault by the 38th and 60th Armies towards Lvov via Zolochev commenced the following day.

Stalin's resources staggered von Mellenthin, who recorded:

> At 0820 on 14 July the great onslaught began. The Red Army employed masses of materiel on a scale never known before; in particular, they flung in thousands of aircraft and for the first time in the

war enjoyed unquestioned command of the air. The preliminary bombardment lasted an hour but was very violent; it was followed by concentrated attacks in two sectors. By 0930 it was clear that two of our infantry divisions had been hit very heavily and would be incapable of mastering the situation on their own, so we asked for the 1st and 8th Panzer Divisions to counterattack.

Resistance by the 1st and 4th Panzer Armies was much better than that conducted by Army Group Centre's shattered armies. Konev threw in his tanks in a two-pronged attack; the right (southern) part forced its way across the Bug and headed north for General Rokossovsky's planned push on Lublin and the Vistula but panzer and SS divisions initially held up its left as it fought its way south towards Lvov. The northern attack ran into the prepared positions of the weak 291st and 340th Infantry Divisions, but these were easily penetrated. To the northwest, into the gap either side of Radekhov, Konev poured Cavalry-Mechanized Group Baranov and the 1st Guards Tank Army. It took the 13th Army two days of tough fighting to surround Brody.

With his defences east of Lvov just about holding, Harpe decided to commit his tactical reserves – the 1st and 8th Panzer Divisions – in an attempt to stifle the Soviet offensive on 14 and 15 July. Although Konev had been ordered by Stalin to hold back the 3rd Guards and 4th Guards Tank Armies until a deep penetration had been made, he knew he must act quickly to exploit the situation.

After some fierce fighting the 1st Panzer Army's 1st Panzer successfully brought the Soviets to a halt at Oleyyov on the 15th. The Germans also counterattacked the 38th Army south of Zolochev, which lay east of Lvov. Unfortunately, instead of striking eastwards along a previously arranged route, the 8th Panzer swung south on the Zlochuv-Jezierna road. General Balck had forbidden troop movements along this route for fear of the Red Air Force. His fears were realized when fighter-bombers swooped and reduced the 8th Panzers' columns to blazing wrecks.

Konev had trouble bringing his tank armies to bear in the Lvov attack because the 15th Infantry Corps from the 60th Army had only managed to hack a narrow corridor – 4–6.5km wide – to a depth of 18km. General P.S. Rybalko, commander of the 3rd Guards Tank Army, took the decision to shove his men down this corridor on the 16th and was followed up by General D.D. Lelyushenko's 4th Tank Army. This was the only time during the war that two entire tank armies were committed to combat on such a narrow front and while their flanks were being counterattacked. With German artillery bombarding this 'Koltiv Corridor', the 1st and 8th Panzer Divisions prepared to counterattack, supported by Freitag's Ukrainian 14th SS.

Once Rybalko's men were in the corridor, General Arthur Hauffe's German 13th Corps knew it must withdraw and fell back to the Prinz Eugen Stellung defensive position. By 17 July the Soviets had captured parts of this strongpoint, which Freitag's Galician Ukrainians attempted to recapture until a number of powerful Soviet IS-2 tanks appeared. The gamble paid off and on the evening of 18 July Konev's 1st Ukrainian Front cut through Harpe's defences to a width of 200km, advanced between 50 and 80km, and surrounded 45,000 men near Brody. Despite pleas to General Hauffe by his subordinates, there was little he could do to help the four divisions in the Brody salient to escape.

The following day the 4th Panzer Army committed the 16th Panzer Division and the 20th Motorized and 168th Infantry Divisions in the vicinity of Zholkov to block the 1st Guards Tank Army's advance towards Lvov. But meeting no serious resistance, the latter continued westwards and did not turn south where the Germans were waiting. By the end of the day its forward detachment had advanced to a depth of between 30 and 40km and was approaching Rava Russkaya.

The 48th and 24th Panzer Corps attempted to reach the 13th Corps but to no avail. On 18 July von Mellenthin, taking command of the 8th Panzer, tried to cut his way through to the trapped men of the 13th Corps at Brody. The Soviets were waiting for him with minefields and concentrated artillery and tank fire. Mellenthin remembered:

> Two days later the bulk of 13th Corps, led by Generals Lasch and Lange, succeeded in fighting their way through to our lines. Thousands of men formed up in the night in a solid mass and to the accompaniment of thunderous 'hurrahs' threw themselves at the enemy. The impact of a great block of desperate men, determined to do or die, smashed through the Russian line, and thus a great many of the troops were saved. But all guns and heavy weapons had to be abandoned, and a huge gap was opened in the front. Marshal Konev's tanks poured through and the whole German position in southern Galicia became untenable.

Those forces remaining in the Brody pocket resisted for four miserable days until it was cut in half and they were finally wiped out on the 22nd.

The Germans suffered 30,000 killed and 15,000 captured, as well as losing 68 panzers, 500 guns and 3,500 lorries. Some 14,000 men of Freitag's 14th SS Division were caught in the Brody area and annihilated.

Just 2,000 or 3,000 Ukrainians managed to escape into Hungary. Those who surrendered could expect little leniency from their captors. Some of those who evaded capture sought sanctuary in the local forests and, along with other Ukrainian nationalists, waged a guerrilla war against the Red Army for several years. Despite the severe mauling of his untested division, there was no doubting Freitag's courage as he was decorated with the Knight's Cross.

Freitag's exhausted survivors were sent to Slovakia to refit. When they crossed into Slovakia, Ukrainian nationalist militia took up their weapons, determined to defend Galicia from the Russians even if the Germans were withdrawing. Freitag's division was slowly rebuilt, this time using captured Soviet Ukrainians, a factor which was reflected in its redesignation to 14th Waffen-Grenadier Division der SS Ukrainische Nr 1.

Hitler was violently distracted from the Eastern and Western Fronts on 20 July 1944 when plotters attempted to kill him at his headquarters near Rastenburg in East Prussia, called the Wolfsschanz or Wolf's Lair. Although four people were killed and five injured as a result of the bombing, Hitler survived with only minor injuries. He spent the following weeks tracking down the conspirators: in total some 5,000 people were arrested and 200 executed by the SS.

The remaining Lvov garrison had no intention of being trapped and on the night of the 26th successfully broke out. It took the Soviets the following day to clear out the rearguard and bitter street fighting raged for 72 hours before Lvov was finally liberated on 27 July. About half of the 40,000 German troops in and around Lvov were killed or captured.

The remains of Himmler's Ukrainische rapidly found themselves involved in security duties, firstly being sent to help crush the Slovak rising in August 1944 and then to engage in anti-partisan operations in Yugoslavia. In the case of Slovakia, an improvised SS-panzer regiment, formed from SS training schools in Bohemia and Moravia, quickly seized Neusohl, the centre of the Slovak rebellion. Operations were also conducted by the 18th SS Panzergrenadier Division Horst Wessel and SS police units, with a regiment of Ukrainians trailing reluctantly along in support. Gottlob Berger was sent by Himmler to cajole the Slovak government back into line. He was then replaced by Hermann Höfle and in the aftermath almost 10,000 Slovak Jews were sent to the concentration camps.

In contrast, in October 1944 Himmler disbanded the ill-disciplined Handschar division and ordered that a kampfgruppe be formed using only the German and Volksdeutsche cadre. The Muslim recruits had mutinied during training in France thanks to the harsh treatment meted out to them by their German SS instructors. They were contemptuous of the volunteers' comic opera fez headgear, special rations and their adherence to their imams. In response to this, several instructors were murdered. This made the Handschar the only SS division ever to mutiny. It should have been disbanded immediately, but instead the ringleaders were shot. Once back in Yugoslavia, the division committed many atrocities, particularly against the Serbs, and the Muslim element was considered a growing liability. This signalled its end.

A second short-lived unit recruited from Bosnian and Croatian Muslims was likewise disbanded in October 1944. Dubbed the 23rd Waffen-Grenadier Gebirgs Division der SS Kama Kroatische Nr 2, it was dissolved before training was even complete thanks to repeated disciplinary problems. Although 9,000 men had been recruited, Himmler decided not to risk another mutiny. The remaining Kampfgruppe Hanke, drawn from both divisions, then fought in Hungary and Austria. Exactly the same fate befell the ill-advised 21st Waffen-Gebirgs Division der SS Skanderbeg. It was raised using 6,000 Muslim Albanians from Albania and Kosovo in the summer of 1944, but over half of them promptly deserted when deployed on security operations. In response to this, an irate Himmler ordered the division to be disbanded and the German cadre to form Kampfgruppe Skanderbeg, which was sent to join the 7th SS Division Prinz Eugen in Yugoslavia.

By January 1945 the Ukrainische was in southern Poland and had been rebuilt to a strength of 13,000 men. However, the men of Ukrainische Nr 1 by this point of the war were not keen on fighting and made a point of avoiding action as much as possible. Their biggest concern was falling into the hands of the Red Army. When the ineffectual 14th Waffen-Grenadier Division der SS Ukrainische Nr 1 moved into Austria in March 1945, it was instructed to hand over all its heavy weaponry to the Luftwaffe's newly forming 10th Parachute Division in the Krems-Melk area. The latter was destined for Czechoslovakia and the Ukrainians were grateful not to be going with it. At the end of the war the Ukrainische surrendered to the British at Radstadt in Austria. The remains of the Handschar battle group also surrendered to the British in Austria.

The two units formed from Russian renegades, the 29th and 30th Waffen-Grenadier Divisions Russiche Nr 1 and 2, proved equally ill-fated experiments in the use of foreign volunteers. The survivors from both divisions were captured by the Red Army and either shot on the spot or sent to the Gulag, which was a fitting punishment in light of all the atrocities they had committed.

Chapter Fifteen

The SS Flatten Warsaw

Following Stalin's hugely successful summer offensive in 1944, Field Marshal Model turned to Himmler's Waffen-SS for assistance in stabilizing the shattered front north of Warsaw. While the 1st SS Leibstandarte Adolf Hitler and 2nd SS Das Reich Panzer Divisions had been shipped west to re-equip after their mauling in the Kamenets Podolskiy pocket, the 3rd SS Totenkopf and 5th SS Wiking Panzer Divisions remained in Romania and Poland rearming.

Although the 5th SS may have been the first and best of the foreign Waffen-SS divisions in terms of combat performance, its behaviour left much to be desired. Wiking, like so many of its SS counterparts, was regularly involved in war crimes throughout the conflict on the Eastern Front. On a number of occasions, the division was responsible for the massacre of Jews. Discipline also proved to be a problem, with the violent mistreatment of Soviet prisoners and civilians, which often led to cold-blooded murder. Complaints were even raised by neighbouring German and Slovak divisions about looting by the 5th SS in the Mius river area.

The 3rd SS Totenkopf was notified to move north as early as 25 June 1944, but disruption to the rail networks and roads meant that it took two weeks to get to northeastern Poland. Arriving on 7 July, it found the Red Amy was already striking towards the Polish city of Grodno, threatening the southern flank of Army Group Centre's 4th Army and the northern flank of the 2nd Army.

Deployed at Grodno, Totenkopf was assigned the task of creating a defensive line for the 4th Army to retire behind. Spectacularly the division held off 400 Soviet tanks for eleven days before withdrawing southwest towards Warsaw. Joined by the Hermann Göring Panzer Division at Siedlce, 80km east of the Polish capital, they held the Soviets for almost a week from 24 July, keeping open an escape corridor for the 2nd Army as it fled towards the Vistula. Three days later the Soviets threw almost 500 tanks to the south and by 29 July were in the suburbs of Warsaw.

Wiking arrived in western Warsaw on 27 July and trundled through the city to take up positions to the east. The next day Stalin ordered General Rokossovsky to occupy Praga, Warsaw's suburb on the eastern banks of the Vistula, and to establish a number of bridgeheads over the river to the south of the city. Rokossovsky at this stage enjoyed a three to one superiority in infantry and five to one in armour and artillery. His front had at its disposal nine armies. Against this, Model's 2nd Army could muster four understrength panzer divisions and one infantry division, while the 9th Army had just two divisions and two brigades of infantry. However, four panzer divisions, the 3rd SS, 5th SS, 4th and 19th, poised to counterattack, now defended the approaches to the Polish capital.

Wiking struck out in a westerly direction from Stanislawow with fifty panzers in an effort to link up with the Hermann Göring and 19th Panzer Divisions, which were fighting a tank battle at Okuniew and Ossow. The two divisions were subsequently repulsed and on the evening of 31 July the Soviets took Okuniew, but could not budge the Germans from their strongpoint at Ossow. North of the Soviet 8th Tank Corps, the 3rd Tank Corps remained unsupported and, like the 16th Corps, had endured a day of heavy attacks from German armour, artillery and infantry. The commander of the Soviet 2nd Army was in an impossible position: his units were enduring heavy casualties, he was short of supplies and his rear was under threat.

Rokossovsky could not fulfil his orders to break though the German defences and enter Praga by 8 August: it was simply not possible. On 1 August at 1610 hours he ordered the attack to be broken off just as Model launched his major counterattack. Model began to probe the weak spot in Rokossovsky's line between Praga and Siedlce. His intention was to hit the Soviets in the flank and the rear, and soon to the northeast of Warsaw the 39th Panzer Corps was counterattacking the 3rd Tank Corps and driving it back to Wolomin.

Totenkopf and three army panzer divisions were to strike south into the unsupported Soviet columns. From Wegrow pushing towards Wolomin came Wiking. At the same time Totenkopf was launched into the fray from Siedlce towards Stanislawow with the intention of trapping those Soviet forces on the northeastern bank of the Dluga.

General Nikolaus von Vormann, appointed to command the 9th Army, brought up reinforcements from the 2nd Army's reserves and also launched a counterattack. Using units of Totenkopf and Wiking attacking from the forests to the east of Michalow, he drove the Soviet 8th Guards

Tank Corps from Okuniew at 2100 hours on 1 August and linked up with the 39th Panzer Corps from the west.

By 2 August the 19th Panzer Division, followed by the 4th Panzer, was in Radzymin and the Soviet 3rd Tank Corps was thrown back towards Wolomin. The following day the Hermann Göring Panzer Division rolled into Wolomin. Pressed into the area of Wolomin, General Vedeneev's 3rd Tank Corps was trapped. Attempts by the 8th Guards Tank Corps and the 16th Tank Corps to reach them failed, with the 8th Guards suffering serious casualties in the attempt.

After a week of heavy fighting the Soviet 3rd Tank Corps was surrounded by the 4th and 19th Panzer Divisions. About 3,000 Soviet troops were killed and another 6,000 captured. The Soviets also lost 425 of the 800 tanks and self-propelled guns they had begun the battle with on 18 July. By noon on 5 August the Germans had ceased their counterattack and the battle for the Praga approaches had come to an end. The 3rd Tank Corps was destroyed and both the 8th Guards Tank Corps and the 16th Tank Corps had taken major losses. The exhausted Soviet 2nd Tank Army handed over its positions to the 47th and 70th Armies and withdrew to lick its wounds. With the Wehrmacht fully tied up fending off Soviet attacks, it was left to Himmler's hated SS police units to stamp out the Polish rising.

Lieutenant General Tadeusz Bór-Komorowski, commander of the Polish Home Army, ordered his men to rise up against the German occupation of Warsaw at 1700 hours on 1 August 1944. Poor communications meant that these instructions were issued staggered, with the subsector commanders being informed at 0800 hours, the district commanders 2 hours later and the unit commanders at midday. Platoon commanders did not get their orders until 1400 hours. This caused delay and confusion, resulting in only a third of their weapons being issued.

SS-Standartenführer Paul Geibel, commander of the SS and police in the city, at 1600 hours received intelligence from a Luftwaffe officer that a general rising was scheduled for 1700. Geibel immediately notified Luftwaffe Major General Reiner Stahel, the garrison commander, who put all German forces on alert. Within an hour Stahel's headquarters in the Brühl Palace came under attack. As a result of this warning the Germans were not taken completely by surprise. Crucially, they held the airport, the police and army headquarters, the radio station and the Vistula bridges. Stahel and his commanders were hampered, though, as they had no contingency plans nor the manpower to deal with such a widespread rising. In consequence, for the first few days their response was ill-coordinated.

At his headquarters in Cracow Hans Frank, the German governor-general of Poland, was alarmed by Stahel's report early in the evening of 1 August. Frank's strong garrison was put on alert in case they were subjected to similar attacks. His main concern, though, was for the German 9th Army's supply routes through Warsaw over the Vistula to the battlefields to the east of Praga. SS-Obergruppenführer Wilhelm Koppe, the SS police chief, who was also in Cracow, telephoned Geibel to inform him that reinforcements were on their way. When Stahel learned of this he decided to go onto the defensive until help arrived.

Stahel's 12,000-strong garrison comprised 5,000 regular troops, 4,000 Luftwaffe personnel (more than a quarter of whom were manning the air defences) and a 2,000-strong security regiment. Wehrmacht forces in the immediate area numbered up to 16,000 men, with another 90,000 further afield. SS-Standartenführer Geibel's police and SS units totalled 5,710 men, supported by 3,500 factory and rail guards. Geibel also managed to borrow four Tiger tanks, a Panther tank, four other medium tanks and an assault gun from Wiking to strengthen his command.

A motley battle group of 12,000 troops under SS-Gruppenführer Heinz Reinefarth, supported by thirty-seven assault guns and a company of heavy tanks, was also assembled to crush the Polish Home Army in Warsaw. SS reinforcements included SS-Brigadeführer Bronislav Kaminski's hated anti-partisan Russian National Liberation Army (Russkaia Osvoboditelnania Norodnaia Armiia – SS-Sturmbrigade RONA). This was also known as the 29th Waffen-Grenadier Division der SS and was one of the worst SS units ever created. Kaminski was supported by SS-Oberführer Oskar Dirlewanger's equally appalling anti-partisan brigade designated the 36th Waffen-Grenadier Division der SS. Both were little more than ill-disciplined militia. Himmler flew to Poznan from his headquarters in East Prussia, and rallied those men under Reinefarth whose support weapons included four heavy mortars and 150 flamethrowers. Additionally, Colonel Wilhelm Schmidt supplied 2,000 men drawn from the 603rd Reserve Regiment plus a grenadier and police battalion and two platoons from the 500th SS Assault Battalion. They were also supported by artillery, fifteen heavy mortars and eight flamethrowers.

All the German forces in Warsaw were placed under SS-Obergruppenführer Erich von dem Bach-Zelewski during the first week of August. A specialist in anti-partisan operations, he had been overseeing the

Léon Degrelle awarding medals to members of his Freiwilligen SS-Sturmbrigade Wallonien in Charleroi, Belgium, who escaped Cherkassy. They held a celebratory dinner in Brussels on 1 April 1944, with Sepp Dietrich just visible second from the left as guest of honour.

During Operation Epsom, launched on 25 June 1944 to the west of Caen, the British came up against teenage Nazis such as these, who had been recruited into the Frundsberg, Hitlerjugend and Hohenstaufen Divisions.

This Hitlerjugend panzer-grenadier barely looks 18. He is armed with the MG42 fitted with the drum magazine.

Young Waffen-SS machine-gunner killed in action. The tube slung around his neck contained a replacement barrel for his MG42 machine gun.

In the foreground is a Das Reich Sd.Kfz.251 half-track caught on the road in Normandy. Hohenstaufen arrived in Normandy with almost 300 of these vehicles.

Two Panzer Mk IVs belonging to Das Reich. These were lost in an encounter with the US Army at St Fromond, just east of the N174 from Carentan to St Lô, on 9 July 1944.

A Panther tank belonging to Hitlerjugend knocked out by the Canadian Army.

Wiking Panther in Poland. In the summer of 1944 Totenkopf and Wiking were instrumental in stopping the Red Army before Warsaw.

Wiking Panzergrenadiers outside Warsaw. The 5th SS deployed to the east of the city in late July 1944 and struck towards Wolomin.

Officers and men of Wiking about to go into action. The division had a full battalion of Panthers at the start of the battle to hold Warsaw.

Polish fighters in Warsaw with a Sd.Kfz.251 half-track captured on 14 August 1944. It belonged to the panzergrenadiers of Wiking.

Assault gun from Sturmgeschütz Brigade 280 supporting troops from Hohenstaufen in Arnhem on 19 September 1944.

Hohenstaufen panzer-grenadiers mopping up the streets of Arnhem.

In the winter of 1944 Sepp Dietrich was ordered to take command of the newly forming 6th Panzer Army, ready to spearhead an attack through the Ardennes and on to Antwerp.

Leibstandarte's Hummel self-propelled guns. At the time of the Battle of the Bulge in the winter of 1944, the 1st SS was short of these. Along with Das Reich, Hohenstaufen and Hitlerjugend, the division formed part of the 6th Panzer Army.

Waffen-SS half-track rolls past a captured American vehicle as Kampfgruppe Peiper advances during the Battle of the Bulge. This was one of a number of battle groups that led Leibstandarte and Hitlerjugend's thrust towards the Meuse river south of Liège.

Panzergrenadiers belonging to Kampfgruppe Hansen, which was responsible for destroying the US 14th Cavalry Group on the road between Poteau and Recht.

Kampfgruppe Hansen panzergrenadiers running past burning American vehicles caught on the open road in the Ardennes.

German propaganda newsreel shot taken on 17 December 1944 showing a Leibstandarte Panzer IV passing American prisoners.

Tiger II of the 501st Heavy SS-Panzer Battalion which supported Kampfgruppe Peiper. Although designed as a breakthrough tank, it was too heavy and cumbersome to be effective in the confines of the Ardennes.

construction of defences on the Vistula near Gdansk. Bach-Zelewski was soon to discover that both Kaminski and Dirlewanger's militias were ill-disciplined. Bach-Zelewski thought the Kaminski Brigade was the lowest of the low, remarking 'The fighting value of these Cossacks was, as usual in such a collection of people without a fatherland, very poor. They had a great liking for alcohol and other excesses and had no interest in military discipline.' In contrast he noted 'Dirlewanger's brigade possessed the highest fighting qualities.'

Just after dawn on 5 August German bombers, without fighter cover, dropped high explosives and incendiaries onto the Wola district. This forced the civilian population towards the city centre. German troops then counterattacked. Dirlewanger and Schmidt's men advanced behind tanks along Wolska and Gorzewska Streets heading for Kercely Square. The tanks blasted the Poles' barricades at close range, then the infantry stepped forward with their flame-throwers. Kaminski's Cossacks struck along Grojecka Street towards Narutowizc Square, to try to seize the area south of Wola. In response Colonel Radóslaw reinforced his defences with two battalions and two captured German tanks. The latter drove into the ghetto and set free 350 Jews held in the concentration camp.

The following morning, 6 August, the Luftwaffe returned with its bombers and fighter-bombers attacking the barricades on the Chlodna-Towarowa crossroads and Kercely Square. Dirlewanger's SS-brigade was soon pushing along Chlodna and Elektoralna streets towards Theatre Square and the Brühl Palace. This drove a wedge through the Polish resis-tance in Wola to the city centre. The Poles, short of weapons and running out of ammunition, had little choice but to fall back to the Palace of Justice in Leszno. Once the Germans had overwhelmed the defences in Chlodna and Ogrodowa Streets, the Poles had to fall back even further towards the city centre. By midday Dirlewanger's men had reached the Saxon Gardens and Theatre Square. Contact was then made with the SS units holding Brühl Palace. They were just in time as General Stahel's men were on the point of giving up.

Dirlewanger, supported by two Tiger tanks and a Poznan police bat-talion, renewed the onslaught on 7 August. The Poles were forced back along Elektoralna. The Germans also pushed along Leszno Street. Kaminski's SS-brigade made faltering progress from Ochtoa towards the city centre. In truth he and his men were more interested in the contents of the Machorka vodka factory. The Poles launched a counterattack towards Wola but were repulsed by a Panther tank and several armoured cars.

By 2000 hours the Germans had secured the Wolska-Chlodna-Elektoralna-Saxon Gardens artery. They had almost reached the Kierbedź bridge. A terrible massacre took place in Elektoralna Street, perpetrated by Dirlewanger and Kaminski's men. It was not the first such incident. At the Marie Curie Radium Institute on 5 August drunken Cossacks had taken part in atrocities against the civilian staff and patients. Rape and murder were followed by the hospital being set on fire.

For two days the renegade Russians ran amok in Wola, the western part of the city centre and Ochota. Atrocities also took place at St Lazarus Hospital and Wola Hospital. At the Ursus factory civilians were herded into the yard and shot. It was estimated that up to 7,000 people were murdered there. After the war the German officers involved disingenuously laid the blame firmly on Kaminski and Dirlewanger. They, however, were in command. Between 5 and 7 August almost 40,000 civilians were executed or lost to the flames.

'They gave no mercy in battle and did not expect any,' said von dem Bach-Zelewski of Dirlewanger's SS-brigade. 'As a result they suffered losses three times as great as those of any other German unit.' He thought little of Reinefarth's Poznan police group in the attack, but noted they were good in defence and much better disciplined than Dirlewanger's men. He was also impressed by Colonel Schmidt's unit, which, while lacking flair, was well led.

General Heinz Guderian, chief of the general staff, was appalled by the conduct of Kaminski and Dirlewanger's men:

> Some of the SS units involved – which incidentally were not drawn from the Waffen-SS – failed to preserve their discipline. The Kaminski Brigade was composed of former prisoners of war, mostly Russians who were ill-disposed towards the Poles; the Dirlewanger brigade was formed from German convicts on probation. These doubtful units were now committed to desperate street battles where each house had to be captured and where the defendants were fighting for their lives; as a result, they abandoned all moral standards.

On 11 August the Germans used for the first time small remote-controlled tanks, known as Goliaths, in Okopowa Street. These comprised a tracked demolition charge operated electrically via a cable from another tank. They could carry up to 75kg of explosives and were ideal for clearing

barricades and other strongpoints. The Germans took the Jewish cemetery but were counterattacked by a Polish battalion when they tried to take
the Catholic cemetery. By the end of the day the Germans had cleared two
districts and started attacks on the Old Town. The Poles clung to the
hope that the Red Army was coming to their aid. However, disturbing
reports were filtering in that Polish officers who had reached the Red
Army east of the Vistula had been arrested.

The fighting, though, was far from over. There remained a force of
about 4,000 Polish fighters in Mokotow, plus forces of unknown strength
in the Old Town and the city centre. Other units were also in the Bielany,
Zoliborz and Marymont districts. Another force of about 3,000 had been
reported gathering in the forests around Warsaw.

To fend off a wider encircling movement by the Red Army to the north,
Field Marshal Model deployed the 4th SS Panzer Corps with the Totenkopf and Wiking Divisions moved into blocking positions. From
14 August the Soviets attacked for a week but the SS successfully held
off fifteen rifle divisions and two tank corps. By 26 August Totenkopf had
been forced back to Praga, but a counterattack by its forces on 11 September thwarted another Red Army attempt to link up with the trapped
Polish Home Army. It was Totenkopf and Wiking which had the dubious
honour of consigning Warsaw to two months of bloody agony. They were
not, though, involved in the suppression of the Warsaw uprising.

After sixty-two days, and the loss of 15,000 dead and 25,000 wounded,
the Polish Home Army surrendered in Warsaw on 2 October 1944. Up to
200,000 civilians had also been killed in the needless orgy of destruction.
The vengeful Himmler expelled the rest of the civilian population and
ordered Warsaw to be flattened. Crushing the Poles had been a pointless
exercise, which cost Hitler 10,000 dead, 9,000 wounded and 7,000 missing.
It was clear from the fatalities outnumbering the wounded that no quarter
had been given. However, German morale was given a much-needed
boost, believing that they rather than Stalin had halted the Red Army at
the gates of Warsaw. The Wiking and Totenkopf Panzer Divisions were
to remain on the Eastern Front until the end of the war. Both fought in
Hungary against the Red Army in early 1945, then withdrew to Austria to
surrender to the Americans.

Chapter Sixteen

Hohenstaufen's Arnhem Victory

After the defeat of the German Army and the Waffen-SS in Normandy in August 1944, Field Marshal von Rundsted CinC West reported, 'At this time, about a hundred tanks are combat ready in Army Group B'. Despite the developing Allied threat to the German city of Aachen, Hitler's intelligence judged that the Allies would strike toward Arnhem, which lay on the northern bank of the Dutch Rhine. A British 1st Airborne Division's intelligence summary noted, 'it is reported that one of the broken panzer divisions has been sent back to the area north of Arnhem to rest and refit; this might produce some fifty tanks.' SS-Obergruppenführer Willi Bittrich and his exhausted 2nd SS Panzer Corps had indeed been withdrawn to the Netherlands having successfully escaped the envelopment at Falaise.

Bittrich did not know that his Hohenstaufen and the Frundsberg SS panzer divisions were in the path of a major Allied airborne and ground attack, which was designed to 'bounce' the Rhine, and overrun the vital industrial region of the Ruhr. He and his divisional commanders assumed that they were in a quiet sector to recuperate, so were not unduly alarmed at the poor condition of their units after the heavy fighting in France. Crucially they lacked manpower and panzers.

Just four days before Field Marshal Montgomery's Operation Market Garden was scheduled to start General 'Boy' Browning commanding the British Airborne Corps issued the following intelligence assessment, 'The total armoured strength is probably not more than 50–100 tanks ... There is every sign of the enemy strengthening the river and canal lines through Nijmegen and Arnhem ... but the troops manning them are not numerous and many are of low category.'

It was at this stage a fatal error of judgement occurred. In wartime generals always have to make very difficult decisions, but on this occasion they grossly underestimated the capabilities of the Waffen-SS. Browning's intelligence on the 2nd SS Panzer Corps was uncannily accurate. Bittrich's command accounted for about half of the estimated total, but just across the German border about forty Tiger Is and IIs were on call. The latter were almost impossible for the paras, armed with 57mm (6 pounder) anti-tank guns, 75mm Pack Howitzers and PIAT man portable anti-tank weapons, to deal with. Their only hope was to lay down such a barrage of fire that it would be enough to persuade the alarmed Tiger crews to break off contact. Such action would require incredible courage. Elements of an assault gun battalion were also to be made available for the Waffen-SS defence of Arnhem. Altogether this would give Bittrich at least 150 tanks and assault guns and other armoured fighting vehicles.

In addition, although Bittrich's divisions were in a poor condition, in Normandy they had proved highly adept at putting together effective kampfgruppen or battle groups using battered front line troops and rear echelon personnel such as clerks and cooks. So not only were the Allies underestimating the potential strength of the panzers that would oppose Market Garden, they also underestimated Bittrich's reaction. A slow response would obviously allow them to steal a lead over the German defenders. A swift response would contest the Allied advance every inch of the way and jeopardise the success of the operation at Arnhem. To make matters worse Bittirch's presence did not filter down to everyone. British glider pilot Alexander Morrison recalled, 'a brief summary of the known troops in northern Holland which, incidentally, made no reference to the two depleted divisions of German armour in the Arnhem area!'

Along the coast once the British were in Antwerp the German 15th Army fell back to a bridgehead blocking the mouth of the Scheldt estuary, thereby barring the sea approach to Antwerp. Dogged German resistance resulted in the Allies wasting almost two months trying to secure the port and the Scheldt, in the meantime much needed supplies had to be driven across Europe from the French ports by the trucks of the 'Red Ball Express.' This meant that everything rested on the performance on Bittrich's exhausted panzer divisions.

Under SS-Obseturmbannführer Walter Harzer the 9th SS Panzer Division Hohenstaufen had barely 6,000 men and around twenty tanks but not all these were operational. Nonetheless, the Hohenstaufen still had large numbers of other armoured fighting vehicles such as armoured cars and self-propelled guns, along with forty armoured personnel carriers to transport its tough panzergrenadiers. This meant that Harzer's division was still more than capable of mobile operations. Under SS-Gruppen-führer Heinz Harmel, the Hohenstaufen's sister division, 10th SS Frunds-berg was much weaker. It retained under 3,500 men and hardly any tanks.

However, Bittrich was soon to be reinforced by elements of a heavy tank battalion equipped with twenty-eight Tiger IIs, a company of twelve Tiger Is and a company of ten assault guns.

Hohenstaufen was deployed in a triangle formed by Arnhem-Zutphen-Apeldorn. They were due to return to Germany for a much needed refit and had been ordered to hand over many of their vehicles to the Frundsberg. Perhaps understandably Harzer was not keen on surrendering his remaining resources and deliberately dragged the process out. The 9th SS had also despatched forces to support Kamfgruppe Walther, part of Student's 1st Parachute Army.

Allied intelligence confirmed the deployment of Hohenstaufen and Frundsberg to the Nijmegen and Arnhem area. This was backed by aerial reconnaissance flights and intelligence from the Dutch resistance. No one though seemed overly concerned. Major Tony Hibbert, British 1st Parachute Brigade attended a meeting with the chief intelligence officer, 1st Airborne Division Major Brian Urguhart noting, 'He went to General Browning, and said that in his view the operation could not succeed, because of the presence of these two divisions.' Browning with just a week to prepare decided that the operation would go ahead.

On the ground carrying out the Garden element Lieutenant General Brian Horrock's British 30th Corps with the Guards Armoured Division, was to drive up Highway 69, followed by the 43rd (Wessex) and 50th (Northumbrian) Infantry Divisions. He was to reach Einhoven on the first day, Nijmegen on the second day and Arnhem by day four. However, British 1st Airborne would end up on its own for nine gruelling days thanks to Bittrich.

The bulk of 1st Airborne landed around Arnhem on 17 September 1944 in complete ignorance of the presence of the SS armour. Harzer was having lunch with SS-Hauptsturmführer Paul Gräbner, commander of the divisional reconnaissance battalion, when Bittrich called. His instruction was for Hohenstaufen to 'reconnoitre in the direction of Arnhem and Nijmegen.' Harzer turned to Gräbner and said, 'Now what are we going to do? The vehicles are dismantled and on the train.' These included forty vehicles from Gräbner's unit. 'How soon can you have the tracks and guns put back on?' Harzer asked his subordinate who was in the middle of his soup. 'We'll be ready to move within three to five hours,' replied Gräbner. 'Get it done in three,' ordered Harzer as he headed for his headquarters. Bittrich had swiftly set in motion reconstituting the very panzer divisions that Allied intelligence so readily dismissed.

After Bittrich was informed of the British airborne drop he immediately called for the bridges at Nijmegen and Arnhem to be brought down to stop them falling into enemy hands, but Field Marshal Model refused claiming that they would be needed for a counterattack. Following some initial confusion Bittrich's two divisions quickly cobbled together various battle groups.

At the same time on 17 September, the artillery of General Horrock's 30th Corps opened fire to support the initial advance of the Irish Guards on a two tanks wide front with infantry from the 231st Brigade from the 50th (Northumbrian) Division. The Guards broke out of their Meuse-Escaut canal bridgehead and rolled into the Netherlands at 1500 hours some 45 minutes after the opening barrage and air attacks. They then ran into elements of two battalions of the 9th SS and two German parachute battalions. These were pushed aside.

Hohenstaufen although preparing to transit home sent its reconnaissance battalion south over the Arnhem highway bridge toward Nijmegen. Another battle group sped westward toward Oosterbeek where most of 1st Airborne was located; this would prevent reinforcements reaching those British paratroops already in Arnhem. The following day Gräbner's unit leaving some self-propelled guns to guard the southern approaches of Nijmegen bridge headed north to Elst. A column of twenty-two vehicles then attempted to force a crossing of Arnhem bridge, the northern end of which was by now firmly in British hands. Half Gräbner's vehicles were destroyed and the SS were driven off amidst a blaze of fire from the paras strongpoints. The bridge was left strewn in debris and burnt out vehicles.

Frundsberg was also despatched to Nijmegen to hold the main bridges against Horrock's advancing armour, this was key to isolating and destroying the paratroops at Oosterbeek. However, with Arnhem bridge in British hands the bulk of the 10th SS was obliged to use the ferry at Pannerden 12km south-east of Arnhem. 'It was 1100 hours on the morning of Thursday 21 September,' according to Geoffrey Powell a company commander with 4th Para Brigade, 'before the Irish Guards received orders to break through to Arnhem Bridge ... Waiting for them were German infantry, by now well dug-in and supported by tanks and SP guns.' 'For three days now,' adds Powell, 'the dogged resistance of Brigadeführer Harmel's SS troops, fighting in the Betuwe between Nijmegen and Arnhem, had slowed the pace of the British advance.'

The Germans had secured the bridge at Arnhem on 20 Setember. In the Oosterbeek pocket Gilder Pilot Louis Hagen was grateful that the 9th SS were not up to full strength, 'If there had not been a sprinkling of first-class and fanatical officers and NCOs in this division, no fight would have been possible. But even with the present state of affairs, it was ridiculous that they did not wipe us out within a few hours.' Hohenstaufen, rein-forced by the 506th Heavy Tank Battalion consisting of powerful Tiger IIs on 24 September, set about eliminating the trapped defenders at Ooster-beek. Luckily for the paras these attacks were initially poorly coordinated with the panzers often operating without adequate infantry support, which left them vulnerable.

Frundsberg were eventually forced back, so Bittrich sent Tiger IIs and a company of Panthers to reinforce them following the landing of the Polish 1st Parachute Brigade at Driel south of Oosterbeek. Geoffrey Powell recalled, 'defeated at Nijmegen, the 10th SS Panzer Division had retired towards Arnhem and was now waiting for 30th Corps' next move.' Horrocks' continually delayed tanks could simply not get through and on 25 September the difficult decision was taken to evacuate the exhausted paratroops trapped at Oosterbeek back across the Rhine. The remains of the British 1st Airborne Division escaped, leaving behind 1,485 dead and 6,414 captured. Bittrich's Waffen-SS panzer divisions suffered 3,300 casu-alties stopping Market Garden from reaching its final objective.

Frundsberg and Hoshenstaufen successfully helped thwart Mont-gomery's attempt to end the war with a thrust into the Rhur and the Allies reverted to their broad front strategy across the whole of Western Europe. Hohenstaufen, following its performance at Arnhem, was sent to Pader-born for a well-earned break and to be re-equipped. Just after Arnhem the Frundsberg were to cause yet more trouble. While trying to destroy the German salient at Geilenkirchen on 15 November 1944 elements of the British 43rd (Wessex) Infantry Division were trapped by Frundsberg around Hoven.

Chapter Seventeen

Budapest Massacre

On 12 December 1944 Stalin ordered the 2nd and 3rd Ukrainian Fronts to take Budapest. The 2nd Ukrainian Front on the left was to attack from Sahy southwards to the Danube north of Esztergom, which would cut off any German retreat to the northwest. The 3rd Ukrainian Front was directed to move northwards from Lake Velence and link up with the 2nd Ukrainian Front near Esztergom. This offensive commenced on 20 December and within six days the two fronts had met, encircling the Hungarian capital.

Budapest was completely cut off by the Red Army once the Budapest-Vienna road was severed on 26 December 1944. Trapped in the city were almost 43,000 German and 37,000 Hungarian troops, along with over 800,000 civilians. Refusing any withdrawal, Hitler declared Festung or Fortress Budapest, which was to be defended to the last.

Trapped in the Budapest pocket was the 9th SS Mountain Corps, comprising the 8th SS Florian Geyer and 22nd SS Maria Theresia Cavalry Divisions, 13th Panzer Division, 60th Panzergrenadier Division Feldherrnalle and 271st Volksgrenadier Division. Hungarian forces in the city included the 1st Armoured, 10th Mixed and 12th Reserve Divisions, as well as elements of six assault artillery battalions and a number of armoured car units. To the south of Budapest the 18th SS Panzergrenadier Division Horst Wessel managed to retreat to safety. Reinforcements sent from Poland comprised the 3rd Panzer Division and the 4th SS Panzer Corps with two tough SS panzer divisions.

Florian Geyer started its career as an anti-partisan brigade conducting operations in the Soviet Union. Initially it was commanded by Willi Bittrich and then Hermann Fegelein. In the summer of 1942 it was expanded to a division and the following year was deployed to Yugoslavia. Under the command of SS-Brigadeführer Joachim Rumhor, it saw action in Czechoslovakia in 1944 and then moved into Hungary. The Maria Theresia Division was essentially its bastard child, having been raised in Hungary using Volksdeutsche and Hungarians in the spring and summer of 1944 under SS Brigadeführer August Zehender. It was formed around Florian Geyer's 17th SS Cavalry Regiment, supplemented by two regiments of Hungarian ethnic Germans. By the time the division went into action at Debreczen only the 17th SS and 52nd SS Cavalry Regiments had been assembled. In October they were joined by the 53rd SS Cavalry Regiment and the whole division fought in the Budapest area until encircled. Similarly, Horst Wessel, which had been formed in early 1944, drew its recruits from the ethnic German community in Hungary.

Defence of the city presented the defenders with a number of problems, not least its differing geography on either side of the Danube. Pest on the eastern bank was flat and hard to fortify while hilly Buda on the western bank, with the Castle Hill government district, offered much better defensive positions. SS-Obergruppenführer Karl Pfeffer-Wildrenbruch, who was appointed garrison commander, would probably have liked to abandon the eastern bank and anchored his defence on the Danube, but tactically and politically this was not possible. Plus, it ran contrary to Hitler's dictate that no ground must ever voluntarily be surrendered to the enemy.

Besides, by late December the Pest bridgehead was considerably larger than the Buda bridgehead. Those forces, including the 8th SS and 271st Volksgrenadiers, west of the Danube were confined to a rectangle that extended north and south of Buda. To the east of the river the remaining defences of the Attila Line, held by the 60th Panzergrenadiers, 13th Panzer, the Hungarian divisions and the 22nd SS, ran in a sizeable arc from Föt in the north through Pécel at its apex to Soroksár in the south. It was only this that gave the defence of the city any depth.

Pfeffer-Wildrenbruch had started his career as a gunner and then became a high-ranking policeman before joining the SS. At the start of the Second World War he commanded the 4th SS Polizei Division before becoming a corps commander. In October 1943 he had been placed in charge of the 6th SS Corps, which included the 15th and 19th Waffen-Grenadier Divisions der SS Lettische Nr 1 and Nr 2. These were formed using Latvian anti-partisan security units. They had proved to be of a higher quality than other comparable forces and were initially gathered together as the Lettische SS Freiwilligen Legion. Both divisions fought with some distinction on the Eastern Front against the Red Army, but their enthusiasm waned after their homeland was overrun in October 1944. Between them they won sixteen Knight's Crosses for gallantry.

In Budapest Pfeffer-Wildrenbruch lacked the infantry with which to properly protect the city. Between them the two SS cavalry divisions could muster around 19,000 men with 46 tanks and assault guns. The SS units included a huge array of foreign 'volunteers' of dubious loyalty. The Hungarian troops knew that their former allies were now their occupiers and that they were trapped between the Nazis and the encroaching Soviets. The Hungarian units defending Budapest were in a sorry state after fighting on the Hungarian Plain. The Hungarians kept two sets of troop manifests, one for themselves and one for the Germans. They reported a ration strength of 55,100 and a combat strength of just 15,050. In manpower terms this equated to two divisions but only the combat strength of a single division. The city militias and police showed no signs of wishing to fight and many of the regular army divisions' soldiers had no inclination to do so either.

By 28 December the Soviets were within 2km of the Danube after capturing János Hospital to the west. They were also the same distance northwest of the German and Hungarian headquarters in the Buda Castle tunnel. Also at risk was Városmajor Grange, the most sensitive point in Buda because if it were to be captured, the Soviets could reach the Castle Hill District and cut the garrison in half. Defence of the Grange was assigned to the Hungarian Volunteer Vannay Battalion.

On 24 December 1944, just before Budapest was cut off, Hitler despatched to Hungary the tough 4th SS Panzer Corps, with Totenkopf and Wiking reinforced by the 1st and 3rd Panzer Divisions from the Warsaw area, plus the 96th and 711th Infantry Divisions, totalling 60,000 men supported by 200 panzers. SS-Obergruppenführer Otto Gille, who had been decorated for breaking out of the Cherkassy pocket at the start of the year, was placed in command. This immediately weakened the German defences on the Vistula, however, enabling the Red Army to reach the Oder. Nonetheless, this development signalled that Hitler was intent on holding Budapest at all costs in order to shield Vienna.

Inside Budapest General Pfeffer-Wildrenbruch and the men of his 9th SS Mountain Corps were under siege and getting desperate. The Red Army shelled and bombed their positions and squeezed them into an ever-shrinking pocket. Ammunition, food and medical supplies were running low and they endured a miserable Christmas. The Luftwaffe attempted to airdrop supplies, but in the face of the Red Air Force and heavy flak this became increasingly impossible to accomplish. Their only hope was relief in the New Year by the 4th SS Panzer Corps marshalling its forces to the west.

Hitler's intention was not so much to rescue the Budapest garrison as to reinforce it. On the table were two options – Operation Paula, which would strike from Székesfehérvár to the southwest of the city, or Operation Konrad from the northwest. Konrad offered the shortest route and, although the terrain was not ideal, was given the go-ahead. The 4th SS Panzer Corps, plus the 1st Panzer Division, did have some chance of breaking through as they had 70 per cent more troops and 140 per cent more armour than the Soviet 4th Guards Army holding the outer ring. However, the Soviets did enjoy a three to one superiority in artillery.

Operation Konrad I, launched on 1 January 1945, saw the 4th SS Panzer Corps strike from Tata north of Budapest. Attacks were also conducted to the west. Martin Steiger, commanding Totenkopf's panzer regiment, recalled: 'Enemy tanks of the type T-34/85 sat in the farms in town [Dunaalmas] and fired at our point vehicles from only 5 metres away.' The Soviet 6th Guards Army blocked the first attempt, which launched from Komárno and initially pushed the Soviets back along the right bank of the Danube. The 6th Guards was ordered to march down the left bank to Komárno, thereby compromising the Germans' flank and rear. The Soviets deployed four extra divisions and the German counterattack was halted on a line Bicske-Mány-Zsámbék, and by 12 January the SS were forced to withdraw having got to within 24km of the city.

Determined to stop the German relief effort, Marshal Tolbukhin redeployed the 2nd Mechanized Guards Army Corps and the 86th Guards Rifle and 49th Guards Army Divisions from the encirclement of Budapest on 3 January. The Soviet 46th Army was also instructed to halt its attacks and ensure that the garrison did not attempt a breakout. Key to preventing this was possession of Mátyás-hegy Hill, which changed hands seven times on 3 January.

German and Hungarian losses between 1 and 7 January 1945 totalled around 3,500 – almost 10 per cent of the 4th SS Panzer Corps' strength – killed, wounded or missing, along with thirty-nine tanks and assault guns destroyed. Tolbukhin meantime had deployed defences blocking both the garrison and the relief force and on 3 January ordered attacks on Buda to stop in order to free up more troops. Three days later seven Soviet divisions were in place to prevent the garrison from breaking out. Despite the hopelessness of the situation, on 11 January 1945 Pfeffer-Wildrenbruch was awarded the Knight's Cross and on 1 February the Oak Leaves.

Konrad II was launched from Esztergom on 7 January, but again was halted just short of its objective at Pilisszentkereszt. Having failed to breach the Soviet lines to the north, the Germans fell back on the southern option. Konrad III, the last part of the operation, commenced on 17 January with the 4th SS Panzer Corps and 3rd Panzer Corps attacking from the south of Budapest near Székesfehérvár with the aim of trapping ten Soviet divisions against the Danube. Again this operation failed, with the Germans getting to within 20km of the city. They were brought to a halt at Zámoly north of Székesfehérvár with the loss of fifty-seven panzers

Hitler reluctantly agreed on the 17th to abandon low-lying Pest in order to hold the hills of Buda. The garrison and the civilian population fled across the five Danube bridges, until the Germans brought them down the following day in the face of Hungarian objections. The SS ensconced themselves in the Citadel on Gellért Hill, while other units defended Buda Castle on Castle Hill, the city cemetery and Margaret Island. Soviet plans were distracted by a renewed German relief effort which was attempted on 20 January to the south of the city. General Balck, commander of the 6th Army seeking to trap the Soviet divisions north of Lake Balaton, summoned the 4th SS Corps south to his assistance, but stiff Soviet resistance also thwarted this effort.

Karl-Heinz Lichte with Wiking witnessed their attack being halted on 20 January 1945. He observed, 'A number of "Josef Stalin" tanks were spotted. The numerically vastly superior enemy bypassed us and attacked our flank. Then, the first of our Panzers was knocked out.' Their commander was killed and Lichte ordered a withdrawal. 'Counterattacks began, and our attack had to be stopped,' continued Steiger of the 3rd SS Panzer. 'The expected enemy tank attack deep into our flanks took place on 29 January from Vertes Aska. It started a huge tank battle near Pettend. Some 200 enemy tanks were knocked out.'

This third attack launched from north of Lake Balaton proved to be the most threatening. The Germans quickly got to the Danube near Dunapentele on the western bank of the river and cut the 3rd Ukrainian Front in two. To counter this, reinforcements had to be transferred from the 2nd Ukrainian Front. From these, two combat groups were formed and counterattacked north and south of the German breakthrough on 27 January. Ten days later they had restored the outer ring.

General der Kavallerie Gustav Harteneck, commander of the German Army's 1st Cavalry Corps, recalled bitterly their role in the relief effort:

While the corps was still in the process of being transferred, we were once again ordered to take up stationary positions, to our great disappointment. The cavalry divisions of the Waffen-SS were fighting in the metropolis of Budapest. Every cavalryman knows that no good could come of that, and, as it turned out, nothing did. The SS divisions were encircled ... Although we managed to fight our way to the city limits, only a hundred or so cavalrymen, under the command of the famous rider Staff Colonel von Mitzlaff, were able to break through to us.

The Konrad operations cost the German and Hungarian relief forces a total of around 35,000 men. This figure comprised around 8,000 dead, 26,000 wounded and about 1,000 captured.

SS-Obergruppenführer Pfeffer-Wildrenbruch gathered his officers on Castle Hill early on 11 February and it was decided they would run the gauntlet of the Soviet cordon and try to escape. It was an almost impossible task as Soviet troops were in the area around Széll Kálmán Square and Széna Square. Just before Pfeffer-Wildrenbruch decided to break out, the Soviet 180th Guards Rifle Division had deployed to Széll Kálmán Square and Olasz Avenue, supported by T-34 tanks dug in along Bimbó Road and at János Hospital. The road between Tinnye and Perbál was cut by another Soviet tank unit in the Dorog area.

Pfeffer-Wildrenbruch's plan was that the first wave, comprising the 8th SS on the right and the 13th Panzer on the left, would leave at 2000 hours. They were to be divided into groups of thirty, each led by a Hungarian guide. The second wave would consist of the 22nd SS and the Feldherrnhalle Panzergrenadiers and the Hungarian units. The attack on Széll Kálmán Square and Széna Square was to drive the Soviets from their positions along Margit Boulevard for a distance of a kilometre. From there they would drive all-out for the fork of Hidegkúti Road and Budakeszi Road some 2.5km northwest of Széna Square. From Remete-hegy Hill it was hoped to escape westwards into the nearby forests and onto Tinnye.

In Széll Kálmán Square and Széna Square the fleeing troops were illuminated by Soviet flares and met by machine gun and mortar fire. Although some broke through the Soviet 180th Guards positions, they were halted with heavy losses 2.5km along Olasz Avenue. Széna Square remained dominated by Soviet machine guns and anti-tank guns and many of those fleeing became casualties or were paralysed by fear.

Colonel General Gerhard Schmidhuber, commander of the 13th Panzer Division, got across Széna Square only to be killed in Retek Street.

SS-Brigadeführer August Zehender, commander of the 22nd SS Cavalry Division, fared no better. A grenade took off his right leg and he promptly committed suicide. The streets became strewn with seriously injured men pleading to be put out of their misery rather than capitulate.

Elements of the Soviet 297th Rifle Division, deployed in Virányos Road, were confronted early in the morning by an enemy column numbering up to 2,000 men taking up the whole width of the street. The Germans were running and firing into the windows and throwing hand grenades as they went. Into this dense mass the Soviet troops fired their weapons and a 120cm mortar began to drop bombs into the column, adding to the carnage. The surviving Germans ran on and straight into Soviet multiple rocket launchers firing at point-blank range. Everywhere the fleeing garrison was massacred.

The Red Army had secured Széll Kálmán Square, which was littered with dead, and parts of the Castle District by the afternoon of 12 February. It took them until noon the following day to move along Olasz Avenue as far as János Hospital. Up to 5,000 men, mainly Hungarians, had been left behind in the Castle District either because they did not get the order to run or the fight had simply gone out of them. In the underground tunnels under Buda Castle and the vault of the National Bank several thousand wounded had also been left behind.

The few Germans who were fortunate enough to break through the Soviet cordons endured a panic-stricken flight that involved ducking and diving away from Red Army units intent on their destruction. All around them their comrades were ambushed and slaughtered. During the night of 12 February the first group reached safety at the Szomor Catholic cemetery. They numbered just twenty-three soldiers, three German officers and a Hungarian officer. SS-Hauptsturmführer Joachim Boosfeld and a companion reached Remete-hegy Hill and joined a group of around a hundred mainly German soldiers. Early on the 13th they got to the front line. Tantalizingly, they could see German positions but were given no covering fire. Between ten and twenty of them crossed over unharmed, with many of the others shot by Soviet snipers.

Pfeffer-Wildrenbruch fled through the sewers only to emerge into the midst of the Red Army. Gravely wounded, he was taken captive. Elsewhere his men were mown down and only 800 men ever reached the German lines. The vengeful Soviets annihilated both SS divisions in the city. During the breakout Florian Geyer's commander Joachim Rumohr was wounded and took his own life rather than face capture; just 170 of his men escaped. In 1949 Pfeffer-Wildrenbruch was sentenced to twenty-five years in a Soviet labour camp but was released in 1955 after Stalin's death.

Pfeffer-Wildrenbruch would have done better to order his garrison to surrender rather than break out as this might have saved more lives. Groups in their hundreds and in some cases in their thousands were cut down by the Soviets as they charged through the shattered city, desperately seeking to escape. He had 43,900 men under his command on 11 February; just four days later 17,000 had been killed and 22,350 captured. Up to 3,000 tried to hide in the surrounding hills but they had been caught by 17 February.

Not all of the Maria Theresia men were lost. About 5,000 Hungarian volunteers had been detached as Kampfgruppe Ney and these men did not share the same fate as the rest of the division. Luckily for them, language problems had led to them being separated from the German-speaking Volksdeutsche. Two battalions of Kampfgruppe Ney had been involved in the abortive Operation Konrad. The surviving Hungarians under SS-Obersturmbannfüher Karoly Ney withdrew westwards to reach Salzburg in Austria, where they surrendered to the Americans.

Chapter Eighteen

Dietrich's Autumn Mist

In late September 1944 the Allies became aware of Hitler withdrawing his armour from the Western Front in order to build up a very large panzer reserve. Alarmingly, his tank strength both on the Western Front and in the reserve steadily expanded to 2,600 tanks compared to 1,500 on the Eastern Front. Signals intelligence indicated that the 1st, 2nd, 9th and 12th SS Panzer Divisions, along with the 17th SS Panzergrenadier Division, were being refitted for renewed combat. Most notably the two SS Panzer Corps were swiftly rebuilt as the strike force of SS-Oberstgruppen-führer Sepp Dietrich's powerful 6th Panzer Army. This was not officially designated an SS army until 1945 as it also included army divisions, but nevertheless, since it was led by the Waffen-SS, it was considered as such.

Previously Himmler had accepted SS divisions coming under army corps commanders and SS army corps and SS armoured groups coming under army commanders, but the Ardennes saw a subordination of a different magnitude. For the first time a whole army was placed under the command of an SS general, with SS units comprising the minority of his command. Dietrich, though, was under an army field marshal. Furthermore, the Waffen-SS was completely reliant on the army's newly raised Volksgrenadier divisions and the Luftwaffe's parachute units fighting as infantry to first seize the ground over which their panzers were to advance.

The two panzer divisions of SS-Gruppenführer Herman Priess's 1st SS Panzer Corps were each brought up to about 22,000 men; Leibstandarte was supplemented with Tiger tanks of the 502nd SS-Heavy Panzer Battalion and Hitlerjugend, now under SS-Brigadeführer Hugo Krass, was rebuilt, although it lacked experienced junior officers. Das Reich, reassigned to SS-Gruppenführer Heinz Lammerding, and Hohenstaufen, reassigned to SS-Brigadeführer Sylverster Stadler, both of SS-Obergruppenführer Willi Bittrich's 2nd SS Panzer Corps, were similarly rebuilt with better than average recruits, although Hohenstaufen lacked transport.

Up until the end of the year Das Reich and Frundsberg helped hold the Siegfried Line, while Hitler built up his counterattack force for the

Ardennes offensive, which had been in preparation from October. This was initially codenamed Watch on the Rhine (Wacht am Rhein) to imply a purely defensive operation, then renamed Autumn Mist (Herbstnebel). Planning was entrusted to Field Marshal Model's Army Group B and he was allocated the very last of Germany's reserves – some ten panzer and fourteen infantry divisions.

After three months the Americans had been unable to punch through the Siegfried Line between Geilenkirchen and Aachen. On 12/13 November 1944 the weak Götz von Berlichingen and 21st Panzer Divisions counterattacked at Sanry-sur-Nied, driving the Americans back, although the Germans were forced to withdraw for fear of encirclement. Götz von Berlichingen was ordered to retreat and escaped being trapped in Metz, which finally fell on 17 November. By the beginning of December the division was down to just 4,000 men and twenty tanks and was no longer available for the Ardennes offensive.

Hitler's massed armed forces included Dietrich's 6th Panzer Army, with a total of 450 tanks, assault guns and self-propelled guns, and von Manteuffel's 5th Panzer Army, with nine divisions supported by about 350 armoured fighting vehicles. The 7th Army with a similar number of divisions under General Erich Brandenberger had a few battalions of tanks and assault guns. Antwerp was their goal. The 6th Panzer Army was to break out between Liège and Aachen and the 5th Panzer Army between Namur and Liège.

On 10 December 1944 Hitler found a convenient way to avoid Himmler being involved in the forthcoming Ardennes offensive. The Reichsführer was appointed commander-in-chief of Army Group Upper Rhine, far from the centre of action. This meant he could not meddle in Field Marshal von Rundstedt's control of the 6th Panzer Army. As C-in-C West, Rundstedt had been particularly irked by Himmler styling himself 'Supreme Commander, Westmark.' It also forced Himmler to commit his Replacement Army to the front; in particular, he plugged a gap in the defences of the German frontier south of Karlsruhe, which was independent of Rundstedt's command.

Dietrich, who nominally answered to Rundstedt, was flabbergasted at the scope of the proposed operation:

Reach the Meuse in two days, cross it, take Brussels, go on and then take Antwerp? Simple. As if my tanks could advance in a bog. And this little programme is to be executed in the depths of winter in a region where there are nine chances out of ten that we will have snow up to our middles. Do you call that serious?

Dietrich hoped to reason with Hitler but the Führer would not see him. Dietrich was acutely aware that although the SS panzer divisions had been rebuilt, they were not what they had once been, and he bitterly observed, 'Out of all the original Adolf Hitler Division there are only thirty men who are not dead or prisoners. Now I have recreated a new panzer army and I am a general not an undertaker.'

Perhaps not surprisingly after its losses in Normandy, Hitlerjugend was only able to field one mixed tank battalion for the offensive, consisting of two companies of Panzer IVs and two companies of Panthers. The other battalion remained in Germany, where it was being reconstituted. The division also committed its two panzergrenadier regiments and its anti-tank battalion. Kampfgruppe Peiper, drawn from Leibstandarte, consisted of a hundred Panzer IVs and Panthers, forty-two formidable King Tigers and twenty-five assault guns.

Elements of Leibstandarte and Hitlerjugend conducted the 6th Panzer Army's main attacks to the north along the line St Vith-Vielsalm on 16 December 1944. They did so under dense cloud, thereby avoiding the unwanted attentions of the Allies' troublesome fighter-bombers. Unfortunately, they were desperately short of fuel so SS-Obersturmbannführer Peiper, instead of pushing westwards, turned north to seize 50,000 gallons of American gasoline at Bullingen.

Hitlerjugend was unable to budge the Americans from the Elsenborn Ridge and had to swing to the left; nor was Panzer Lehr able to get to Bastogne before the Americans reinforced the town. On the northern shoulder Hohenstaufen headed northwards after breaking through the Losheim Gap; frustratingly, only the artillery regiment and reconnaissance battalion were committed, although once St Vith was captured, the rest of the division was brought in. On 18 December Hohenstaufen reached its official start line and fought its way towards Manhay and Trois Ponts before being replaced by the 12th Volksgrenadier Division, which got as far as Salmchateau, less than halfway to the Meuse.

Meanwhile the 116th Panzer Division drove between Bastogne and St Vith, but the Americans holding out in Bastogne delayed the 2nd Panzer Division's advance. Crucially, the failure to take Bastogne greatly slowed von Manteuffel's drive on the Meuse. St Vith fell on 21 December, although American artillery fire forced the 6th Panzer Army to become entangled with the 5th Panzer Army. Hitler felt that even if Antwerp were not taken, keeping his panzers in the hard-won bulge would slow down the Allies' push on the vital Ruhr. To secure the bulge, Bastogne had to be taken and Hitlerjugend was shifted south to help capture the town.

By 22 December Hohenstaufen had been committed to the southern flank of Leibstandarte, but was unable to reach Kampfgruppe Peiper. His force was eventually surrounded and destroyed, leaving forty-five tanks and sixty self-propelled guns north of the Ambleve river. At the end of the month Hohenstaufen was replaced by the 12th Infantry Division and also moved south to help with the assault on Bastogne. However, once the weather cleared Allied fighter-bombers began to attack the panzers in a repeat of the Falaise battle. Exposed on the snow-covered landscape, many were easy targets. Lacking fuel, the 2nd Panzer got as far as Celles, just 6.5km short of the river Meuse before American armour moved in. American tanks also halted Das Reich, and the 116th and Panzer Lehr Divisions were stopped short of Marche.

Even in the face of defeat Das Reich continued to inflict heavy losses on the Americans. Normandy survivor SS-Untersturmführer Fritz Langanke recalled taking his Panther tank into battle just before Christmas:

> Thanks to our preparations, we knocked out the first five Sherman tanks in quick succession despite the poor visibility. They moved at a steep angle to us, down the slope, half-right. The firing distance between us was 500 and 700 metres. The other tanks then turned around and drove back. Thereafter it was quiet and dusk set in soon.

The US 6th Armored Division launched an attack near Bastogne on 2 January 1945. Although its tanks were driven off, its infantry broke through the positions of the 26th Volksgrenadier Division and reached Michamps. Hitlerjugend's escort company and the 1st Battalion, 12th SS-Panzer Regiment, were sent to counterattack under the command of Normandy veteran SS-Obersturmführer Rudolf von Ribbentrop. He recaptured Michamps and Obourcy; in the fighting there and at Arlencourt Hitlerjugend accounted for twenty-four American tanks. The German attackers were then thrown at the northeast outskirts of Bastogne on the 4th, but the Americans turned back every attack. Shortly afterwards, the 12th SS was withdrawn to Cologne. By now Hohenstaufen and Hitlerjugend only had fifty-five tanks left between them.

Early in the New Year Dietrich was dismayed to learn that his SS panzer divisions had been handed over to the army to help take Bastogne.

Initially Leibstandarte and then the whole of the 1st SS Panzer Corps were assigned to von Manteuffel. By 4 January 1945 Hohenstaufen had also been reassigned, leaving Dietrich with just Das Reich as his sole armoured unit. Within four days both generals were in full retreat, heading back to their start lines. Field Marshal von Rundstedt counselled Hitler to withdraw the two battered panzer armies east of Bastogne, ready for the inevitable Allied counterattack. On 8 January Hitler finally ordered a partial withdrawal. The 6th Panzer Army was now needed on the Eastern Front, following a major Russian offensive.

Meanwhile Himmler, with his first combat command, wanted to launch a major offensive across the Rhine. To the south in Alsace, to distract attention from the Ardennes, he conducted Operation Northwind (Nordwind), involving ten divisions including the Normandy veterans Frundsberg and Götz von Berlichingen. It was simply too late to have any bearing on the fighting in the Ardennes. Undoubtedly for Himmler himself this was a matter of SS prestige over the army. While the army high command had floundered on the Ardennes battlefield, Himmler naively believed he could be the conqueror of Alsace if he could retake Strasbourg. He wanted to be the civilian who had won a victory defending Germany where the army had failed. This conveniently avoided the embarrassing truth that Sepp Dietrich and the 6th Panzer Army had also failed, even if it had been under the direction of the army.

Himmler's planning was flawed from the start because his offensive was to comprise three generally unrelated local offensives that could be contained piecemeal. His SS staff dominating Army Group Upper Rhine proposed a swift advance to the Saverne Gap by three panzer divisions, including Frundsberg, supported by Volksgrenadier divisions to the north and south. This would cut the US 7th Army in two, the southern portion of which would be destroyed, allowing Himmler's offensive to sweep the French army out of Strasbourg.

The Panzergrenadiers of Götz von Berlichingen, along with the 36th Volksgrenadier Division, attacked the US 44th and 100th Infantry Divisions near Rimlingen on 1 January 1945. Within a week they had been thrown back and the Americans on 13 January recaptured Rimlingen. It was only after the Americans had withdrawn in good order towards the river Moder south of the Forêt de Haguenau that Himmler launched his secondary attacks in the centre around Gambsheim and to the south around Erstein.

Frundsberg achieved some success in its attack from Offendorf to Herlisheim on 17 January. Although this lost momentum, SS-Obersturm-führer Bachmann, adjutant of the 1st Battalion, 10th SS-Panzer Regiment, remembered, 'Everything went according to plan. The two panzer crews cooperated in a first-rate fashion. Panzer 2 opened fire while Panzer 1 raced into the junction and knocked out the first Sherman. More US tanks were knocked out, and a white flag appeared.' Bachmann's tank crews were rewarded with Iron Crosses, with Bachmann gaining the Knight's Cross. This success posed a threat to Strasbourg, forcing the Allies to counterattack and clear the Germans from the west bank of the Rhine. Although Himmler's Northwind caused a crisis, it also wasted away more of Hitler's already meagre reserves.

By the end of January 1945 Hitler's Ardennes bulge had gone for the loss of 100,000 casualties and most of the armour: the 5th and 6th Panzer Armies lost up to 600 tanks. Hitler's great gamble had not paid off, although in five weeks of fighting twenty-seven US divisions suffered 59,000 casualties thanks to the reconstituted panzer divisions. However, Hitler achieved what Falaise had failed to do: the near-total destruction of his panzer forces in the west. This time there could be no miraculous recovery. Field Marshal von Rundstedt did all he could to make the Waffen-SS shoulder the blame for the failure of the Ardennes offensive: 'I received few reports from Sepp Dietrich of the 6th Panzer Army and what I did receive was generally a pack of lies. If the SS had any problems, they reported them directly to the Führer.'

In late January 1945 Himmler was posted to the Eastern Front to command Army Group Vistula. General Westphal, one of Himmler's bitterest critics, viewed the Reichsführer's organizational abilities as shambolic. Upon his departure Westphal wrote, 'There was naturally no question of an orderly transfer', as Himmler left behind 'a laundry-basket full of unsorted orders and reports.' The Reichsführer took with him Heinz Lammerding as his chief of staff. Lammerding, the former commander of Das Reich, had the blood of the Oradour-sur-Glane massacre and the Tulle executions on his hands. Himmler did not care.

Paul Hausser assumed command of the Upper Rhine, which came under von Rundstedt as CinC West. Hausser found himself with the unenviable and impossible task of trying to hold the Colmar pocket with much-depleted forces.

Chapter Nineteen

Himmler's Winter Solstice

After the failure of Hitler's Watch on the Rhine offensive, it was widely assumed that the remaining tanks of Sepp Dietrich's 6th Panzer Army would be withdrawn to the east to help fend off the Red Army, which was already encroaching over the Oder. Instead, much to his generals' dismay, Hitler decided they would be sent to Hungary to spearhead an attack there. The defence of Berlin fell to Himmler's Army Group Vistula, cobbled together from the remains of two other army groups. Deep down, the Reichsführer must have worried that the Waffen-SS's glory days were past – the failure of his armoured divisions to gain victory in the Ardennes and Alsace had seen to that. Furthermore, he must have been aware that he kept being sidelined and that his star within the Nazi hierarchy was rapidly waning.

The Soviet salient over the Oder was to be pinched off by simultaneous attacks conducted by Himmler in Pomerania and General Schoerner in Silesia. Rather optimistically, over 1,200 panzers from the 3rd Panzer Army were earmarked for Operation Solstice (Sonnenwende). Even if such inflated numbers had been available, there were insufficient trains to move them and little or no fuel and ammunition. Also the 3rd Panzer Army was needed to hold the banks of the Oder to the north of the strategic Seelow Heights, which dominated the approaches to Berlin.

Himmler's attack was to be conducted by SS-Obergruppenführer Felix Steiner's newly created 11th SS Panzer Army, which consisted – on paper at least – of three corps. These included the volunteer Nederland, Nordland and Wallonien Waffen-SS panzergrenadier divisions that had originated in Scandinavia and the Low Countries. This operation was to be one of the last major German armoured offensives on the Eastern Front and, like the attack in Hungary, it was dominated by the SS.

The grand-sounding 11th SS Freiwilligen Panzergrenadier Division Nordland had been formed in 1943, with the intention of using Danish, Dutch and Norwegian SS volunteers. However, the Dutch Nazi leader Anton Mussert objected and insisted on a separate force for his countrymen. The resulting shortage of numbers meant that Nordland had to be fleshed out using Germans and Hungarians. After limited combat experience against Yugoslav partisans in Croatia, the division, under the command of SS-Brigadeführer Joachim Ziegler, had been shipped to the Eastern Front and the Narva area. Mussert's Dutch Nederland panzergrenadier brigade, which had fought at Leningrad in late 1944, was given unwarranted divisional status as the 23rd SS Freiwilligen Division Nederland. It was commanded by SS-Brigadeführer Jurgen Wagner. Likewise, the Belgian-raised 28th SS Freiwilligen Panzergrenadier Division Wallonien under SS-Sturmbannführer Leon Dégrelle was upgraded at the same time, but never reached anything like full strength.

Hohenstaufen throughout January 1945 conducted a fighting withdrawal to the German border. It was then sent to the Kaufenheim-Mayen area to be re-equipped before being sent to Hungary. Frundsberg, which had also faithfully served the 2nd SS Panzer Corps throughout the Normandy campaign, at Arnhem and in the Ardennes offensive, was now detached from its sister division and sent to the Vistula sector. Its remaining thirty-eight Panzer IVs and fifty-three Panthers would not rejoin the now officially designated 6th SS Panzer Army for Hitler's forthcoming Hungarian offensive. Instead they would spearhead Himmler's Operation Solstice.

Of the other Normandy SS veterans, the 502nd SS Heavy Panzer Battalion (formerly the 102nd) was refitted at Sennelager, while the 503rd SS Heavy Panzer Battalion's 1st Company moved to Bentfeld, the 2nd to Eilsen and the 3rd to Hovelhof. The 500th Panzer Training and Replacement Battalion at Paderborn provided much-needed crews and between 19 and 22 September 1944 the 503rd received forty-five new Tiger IIs. The following month it was shipped to Hungary and subordinated to the Feldherrnhalle Panzer Corps and assisted in the futile defence of Budapest.

The 503rd SS Heavy Panzer Battalion was back in Germany by January 1945. It was split in two, with one group sent to the Arnswalde-Pomerania area and the other to the Landsberg-Küstrin area. Arnswalde's strategic position protecting Stargard and the sea port of Stettin meant that there was a strong German garrison defending the town. The first group, under SS-Obersturmbannführer Fritz Herzig, along with a panzer support battalion, 1,000 troops and 5,000 civilians, were trapped in Arnswalde on 4 February. Herzig's Tiger II could have fought its way out but that would have meant abandoning everyone else to their fate. Three days later

SS-Untersturmführer Fritz Kauerauf set out with three Tiger IIs from Stargard for Arsnwalde via Reetz. He then became involved with the 11th SS trying to stop the Soviet advance to the Baltic.

On 13 February 1945 the chief of the general staff, General Heinz Guderian, along with Sepp Dietrich, met in conference with Hitler; hoping to keep the German 2nd Army's lines of communication between East Prussia and Pomerania open, they advocated a pincer movement against the advancing Soviets. To the displeasure of Himmler, who also attended the meeting, the SS attack was to be directed by army general Walther Wenck, Guderian's second-in-command.

Guderian had great respect for the Waffen-SS panzer divisions, remarking, 'They fought shoulder to shoulder with the panzer divisions of the army, and the longer the war went on the less distinguishable they became from the army.' He felt that much of this professionalism was thanks to the work of former army general Paul Hausser. In contrast he was not impressed by the Reichsführer, stating, 'In military matters Himmler proved an immediate and total failure. His appreciation of our enemies was positively childish.'

Dietrich was aghast that his panzer army was being sent to Hungary; to him, it made no sense in light of the imminent threat to Berlin. He also had a very personal reason to be against such a move, as his family were living near the Oder. Later Dietrich had them moved to safety at the Nazi Ordensburg at Sonthofen but at the time he was very worried. Having said his piece, he remained sullen and hostile for the rest of the meeting, while Hitler and Guderian argued over appointing Wenck as Himmler's chief of staff.

Guderian had no confidence in Himmler's choice, SS-Gruppenführer Lammerding, the former commander of Das Reich, whom he considered merely a policeman and amateur divisional commander. Before becoming a divisional commander at the age of 39, he had previously served as the chief of staff of Totenkopf in Russia. Lammerding had lasted as Himmler's chief of staff for just two months. He now found himself packing his bags, having been sacked.

Initially Hitler stated that Himmler was 'man enough to carry out the attack on his own' but after two hours of arguing he turned to an embarrassed Reichsführer and said 'Very well, Himmler, Wenck is coming to you this evening and will take charge. The attack begins on the 15th.' It was decided to relieve Arnswalde and attack in the Landsberg-Küstrin area. Frundsberg and half a dozen other Waffen-SS divisions, serving with

Steiner's 39th Panzer Corps, 3rd (Germanische) SS Panzer Corps and 10th SS Army Corps, were to take part in the counterattack on Marshal Georgi Zhukov's advancing 1st Belorussian Front.

Himmler, regardless of the military situation, felt completely humiliated and retired to hospital at Hohenlychen. He knew that the Waffen-SS had been taken away from him, and perhaps he also finally appreciated he was not fit to command. From Hohenlychen he 'bravely' issued the order of the day extolling the Waffen-SS 'Forward through the mud! Forward through the snow! Forward by day! Forward by night! Forward to the liberation of German soil!' The truth was Himmler had no actual military aptitude and had always been reliant on his skilled SS generals, such as Bittrich, Dietrich and Hausser, to secure the victories that impressed Hitler so much.

In the event, elements of just four weak SS armoured divisions, comprising the 4th SS Polizei, Nordland, Nederland and Frundsberg, plus around four army divisions, were thrown into the short-lived attack on 15 February between Stargard and Arnswalde. Polizei had mainly been on security duties up to this point and Frundsberg was completely exhausted by constant combat. Nordland at the start of the year included a powerful armoured unit, the 11th SS Panzer Battalion Hermann von Salza, and was a well-equipped full-strength division. After constant battles along the Baltic, though, it had been considerably weakened. Nederland was a paper division and remained at brigade strength. Many of its men were lost when their transport ship *Moira* was sunk on the way to Danzig. Elements of two other SS divisions, Wallonien and Langemarck, were also involved. Between them these forces could muster fewer than 300 panzers and tank destroyers. Almost 10,000 infantry allocated to support the operation were still en route from Norway when Sonnenwende started.

Steiner's so-called 11th SS Panzer Army, led by Nordland, initially made good progress on the first day, penetrating the Soviet envelopment of Arnswalde and rescuing the German garrison. The following day the rest of the 3rd (Germanische) SS Panzer Corps fought to enlarge the corridor. However, the panzers and the infantry were on their own as they had hardly any air cover from the Luftwaffe or artillery support. It was only a matter of time before the Red Army and Red Air Force recovered and responded.

The 503rd Heavy Panzer Battalion's Tiger IIs were instrumental in holding the corridor open as the wounded and civilians were evacuated and fresh troops sent in. During the fighting in the Danzig-Gotenhafen area Tigers of the 503rd destroyed sixty-four Soviet tanks, while Soviet troops were also expelled from Brallentin and two villages. The Germans then cut into Marshal Bogdanov's 2nd Tank Army to retake Pyritz. However, by this stage of the war the Tiger's dominance of the battlefield was no longer assured.

The 11th SS Panzer Army's short-lived success was to swiftly come to a halt in the face of the Red Army's superior firepower. Although the Tiger II was armed with an even more powerful 88mm gun than the Tiger I, the Joseph Stalin tank was more than a match. The IS-2 heavy tank carried a 122mm gun and the previous year had proved itself a worthy adversary of the Tiger. The latter could do little once the 2nd Soviet Guards Tank Army brought up these tanks on 17 February. In addition, the ground began to turn to mud as the frost thawed, which the Soviet tanks with their wide tracks were better equipped to cope with.

On the same day Wenck, returning from Hitler's evening briefing, was injured in a car crash and the momentum of the operation was completely lost. Steiner called off the assault, pulling back his 3rd (Germanische) SS Panzer Corps to the Stargard and Stettin area on the northern Oder. The few remaining panzers were moved to the Oder front. The least damaged unit, Polizei, was shipped by sea to help in the defence of Danzig before being sent to Berlin.

By 19 February the Red Army had recaptured Arnswalde, surrounded Graudenze and destroyed the German base at Stargard. The ill-conceived Operation Sonnenwende cost Himmler's Army Group Vistula considerable casualties amongst the few SS divisions that could still be relied on. The remnants of Nordland withdrew to Berlin to help with the city's defence. The survivors of Nederland eventually reached Fürstenwalde, where they surrendered to the Americans. Leon Dégrelle and some of his Wallonien withdrew to Denmark. From there Dégrelle, who was the most decorated non-German volunteer in the Waffen-SS, escaped to Norway and on to Spain and exile. Other members of the division were not so lucky and were caught by the Red Army at Schwerin.

In reality the Stargard operation constituted little more than a nuisance to the Red Army. Hitler and Himmler achieved nothing save grinding down those few units still capable of conducting offensive operations on the Eastern Front. For the forthcoming battle of Berlin, the discredited Reichsführer found himself replaced by Colonel General Gotthard Heinrici as the commander of Army Group Vistula. Nonetheless, the operation caused enough alarm in the Red Army for the Soviets to halt their main offensive towards Berlin and lose some six valuable weeks while they cleared Pomerania of German forces.

Steiner's actions at Arnswalde also convinced Hitler that he was the man to rescue Berlin. But Steiner, with just 11,000 men, refused to obey orders, much to Hitler's fury. After the failure of Dietrich's 6th SS Panzer Army in the Ardennes and Hungary, in Hitler's mind Steiner's insubordination was the final betrayal by the Waffen-SS. The Führer even threatened Steiner with death but it did no good: Steiner's loyalty was to his surviving men.

Chapter Twenty

Humiliation in Hungary

SS-Oberstgruppenführer Dietrich in late January 1945 was summoned to Berlin, where he met General Heinz Guderian, the army chief of staff. They both agreed that all available troops should be sent immediately to defend the Oder. The Red Army was already over the river at Wriezen near Küstrin, just 72km from Berlin. They had got a hundred tanks across the river before the Germans moved to seal off the developing bridge-head. The anticipated Soviet offensive towards Berlin would not come for another two-and-a-half months, giving the defenders a much-needed breathing space. Guderian in the meantime wanted the occupying divisions redeployed from Kurland, Italy, Yugoslavia, Norway and Denmark to protect Berlin. He also argued that the 6th Panzer Army's armour was desperately needed on the Oder. But Hitler had other plans for Dietrich and his panzers in Hungary.

Hitler was convinced that if the Soviets were caught by surprise, they would be sent reeling. He wanted to attack between Lake Balaton and Lake Velence to split Marshal Tolbukhin's 3rd Ukrainian Front in two, in an operation dubbed Spring Awakening (Fruhlingserwachen). Under Army Group South's direction, the now officially dubbed 6th SS Panzer Army and 6th Army, supported by the Hungarian 3rd Army, were to attack, while the 4th SS Panzer Corps, with Totenkopf and Wiking, held the Margarethe defences around Balaton. The German 8th Army north of Budapest was to remain on the defensive. At the same time Army Group South's 2nd Panzer Army, equipped only with assault guns, would employ its four infantry divisions to attack in an easterly direction south of Balaton. This was to be coordinated with a supplementary attack by General Lohr's Army Group E in Yugoslavia, which was to launch three divisions from the direction of the Drava to link up with the 6th SS Panzer Army.

The 6th SS Panzer Army fielded six panzer, two infantry and two cavalry divisions as well as two heavy tank battalions equipped with about sixty Tigers IIs. The 6th Army had five panzer and three infantry divisions, and the 3rd Hungarian Army had one tank, two infantry and one cavalry divisions. On paper the 6th SS Panzer Army was a formidable formation that included four veteran SS panzer divisions, with Leibstandarte and Hitlerjugend grouped into the 1st SS Panzer Corps and Das Reich and Hohenstafen forming the 2nd SS Panzer Corps. In reality these units had been exhausted during the Ardennes offensive. However, the Germans enjoyed a local 2:1 superiority in tanks. The Soviet forces in Hungary were weak in armour, which meant they would have to rely on anti-tank guns as their principal defence against the 900 panzers and assault guns about to be thrown at them.

Tolbukhin was ordered to hold the Germans while the Red Army prepared its own offensive. His men established three main defensive lines of considerable depth. He had 407,000 men under his command equipped with 400 tanks and self-propelled guns, 7,000 guns and mortars and 965 aircraft. Soviet suspicions regarding the direction of Hitler's attempts to stop their advance were confirmed on 2 March when Hungarian deserters told their captors of a German assault due in three days' time in the Balaton-Velence sector. Fully prepared, Tolbukhin sat back and awaited the enemy offensive.

To begin with, the 1st SS Panzer Corps struck the 7th Guards holding the Hron bridgehead on 17 February 1945 with up to 150 tanks and assault guns. Seven days later the Soviets lost their foothold there, with the loss of 8,800 men and most of their equipment. However, this victory cost the Germans 3,000 casualties and confirmed to the Soviets that a major counteroffensive was looming. Although the 1st SS Panzer Corps' preliminary attack got off to a good start by destroying the Soviet bridgehead around Esztergom, once Tolbukhin had established that the attack was being conducted by Hitler's elite forces, it was obvious what was happening.

On the morning of 6 March 1945, after a 30-minute artillery bombardment, the 6th SS Panzer and 6th Armies, supported by the Luftwaffe, struck Tolbukhin's defences. As planned, the Germans launched a furious three-pronged offensive, with the 6th SS Panzer Army striking in a southeasterly direction between Lakes Velence and Balaton. The Hungarian plain between the northern extremity of Balaton and the Danube was not good tank country because it was bisected by canals and drainage ditches. Dietrich was furious with General Wohler, who had given assurances that the ground in front of his two panzer corps was passable. The mud claimed 132 tanks and fifteen Tiger IIs, which sank up to their turrets. The SS Panzergrenadiers were dropped off 16km from their starting points, ironically so that the Soviets were not alerted by their half-tracks. To make matters worse, the 2nd SS Panzer Corps found itself in a sea of mud and penetrated the Soviet defences to a depth of just 8km, although the 1st SS Panzer Corps made much better progress, covering some 40km.

Das Reich joined the fight with 250 tanks on 8 March 1945, followed by Hohenstaufen the next day, bringing the total of panzers committed to the battle up to 600. However, Dietrich was rapidly running out of time and resources. On 11 March he contacted Hitler's headquarters requesting permission to call off Spring Awakening; he repeated his request three days later. His pleas to save his command from complete destruction fell on deaf ears.

The 6th Panzer Division with 200 tanks and self-propelled guns, Spring Awakening's last reserves, were thrown into a desperate push for the Danube on 14 March. They attacked resolutely for two days and almost reached the Soviet rear defence line, but Tolbukhin's men held fast. Just as Hitler's Ardennes offensive had expended the last of his military resources on the Western Front, so Spring Awakening exhausted his remaining strength on the Eastern Front. By 15 March 1945 Sepp Dietrich had lost over 500 panzers and assault guns, 300 guns and 40,000 men trying to breach the Soviets' well-prepared defences. Using the excuse of protecting Vienna, Dietrich tried to rescue his battered forces.

Whilst Spring Awakening slowed the Red Army's attack on Vienna, ultimately it did not greatly affect the Soviet's plans, although the main axis of their forthcoming offensive was now moved south of the Danube to Tolbukhin's command. He was still weak in tanks, which numbered just 200, while the mauled German panzer units could still scrape together some 270 tanks and self-propelled guns. To bolster Tolbukhin's attack, the 6th Guards Army from Malinovsky's command joined him, bringing 400 tanks and self-propelled guns. Their job was the final destruction of the remnants of Dietrich's 6th SS Panzer Army. Two infantry armies, the 9th and 4th Guards, were assigned the task of cutting off the German armour.

The Soviets launched their counterstroke on 16 March along the entire front west of Budapest and Dietrich's spearhead was smashed. The weight of the attack fell on General Balck's 6th Army and the Hungarian 3rd Army north of Lake Velence. Soviet tanks and motorized infantry poured through a breach, which Hitlerjugend was hastily sent to seal. Instead of throwing the Red Army back, the 6th SS Panzer Army and 6th Army found themselves in danger of being cut off and a huge battle ebbed and flowed around Lake Balaton. In a repeat of the disaster at Stalingrad, Hitler's forces were once again let down by their Eastern Front allies. The inadequately equipped Hungarians on the 2nd SS Panzer Corps' left flank defected, with inevitable results.

There was nothing Dietrich could do to save the situation. 'Up to this time the morale of the SS divisions had been good but now it cracked,' observed Guderian. 'The panzer troops continued to fight bravely but whole SS units, taking advantage of the cover thus offered, proceeded to retreat against orders.' Under pressure Leibstandarte gave ground, exposing Balck's flank. Six days after the Soviet counteroffensive commenced, the 6th SS Panzer was faced with complete encirclement south of Székesfehérvár, with just a 1.5km-wide escape corridor that was already under heavy enemy fire. Four panzer divisions and an infantry division fought desperately to keep the Soviet pincers apart and the 6th SS Panzer Army only just escaped. Against orders Dietrich retreated and when Hitler was informed of this he flew into a rage. 'When Hitler heard of this he almost went out of his mind,' recalled Guderian. 'He flew into a towering rage.'

Hitler could not believe that Himmler's elite Waffen-SS had failed him during their last-ditch Hungarian campaign. 'There could be no more reliance placed on such divisions,' said Guderian. A furious Hitler declared, 'If we lose the war, it will be his, Dietrich's, fault.' In a fit of further ingratitude, he ordered General Guderian to fly to the front to instruct the exhausted troops of Leibstandarte, Das Reich, Totenkopf and Hohenstaufen to remove their SS arm-bands. It is claimed that Hermann Fegelein urged Hitler to give the order to deliberately undermine Himmler's standing with the Waffen-SS. 'Fegelein, at the end,' said Guderian, 'made the most displeasing impression.' Guderian was appalled by Hitler's instructions and pointed out that these divisions were under the jurisdiction of Reichsführer Himmler, not the Wehrmacht. Instead the spineless Himmler sent a message, but Sepp Dietrich chose to ignore it. Guderian noted that 'Himmler did not win himself much love from the Waffen-SS over this affair.'

Upon receiving the teletype order, Dietrich remarked with bitterness, 'This is thanks for everything.' He summoned his four divisional commanders and threw Hitler's message on the conference table, saying, 'There's your reward for all that you have done the past five years.' Dietrich instructed them not to pass the order on, but word of it quickly spread through the tattered ranks of his SS panzer divisions. Removal of unit insignia was largely symbolic, as they had already been removed when the 6th SS Panzer Army moved secretly into Hungary prior to Operation Spring Awakening. Nonetheless, Hitler's order was still seen as an insult by surviving SS veterans.

Dietrich's response was to inform Berlin that he would rather shoot himself than carry out the order. When he received no reply, he reportedly sent all his decorations back to Hitler, though it is doubtful that the Führer, amidst all the chaos in Berlin, ever received them. As a result of this a subsequent rumour arose that angry Leibstandarte officers also sent their decorations back in a chamber-pot along with a severed arm wearing an Adolf Hitler arm-band. Setting Dietrich's war crimes and political beliefs aside, this was appalling ingratitude for a general who had served Nazi Germany so faithfully.

By 25 March 1945 Malinovsky's offensive had torn a 96km wide gap in the German defences and penetrated more than 32km. He then prepared to strike towards Bratislava. Hungary was lost. In the meantime, the 6th SS Panzer Army and 6th Army attempted to hold the river Raab, south of Vienna, and Lake Neusiedler against the Red Army. The Soviets crossed the Raab on 28 March and brushed aside the exhausted defenders. Vienna now lay wide open to the Red Army. Once more Hitler was incensed. Austrian by birth, he knew the implications of his defeat in Hungary.

The battle for Budapest significantly contributed to Hitler's downfall. By the end of the war the once-mighty 6th SS Panzer Army and the 4th SS Panzer Corps had ceased to exist because of his obsession with Hungary's capital. At the end of March 1945 Hitler's defences in Hungary lay smashed. All the blood shed at Debrecen, Budapest and Balaton had achieved nothing. 'The 6th SS Panzer Army is well named, all right,' said Dietrich. 'It's only got six panzers.'

Dietrich, after the fall of Hungary, was assigned to General von Buenau, the battle commander of Vienna. Both men knew the defence could last little more than a few days. By his own admission, Dietrich's defensive measures round his command post were designed to protect him from Hitler as much as the Soviets. The Red Army pressed home its attack, pushing towards Papa and Gyor, and by 2 April had reached Lake Neusiedler on the border between Hungary and Austria.

Vienna fell eleven days later, with the loss of 125,000 prisoners. The 6th SS Panzer Army's message to Berlin read, 'The garrison of Vienna has ceased to exist. Despite their exhaustion, the troops are fighting with exemplary courage.' Within a month the war was over and Hitler was dead. Following the fall of the Austrian capital, Dietrich withdrew west to the River Traisen, where 10,000 men gathered from local training units reinforced his forces, and he held the Soviets for several weeks. The Red Army, though, had shifted its main attention to capturing Brno, an important industrial centre in Czechoslovakia.

Dietrich's priority was now to save the remains of his SS divisions from Soviet captivity. Leibstandarte, totalling just 1,500 men and sixteen panzers, as well as the remnants of Hohenstaufen, surrendered to American forces at Styer in Austria in May 1945. However, the pursuing Soviets captured some of Leibstandarte's rearguard. Hitlerjugend, with just 455 men and one panzer, also capitulated to the Americans in Austria. The bulk of the division gave up their arms to General Patton's US 65th Infantry Division, near Amstetten. Those who had survived Falaise and the Ardennes must have felt bitterly that it had all been for nothing. Survivors from Das Reich surrendered to American forces in Slovakia after fighting the insurrection in Prague.

At the time of its surrender to the Americans, Totenkopf numbered just 1,000 men with six panzers. Most of Wiking was caught in Czechoslovakia, although its 5th SS Panzer Regiment managed to march through Austria to surrender to the Americans in southern Germany. Prisoners from both of the 4th SS Panzer Corps' divisions were, though, subsequently handed over to the Soviets. A few men from Wiking eluded capture and ended up serving in the French Foreign Legion. Frundsberg after fighting in Pomerania, was eventually forced to surrender to the Red Army at Schönau. The survivors from Götz von Berlichingen were driven back into Bavaria via Rimlingen and Nürnberg and finally surrendered to the Americans near Achensee.

Desperately the Waffen-SS continued to form divisions until the very end. The last appeared on 27 March 1945 with the formation of the 38th SS Waffen-Grenadier Division Nibelungen. Despite its designation, it is doubtful whether the division had any tanks and what vehicles it did have lacked fuel. It consisted of men scraped together from the SS Junkerschule at Bad Tölz and former members of the hated 30th SS Division. Its ranks included at least one Belgian and thirty-six Dutch officer cadets. In all some 8,000 men were rounded up, but by 7 April its infantry battalions could only muster 2,700. They briefly saw combat in upper Bavaria, and just 935 men, including 218 Hungarian labourers and 151 Volkssturm, surrendered to the Americans in the Alpen-Donau region in early May.

One of the Dutch officers philosophically told his captors, 'The Nibelungen myth was lost on the Rhine; the Nibelungen Division was lost in Donau.' This marked the end of Himmler's private army and the armed SS.

Stalin cared little about the fate of Kaminski and Dirlewanger's renegade Russians or indeed the myriad of other foreign units who had signed their own death warrants by serving with the Waffen-SS and the Wehrmacht. By 1945 the Dirlewanger Brigade was in Hungary. When the 8th Panzer Division north of Budapest failed to stop the Soviet advance, it fled. The survivors surrendered to the Red Army on 29 April 1945, and when the Russians discovered their identity they massacred the lot. Dirlewanger died of unspecified causes whilst under arrest in June 1945. The SS-Cossack Cavalry Corps withdrew into Austria and was handed over to the Red Army. Remarkably, a group of Ukrainian deserters from the 14th SS Division made it to the American Zone in Germany and safety as late as 1946–47.

Chapter Twenty-One

Skorzeny's Commandos

The SS tried to emulate the army by creating its own covert units. Although the Sicherheitsdienst, the SS security and intelligence service, conducted special operations in the early part of the war, it did not set up dedicated special forces until 1943. The aim was to copy the army's successful Brandenburg regiments, which specialized in operating behind enemy lines, often wearing enemy uniforms. One man in particular was to gain notoriety for leading Himmler's tough SS commandos. Austrian-born Otto Skorzeny came to notice after he helped prevent a countercoup in Austria following the Anschluss in 1938.

Skorzeny wanted to join the Luftwaffe but was told he was too old. It is more likely that at over 6ft tall his height was a factor. Instead he was posted to the Waffen-SS as an engineer officer cadet. He was involved in the invasion of France serving as a transport officer with Leibstandarte's heavy artillery battalion. Skorzeny was surprised by the reaction of the French, observing 'there had been no sign of hostile reaction by the civil population towards German soldiers'. He went on to see action as an SS-Untersturmführer with Das Reich during the invasions of Yugoslavia and the Soviet Union. He was also involved in the dramatic capture of Belgrade, where he remarked dryly, 'It was seldom that a friendly smile greeted us.'

After becoming sick in late 1941 and subsequently being deemed fit only for home front service, Skorzeny was sent to a depot in Berlin on light duties. He was, though, highly ambitious and set about getting himself transferred to Totenkopf's panzer regiment as an engineer officer. A meeting with Dr Ernst Kaltenbrünner provided him with a golden opportunity when Kaltenbrünner, a fellow Austrian and chief of the Sicherheitsdienst, revealed that the SS was planning to form a new commando unit. Skorzeny wanted to be involved.

He got his way when on 20 April 1943 he was promoted to SS-Hauptsturmführer and placed in charge of the newly created department for special troops. Although technically not part of the Waffen-SS, it would draw on SS officers and men. Setting up his headquarters at Friedenthal Castle near Oranienburg, Skorzeny found himself starting almost from scratch. His tasks included establishing a training camp for what eventually became the 502nd SS-Jagdverbände Battalion, which conducted covert operations for the SS. Regional SS-Jagdverbände were to be set up with an Eastern battalion designed to operate in Russia, a Southeastern battalion in the Balkans plus Central and Western European battalions. It was also decided to establish SS airborne forces, thereby duplicating the Luftwaffe's, and Skorzeny found himself in charge of the 500th SS Fallschirmjäger Battalion.

When Skorzeny received orders authorizing the establishment of the 502nd SS-Jagdverbände Battalion, he was dismayed by the proviso that 'SS Headquarters must, however, make it clear that the allotment of personnel or materials is not to be counted on.' Skorzeny, already short of resources and men, had little choice but to broaden his recruitment outside the confines of the SS. 'To this latter decision I owe the fact,' he said, 'that the army, the navy, the Luftwaffe and the Waffen-SS were all represented in my formations, fought side by side and acquitted themselves brilliantly.' In the Netherlands a school for agents had been set up teaching espionage and counterespionage under SS-Standartenführer Knolle. This likewise came under Skorzeny's remit. Knolle gave him great insight into the techniques and equipment of the British Special Operations Executive.

Skorzeny's first mission was to train a small team that was to be dropped into Iran to foment revolt in order to disrupt the Allied supply lines to the Soviet Union. This operation failed miserably when all its members were caught and its commanders committed suicide. However, Skorzeny was greatly encouraged when he was approached by eleven disgruntled officers from the Brandenburg Division who wanted to join him. Much to his annoyance, they were not released until November 1943. Amongst them was Oberleutnant Adrian von Foelkersam. 'I immediately took a great fancy to von Foelkersam, both as a man and as a soldier,' recalled Skorzeny, 'and felt sure that in a tight corner I would certainly find him an experienced and valuable helper.' Skorzeny ensured von Foelkersam was commissioned into the SS and appointed as his chief of staff.

The formation of the SS commandos did not go unnoticed and Hitler summoned Skorzeny to his headquarters in East Prussia in late July 1943. The Allied landings in Sicily had triggered a political crisis in Italy and the Italian leader Benito Mussolini had been overthrown and imprisoned.

To prevent him being freed, his captors regularly moved him. Although the Luftwaffe's airborne forces were tasked with locating and rescuing Mussolini, Skorzeny, who knew Italy, was instructed to help. Before he left, Hitler shook his hand and said, 'I hope I shall hear from you soon and wish you the best of luck.'

Afterwards Skorzeny met with Luftwaffe general Kurt Student, commander of the airborne forces, and Reichsführer Himmler to discuss their plans. Himmler was of the view that the Italians were traitors and that the new Badoglio government was about to abandon the Axis. When Skorzeny attempted to smoke, he incurred the Reichsführer's displeasure. 'Can't you do anything without a cigarette in your mouth?' said Himmler curtly. 'I can see that you're not at all the sort of man we need for this job!' For a moment Skorzeny thought he had been sacked, but he still flew to Rome along with fifty of his men. He knew this would be an opportunity to shine with both Hitler and Himmler.

After much searching, Mussolini was found in a mountain-top hotel at Gran Sasso. Student decided to conduct a glider operation to snatch him from his guards. Another group would secure the cable car station at the foot of the mountain to prevent reinforcements trying to interfere. Skorzeny persuaded Student to allow him and eighteen of his men to accompany the glider force. The Waffen-SS, in an act of bravado, adopted 'Take it easy' as their password. Skorzeny noted 'that battle-cry remained the watchword of the SS commandos right up to the end of the war'.

The glider team took off on 12 September 1943 and, fortunately for Skorzeny, he landed before Oberleutnant von Berlepsch, the parachute company commander, leaving him in charge. As a result, he and his men grabbed all the limelight. It was Skorzeny and his commandos who sped forward from their glider to liberate the fallen Italian dictator and disarm his surprised guards. 'I knew my friend Adolf Hitler would not leave me in the lurch,' said a grateful Mussolini, embracing Skorzeny. When a light plane arrived to whisk Mussolini to safety, much to the pilot's alarm Skorzeny insisted on squeezing himself on board as well. After flying to Rome, they transferred to a larger aircraft and flew on to Munich via Vienna. A highly delighted Hitler immediately awarded Skorzeny the Knight's Cross. General Student rightly felt snubbed by the SS taking all the glory thanks to Skorzeny's outrageous grandstanding.

To transport Skorzeny's expanding commando forces the Luftwaffe created the 200th Kampfgeschwader (KG 200), which was formed on 20 February 1944. Although it was a Luftwaffe unit, it largely answered directly to Skorzeny on a day to day basis. Its aircraft included Heinkel He 177 long-range bombers, Junkers Ju 290 and 352 troop carriers and Arado 232 heavy transport aircraft. The latter was known as the Tausend-füssler (Millipede) because of the large number of wheels on the lower fuselage. These aircraft were used to deploy special forces teams and agents far behind enemy lines. The air wing's outstations included 'Carmen', which covered the Western Mediterranean, and 'Olga', which covered Western Europe. Leutnant Josef Thurnhuber gained the Knight's Cross while flying dangerous missions from the former.

In the meantime, Skorzeny's next operation was to capture Josip Broz, better known as Tito, who was leading the Communist partisans fighting against the German occupation of Yugoslavia. Tito's forces were well organized and all previous attempts to capture him had failed. The 500th SS Fallschirmjäger Battalion was to land by glider around Tito's headquarters at Drvar, this time, though, without Skorzeny. The assault team was also to destroy the American, British and Soviet military missions supporting Tito's war effort. At the same time a ground operation, involving elements of the 7th SS Freiwilligen Gebirgs Division Prinz Eugen, was to distract the partisans and relieve the airborne forces.

Prinz Eugen comprised Volksdeutsche conscripted in the Balkans and the division had gained a reputation for brutality in Yugoslavia since its inception in 1942. Their commander, SS-Obergruppenführer Artur Phleps, was a former Romanian army general. After resigning his commission, he initially served with Wiking until Himmler offered him a divisional command. Prinz Eugen included officers and non-commissioned officers recruited in Austria and southern Europe, as well as the German-speaking Croatian Einsatz Staffel, Croatia's answer to the SS. Other pro-Nazi Croatian troops were to support the attack.

Skorzeny's plans, though, were compromised by the conspicuous gathering of the ground forces and when his gliders landed on 24 May 1944 they were given a hot reception. Tito escaped to the island of Vis and the SS commandos were almost wiped out before the ground column reached them. The operation cost the Germans 250 dead and 880 wounded. It was an embarrassing failure that Hitler and Skorzeny preferred to forget.

The defection of Romania in August 1944 posed a threat to the German right flank. Should the Romanians close the passes in the Carpathian Mountains, this would trap Army Group South. Therefore, two platoons of SS-Jagdverbände Southeastern were sent to secure the passes. This was achieved and the men remained in place until the German withdrawal had been completed. The commandos then had the task of escaping through enemy lines. To achieve this the platoons were divided into four groups. Each adopted a different disguise in order to elude the Soviets. One group decided to don Romanian uniforms as they had a Romanian speaker in their ranks but this plan did not succeed as they were stopped at a road-block and their identity revealed. Marched off to a quarry, they were promptly executed as spies. Another group dressed as civilians simply joined the great throng of refugees heading westwards. A third group disguised themselves as a fleeing Hungarian tank crew desperate to get home.

Around the same time SS-Jagdverbände Eastern was sent to the Minsk area on a fruitless rescue mission. Following the collapse of Army Group Centre in Byelorussia, German forces had been trapped in numerous pockets and were either massacred or forced to surrender. According to a Soviet agent, a group of 2,000 survivors was still holding out almost 800km behind enemy lines. The Eastern battalion was ordered to link up with the pocket and try to lead the men to safety. The commando team consisted of four groups, each comprising two Germans and three Soviet collaborators. Dressed in Red Army uniforms, they were to parachute in as close to the pocket as possible.

The first group landed to the east of Minsk at the end of August and immediately ran into trouble. They encountered a strong Soviet patrol and were quickly overrun. The second group successfully located Oberst-leutnant Scherhorn, the commander of the trapped troops. They radioed back their location and reported the terrible condition of the survivors, who had almost run out of food, medicines and ammunition. A doctor was parachuted in to try to help, but he landed heavily and broke both ankles. A second doctor was sent in, along with food and ammunition. Skorzeny instructed Scherhorn to build an airstrip so that KG 200 could airlift out the seriously wounded. However, when the Soviets discovered the cleared ground, they quickly occupied it. The third special forces team simply vanished and was never heard of again. The fourth, unable to locate the pocket, miraculously managed to make their way back to German lines.

When Hitler discovered that Admiral Horthy, the Hungarian leader, was planning to defect, he ordered Skorzeny to swiftly install a puppet government. While the newly raised 22nd Freiwilligen Kavallerie Division der SS Maria Theresia moved into Budapest, Skorzeny's commandos were to seize the citadel at Buda Castle. His strike force consisted of the 500th SS Fallschirmjäger Battalion, SS-Jagdverbände Centre and four enormous Tiger II tanks from the 503rd Heavy Panzer Battalion. This was hardly a subtle operation and after the tanks barged their way into the citadel, the surprised Hungarian garrison quickly laid down their weapons. Skorzeny was vexed to discover Horthy had already surrendered himself to a senior SS officer elsewhere in the city. For a while the Hungarians were forced to continue fighting alongside the Germans.

Once both Romania and Hungary changed sides, the only hope for Oberstleutnant Scherhorn and his men to reach safety was to try to march to Dünaburg in Lithuania. From there KG 200 could airlift them out. The Luftwaffe, though, had much greater priorities and the vital supply drops began to diminish drastically. Furthermore, the fleeing German soldiers lacked warm winter clothing and once the cold weather began to set in their situation would be much worse. On 15 November 1944 two columns set off on the long trek, but neither ever reached Dünaberg. Remarkably, in early May 1945, just as Germany was surrendering, Skorzeny's headquarters received a message saying Scherhorn and his remaining men had finally been captured.

Skorzeny, promoted to SS-Obersturmbannführer for his escapades in Hungary, was next instructed personally by Hitler to form the 150th Panzer Brigade. Pretending to be an American unit, it was to spearhead the Führer's ambitious Ardennes offensive on 16 December 1944 and secure the bridges over the Meuse. This was to prove an almost impossible task. The brigade was not an SS unit, and although it included three companies from the now renumbered 600th SS Parachute Battalion and SS-Jagdverbände Centre, most of the men were drawn from the army and Luftwaffe. Two Luftwaffe parachute battalions previously attached to KG 200 were sent to join the brigade as the Sonderverbände Jungwirth. Skorzeny only received about 2,500 men in total and just a fifth of these came from the Waffen-SS. The secrecy of Skorzeny's operation was immediately compromised when a general request was issued to the German armed forces for English speakers, who were to report to his headquarters.

Although this ad hoc panzer brigade was supposed to masquerade as American, there were never enough captured uniforms, weapons and vehicles to equip it properly. 'There were only enough American arms for the commando company,' grumbled Skorzeny. 'None of the volunteers selected for this unit had ever had any experience in that line.' Even his tanks were German, crudely converted to look like American ones. The unit was divided into three kampfgruppen, but only one of these was commanded by an SS officer, SS-Obersturmbannführer Willi Hardieck. When he was killed by a mine he was replaced by SS-Haupsturmführer von Foelkersam, who had come from the Brandenburg Division. 'I knew', said Skorzeny, 'that he would make a fine job of it.'

In the event the brigade, snarled up in the confusion of the German advance, ended up fighting as regular infantry. Only the English-speaking Einheit Stielau commandos, dressed as Americans, enjoyed some limited success by causing confusion behind enemy lines. Skorzeny, with his mission in tatters, was hit in the face by shrapnel and had to have the splinters extracted. He subsequently endured more painful treatment when the wound became infected, threatening his right eye. After the Germans lost the Battle of the Bulge his 150th Panzer Brigade was quickly disbanded. Skorzeny was heartened when he learned that most of the volunteers had remained with his commando units. Indeed, these were still getting more applicants than they could accept.

On Himmler's orders, in January 1945 Skorzeny's SS-Jagdverbände battalions were grouped into a so-called division and thrown into the battle for the Schwedt bridgehead on the Oder. Fighting as infantry against the Red Army meant that all their special forces expertise was completely wasted. Standing in trenches and fending off enemy tanks was not what they were trained for.

Skorzeny could only muster his Centre and Parachute battalions, plus a single company from the Northwest battalion. 'In our commandos we had Norwegians, Danes, Dutchmen, Belgians and French,' said Skorzeny, 'and it could almost be said that we were a European division.'

Upon arrival at Schwedt he was promised three depot battalions and a pioneer battalion. However, he was under no illusion about how effective these units would be, as he was warned that 'they were mainly elderly invalids'. In order to delay the Soviets, he deployed his parachutists east of Königsberg, while the Centre troops held the inner defence line. The Königsberg defences were also held by two militia battalions, only one of which was any good. This had come from Hamburg and was well equipped. Desperately short of men, he also resorted to press-ganging fugitives who came his way, which included three Luftwaffe companies and three anti-aircraft sections. Skorzeny was informed that his battle group was to be known as the Schwedt Division. He knew that the core of his defence rested on his special forces, but whether they could withstand the Soviet onslaught was another matter.

Skorzeny was ordered to mount a special operation to rescue or destroy sensitive Nazi Party documents that had been abandoned in two trucks in the woods to the east of Bad Schönfliess. He personally led a nine-man commando team on this dangerous mission. On reaching the town they discovered that for the past two days it had been occupied by about fifty Soviet tanks, which were guarding the railway station. Soviet infantry was also camped to the south and east of Bad Schönfliess. Skorzeny knew that this meant it would be impossible to reach the two trucks and returned empty handed to his lines.

That evening one of Skorzeny's parachute companies at Königsberg came under attack by forty Soviet tanks. His SS men drove off the first attack but suffered heavy casualties and the Soviets broke through into the town. Fierce street fighting followed, with the SS stalking the enemy tanks at close quarters. By 5 February 1945 Skorzeny had lost almost all his forward positions and the Soviets began to close in on the bridge over the Oder. Again and again Skorzeny's men bravely took out enemy tanks using just hand-held panzerfausts. 'The men fought and behaved superbly,' observed Skorzeny. At Nipperwiese, when one of his Luftwaffe companies gave ground, he was ordered to court-martial or shoot its unfortunate commanding officer. Viewing this instruction as ridiculous, he ignored it. He then went forward to Grabow where he witnessed his SS paratroopers beat off yet another attack.

An angry Himmler summoned Skorzeny to Prenzlau to explain why he had disobeyed a direct order regarding Nipperweise. Arriving late, Skorzeny stood to attention while Himmler ranted, accusing him of impudence and disobedience. 'The officer withdrew to the bridgehead on orders from me,' replied Skorzeny firmly. He then explained how his men were working miracles despite being starved of supplies and bombarded with unhelpful orders from the local corps commander. After listening to his report the Reichsführer promised him a few tanks and offered him dinner. Skorzeny was grateful for the support of the tank detachment, but it stayed with his division for only ten days before being redeployed.

Himmler was not the only one keeping an eye on Skorzeny. Reichsmarschall Hermann Göring's country estate at Karinhall was just west of Schwedt. His staff regularly called Skorzeny for updates on the fighting and to ask if he wanted anything. When Skorzeny requested reinforcements he was sent a newly raised battalion of Luftwaffe soldiers under the command of a major. Skorzeny was horrified to discover that the major was a former fighter pilot and most of his troops were former aircrew without any infantry training. He quickly decided that 'it would have been a crime to use them as a unit under such circumstances'. Skorzeny resolved to break up the battalion and send the airmen forward as reinforcements in order to gain combat experience fighting alongside his commandos and paratroopers for a couple of weeks. When the battalion was brought back together the major was immensely grateful that his men had been given such a valuable opportunity.

Skorzeny was ordered back to Berlin at the end of February and he gained the Oak Leaves to his Knight's Cross on 8 March 1945. He discovered that there was still urgent work for his special forces. One of his frogmen commando teams was ordered to Remagen to try to destroy the bridge over the Rhine, which the Americans had captured. When it was learned that the bridge had collapsed, they were sent instead to attack a pontoon bridge. The attack failed and the men were either killed or captured. Undeterred, his men continued to mount other special operations. 'Two commando attacks on two important road bridges behind enemy lines were considered and approved,' noted Skorzeny. 'In the week following, they were successfully carried out.' SS-Obersturmführer Girg and a team of twelve Germans and twenty-five Russians were sent into Poland to disrupt the Red Army's supply lines. Disguised as Romanians, they set off from East Prussia to cover 800km. After launching a number of raids, they then fought their way back to German lines.

The paratroops of Skorzeny's SS Parachute Battalion by March 1945 found themselves fighting as infantry in the German bridgehead at Zehden on the east bank of the Oder. Numbering some 800, they valiantly held out for three weeks in the face of relentless Soviet attacks. Just thirty-six of them escaped back over the Oder on 26 March. These lucky survivors formed the cadre for a new battalion, which used volunteers from the SS training schools and convalescents. This unit was sent to defend Neuruppin. It beat off repeated Soviet tank attacks until there were just 180 men left. They withdrew westwards and nothing more was heard of them.

In early April Skorzeny and two companies of commandos from his Centre battalion were ordered to the Alpine fortress from where the Nazis planned their last stand. Skorzeny ended up in Vienna, which was under attack by the Red Army, but managed to escape into upper Austria. He instructed his surviving commandos from the Southeast and Southwest battalions to go into hiding and await further instructions. The daring Skorzeny was captured by the Americans and afterwards was tried for ordering his men to fight in American uniforms. He was acquitted and eventually moved to Spain. There he proceeded to fuel the legend of the SS commandos by writing his memoirs and overseeing Odessa, the clandestine Nazi escape network.

Chapter Twenty-Two

Hitler's British Nazis

Reginald Cornford was killed on 27 April 1945 fighting not the Germans but the Soviet tanks assaulting Berlin. His body was discovered wearing a Waffen-SS uniform bizarrely bearing a Union Jack arm-shield. A day earlier Marshal K.K. Rokossovsky's 2nd Byelorussian Front had clashed with SS-Standartenführer Walter Harzer's 4th SS Polizei Panzergrenadier Division in the Stettin area. On taking the city they captured not only bedraggled elements of the 4th SS, but also another Briton, Edward Jordan, dressed the same as Cornford. These men were members of the Britische Freikorps (British Free Corps), Hitler's little known British SS volunteers. Both, not surprisingly, were using aliases.

During the war there had been extravagant talk in senior German military circles of a 2,000-strong British SS brigade and of 150,000 Nazi sympathizers in England waiting to join it. The implications were clear: these men could have formed the vanguard of Hitler's threatened incorporation of the United Kingdom into the Third Reich. The Britische Freikorps represents Britain's only instance of uniformed collaboration with Nazi Germany. Although some recruits served with a number of SS divisions and the SS-Standarte Kurt Eggers propaganda regiment, most of its members had an extremely inauspicious career in comparison to the many other European foreign volunteer legions. Initially used for propaganda purposes, such as touring prisoner of war camps and German cities, this collection of misfits and losers soon became an embarrassment even to the Germans.

Britain, though, was never occupied, so what motivated British citizens to betray their country and serve the SS? Was there a link between the Britische Freikorps and the strong Fascist movement that existed in Britain during the 1930s? Certainly the influence of the far right British Union of Fascists (BUF) is irrefutable. Initially called the Legion of St George, the Freikorps was raised from former BUF blackshirts and men of mixed British/German parentage.

Berlin's infamous leading British propagandist, William Joyce (alias Lord Haw Haw), was once the propaganda chief for the BUF. Leading Freikorps officials Thomas Haller Cooper and Francis George MacLardy were both members of the BUF, as were Peter Butcher and Walter Purdy (who was a member of the Ilford branch). In England former leader of the Imperial Fascist League Arnold Lease's sympathies were such that he even tried to help Dutch SS prisoners of war to escape in 1945.

The BUF was formed by Sir Oswald Mosley in October 1932, the year before the Nazis came to power, and was supported by the black-shirted paramilitary ex-youth movement called the Fascist Defence Force (FDF). This was the organization's muscle, similar to Hitler's early Brownshirts, before they were subsumed by the SS. The BUF took to the streets with its anti-Jewish message. Somewhat unfairly portrayed as a bunch of gangsters, the BUF's image was severely tarnished by the violence at the Earls Court Olympia rally in June 1934 and the Battle of Cable Street in October 1936.

The lure of continental Fascism did not seem that great. During the Spanish Civil War only about a dozen British fought for Franco's nominally Fascist Nationalist cause whereas up to 2,000 fought for the nominally Communist Republicans. Initially, during 1934, with the support of the *Daily Mail* newspaper, the BUF's membership is believed to have risen from 15,000–20,000 up to 40,000–50,000. After the Olympia rally resulted in violence and the paper withdrew its backing, the movement, which was already suffering financial problems and internal feuding, fell into steep decline. It was forced to reorganize. Fear of war enhanced the appeal of the new British Union, although the East End's working-class anti-Semites had left the cause because they disliked the Germans as much if not more than they hated Jews.

In the face of continuing Nazi aggression in Europe, the new Union's appeal in Britain plummeted further. With the onset of the Second World War BUF membership was believed to have dropped by 75 per cent, from 40,000 in 1934 to 9,000 in 1939. However, it has been estimated that total membership including passive members of the BUF in 1939 was actually around 22,000–40,000, roughly the same as at its peak in 1934. This is at odds with how many saw its development and subsequent decline after the mid-1930s.

Whatever its strength, the BUF was deemed a threat to national security. Mosley and his leadership, including his lieutenant John Beckett, were arrested and imprisoned under the Emergency Powers Defence Act of 1939 for the duration of the war. It is likely that other BUF members volunteering for the British armed forces would have been prevented from joining combat and intelligence units. This was certainly the case with members of the left wing. Historian Eric Hobsbawn, a known Communist, was given a clerical job on joining the British Army.

In Nazi Germany an associate of William Joyce, John Amery, eldest son of Leo Amery, the former Secretary of State for India, founded the Legion of St George in 1943. Inspired by the French anti-Communist legion raised to fight the Russians, Amery had travelled from France to Berlin the previous year. It has been claimed that Amery and Joyce were endeavouring to raise a corps similar to the 5th SS Panzer Division Wiking. However, Amery appears to have been a dissolute and disillusioned playboy rather than a fiery political ideologue. After approaching the Wehrmacht, which was not very receptive, he later tried Gottlob Berger, head of SS recruitment. Berger was very keen on the idea of recruiting from among the thousands of British prisoners of war captured in France and the Mediterranean during 1940 by appealing to anti-Semitic sentiment.

Amery recruited Frank Wood, a Lancashire pharmacist, who drafted a leaflet to be distributed in the camps. Calling on 'Fellow Countrymen!' it stated:

> We of the British Free Corps are fighting for YOU! We are fighting with the best of Europe's youth to preserve our European civilisation and our common cultural heritage from the menace of Jewish Communism ... Most of us have fought on the battlefields of France, Libya, Greece, or Italy, and many of our best comrades in arms are lying there – Sacrificed in this war of Jewish revenge ... We must unite and take up arms against the common enemy.

But the appeal fell on deaf ears and most of the leaflets were suitably deployed for latrine duty. German internal security forces also resorted to crude blackmail. Many British, American and Canadian prisoners were sent out as work parties (Arbeitskommando) to clear up the bomb damage. Some deserted, being turned by women or financial inducements to become 'stool-pigeons' (camp informers) or in the case of the Legion members, traitors. Only a handful of men signed up for ideological reasons having been BUF members, or were just vehemently anti-Communist. Many though were blackmailed for consorting with German women or for petty misdemeanours.

One such case was Private John White of the British army. Assigned to an Arbeitskommando working in a sawmill, he was seduced by the owner's daughter and arrested by the Gestapo. White was told that if he did not collaborate he would be shot, so he joined the Freikorps. Seaman Ronald Barker was another victim of this ploy. After an association with a German girl he was told he might be sent to a concentration camp. Then a German security officer suggested that instead he could join the Britische Freikorps. Private Reginald Heighes also claimed that he was threatened with court-martial or a concentration camp if he refused.

Civilians Dennis Leister and Eric Pleasant fled to Jersey in May 1940 to avoid military service. After the occupation of the Channel Islands they were sent to Germany and in July 1944 decided to join the Britische Freikorps. The pair of them, along with five others, were sent to a punishment camp for five weeks after complaining about conditions. By February 1945 there was talk of them being sent to the Eastern Front. Leister went sick and escaped to Italy with his German girlfriend.

Jersey seemed a rich recruiting ground for the Germans. Charles Gilbert, a journalist from Sandhurst, was also on the island when the Germans invaded. He was sent to Berlin and interviewed by Joyce for the Foreign Broadcast Department. Schoolteacher Pearl Vardon, a native of Jersey, was likewise recruited to broadcast for the Germans. Another recruit, Walter Purdy, a junior engineer officer on HMS *Vandyke*, was captured on 10 June 1940 when his vessel was sunk off Narvik, Norway. Purdy allegedly knew Joyce from before the war. He was moved to a 'holiday camp' near Berlin on 10 May 1943 and recruited to 'Radio National'. Another journalist, Patrick Dillon, after his ship was sunk by a German raider in the Indian Ocean, was imprisoned in Bremen in March 1943. He was recruited to work for Radio Luxembourg broadcasting German propaganda to southern Ireland.

Gerald Percy Hewitt was an English teacher living in Paris with his mother when the war broke out. When the city was about to fall, he and his mother escaped to the unoccupied zone. Between December 1942 and June 1944 he busied himself supplying broadcast scripts and making broadcasting records for the Germans. In 1943, at the behest of Professor Haferkorn, head of the propaganda branch at the German Foreign Office, he returned to Paris to broadcast once a week under the name of Smith.

Warrant Officer Raymond Davis Hughes, RAFVR, was shot down over Peenemunde on 18 August 1943. He was held with Squadron Leader Carpenter (also known as Carter and John Charles Baker) and Sergeant

Alcock. Hughes and Carpenter were sent to Berlin in October 1943 to see if they were any good at writing propaganda and whilst there they met Walter Purdy masquerading under the name of Wallace. Hughes was also introduced to Norman Baillie-Stewart and three other men named Boldey, Hewitt and McCarthy. Baillie-Stewart, a former naval cadet and ex-Seaforth Highlander, had been court-martialled back in 1933 for conveying military information to the Germans. After serving a five-year sentence, he went to Austria and then to Berlin in August 1939.

Whilst in Berlin, Hughes advised the German Air Ministry on how best to defend against Allied air attacks. He also drafted anti-Semitic propaganda and broadcast for Radio Metropole in Welsh to the troops in Italy. After being arrested in the street following a particularly heavy air raid, he was held by the Gestapo from 28 March to 10 April 1944. In late 1944 Baillie-Stewart brought Frank MacLardy and a man named Collander to see Hughes and offered him a commission in the Britische Freikorps.

Hughes recalled at his trial:

> It was not intended to fight in the front line of the Russian Front, but to fight against partisans who were assisting the Russians.
>
> They told me there were 2,000 men waiting to join the corps, and Brig-General Patterson [acting Brigadier Parrington] of Crete, was waiting to take over.

Hughes was sent to a Britische Freikorps billet where there were ten or twelve other men, including Eric Wilson of 3 Commando and a Canadian called Corporal Martin.

In total 300 'volunteers' were despatched to a Berlin 'Holiday Camp' for two or three weeks of indoctrination and education in 1943. However, only about fifty men were eventually deemed suitable to be granted full membership of the Britische Freikorps, including John Amery, Thomas Heller Cooper, Eric Durin (Duran), John Galaher, Edward Jordan, John White and an American called Lieutenant Tyndall.

The Freikorps was run by the 'Big Six', who included Sergeant MacLardy of the Royal Army Medical Corps. He was a member of the BUF from 1934 to 1938 and was subsequently taken prisoner in 1940. In September 1943 he applied to join the Waffen-SS and it was allegedly on his proposal that the Britische Freikorps was set up. After preparing propaganda leaflets, he then applied to join the SS medical services. Eric Wilson was also alleged to have been at one time in control of the Britische Freikorps. Lance Corporal Nicholas Courlander, a Londoner serving with the New Zealanders, also claimed he had interested the Germans in the formation of the Freikorps. In early 1944 he set out on a recruiting tour, visiting some nine prisoner of war camps. After the allied invasion of France, he left the Britische Freikorps and joined the SS as a propagandist and war reporter.

According to Courlander's testimony, in 1945 the Nazis proposed setting up a provisional government in Britain and the Channel Islands. Arrangements had been made by the German Foreign Office for Amery to be a leading member. However, the plan was conditional on the Freikorps raising 1,500 men. Courlander alleged that he expected to be second in command to a man named Cooper, who was to be the Führer of England. He also claimed that there were up to 150,000 Nazi sympathizers in England waiting to join the Britische Freikorps.

Americans, Australians, Canadians, New Zealanders and South Africans also joined the SS. Lieutenant Tyndall of the USAAF, born in Texas of an English father and French mother, joined the Britische Freikorps working in US prisoner of war camps handing out propaganda literature. Becoming bored with this, he volunteered for active service and disappeared on the Eastern Front. Corporal John Galaher of the Canadian Army was a 'stoolie' gaining money and whores in return for his services, and signed up for reasons of personal safety.

Some men joined other SS units. An early recruit was Thomas Haller Cooper; of mixed parentage, he joined the SS serving with Leibstandarte or Das Reich on the Eastern Front. Cooper joined the BUF in 1938 and went to Germany before war was declared. In February 1940 he volunteered for the Waffen-SS and served on the Russian front, according to evidence at his trial, with Leibstandarte. By his own admission he killed Jews and ordered Russian prisoners of war to be shot. He was the only Englishman to gain a German combat decoration, whilst attached to the 4th SS Polizei Division in 1943. Cooper then joined the SS as a propagandist and war reporter in August 1944. Obersturmbannführer Gerd Bremer of Leibstandarte remembers two Englishmen – a London bus driver and a mechanic – captured in Greece, who fought with his unit in Russia. Ironically, whilst on leave in 1944 they were stopped by a border official, ordered out of Leibstandarte and returned to prison.

Large numbers of Allied prisoners were also sent to special camps as potential recruits. About 6,300 South Africans, many from the unfortunate 2nd South African Division, part of the 33,000-strong garrison captured at Tobruk under the hapless Major General Klopper in June

1942, were gathered at Luckenwalde. A few were also possibly from the 1st South African Division taken during the retreat from Gazala. Gottlob Berger thought they had particular potential, hoping to appeal to their Afrikaans nationalism as well as their German and Dutch antecedents. These operations were a complete failure, however, and the men were returned to their prison camps. Only a handful signed up, including Theo Martens, who could only speak Afrikaans, Douglas Hodge and Adrian Smith.

Nearly 1,000 Irish from the Irish Republic, the UK, the Commonwealth and the US were likewise collected together at Luckenwalde. A Swiss SS-Standartenführer, using the pseudonym McGinty, and several IRA representatives tried to appeal to these men, but the operation was again a failure and they were returned to their prisoner of war camps.

The only success the Germans had in recruiting Commonwealth troops in large numbers was with the Free Indian Legion. The nationalist leader Subbas Chandra Bose persuaded the Wehrmacht to recruit Indian troops captured in North Africa. Some 2,000 were formed into the Legion Freies Indien by 1942 and were stationed in Europe; withdrawn in 1944, they came under the Waffen-SS but never saw combat. Bose also assisted the Japanese to organize the Indian National Army, which fought at Imphal and by 1944 numbered 7,000.

By December 1943 there were fewer than twenty volunteers gathered at Pankov/Berlin, including Able Seaman Walter Lander RN, three gunners (Clifford Haggard, Nobby Clark and Rudyard Meredith), three privates (William Bryant, Alfred Robinson and Harry Davis), Canadians Arthur Tilbury and Edwin Bartlett, and New Zealander Roy Regan. Amery, the instigator of the Freikorps had little contact with his creation after 1943, giving credence to the claims of others that they indeed founded or shaped the unit. Instead, ever the playboy, Amery toured Europe with his girlfriend.

The SS officially took responsibility for the Legion of St George on 1 January 1944 when it became the Britische Freikorps. It was placed under SS-Hauptsturmführer Johannes Roggenfeld from the Wiking division, who had lived in America before the war. As the reality of their actions sank in, many volunteers – including Lance Corporal Vance, Privates Bryant, Robinson and Street, Gunners Clark, Haggard and Meredith, Arthur Tilbury and Percy Norman – opted to return to their prisoner of war camps. There remained about fifty volunteers gathered at Hildesheim, a far cry from the impressive force of 2,000 men which had been suggested.

Berger reported to Himmler on 3 March 1944 that the volunteers had requested that 'Brigadier General Parrington' (also known as Patterson and Passavant) be appointed their commander. Acting Brigadier Parrington had the misfortune to be the senior officer in Kalamata, Greece, and with 7,000 Commonwealth troops had gone into the 'bag' on 29 April 1941. According to Berger, Parrington had 'the reputation of being both enthusiastically and sincerely devoted to the Führer'. His name may have been put forward after an inspection visit to the 'holiday camp' at Genshagen. Roy Regan had been captured at Kalamata and probably knew of Parrington. However, all was not well with the project for even Berger acknowledged there would be difficulty getting the volunteers to swear an oath of allegiance to Hitler and requested that Himmler's adjutant 'ask the Reichsführer-SS whether the … soft formula is appropriate'.

Brigadier Leonard Parrington MC was ignorant of the Britische Freikorps and innocent of Berger's enthusiastic claims. He had an impeccable career, having been mentioned four times in dispatches during the First World War. Everything pointed to an ill-conceived recommendation. Born on 24 February 1890, Parrington was commissioned into the Royal Artillery in August 1914. Whilst acting major, he had been awarded his Military Cross in the *London Gazette* on 26 September 1916. Between 1919 and 1937 Parrington served in staff posts and in India. Then, as a colonel, he was a member of the British Military Mission to Egypt from March 1937 to March 1941 and subsequently an acting brigadier from March 1941 to May 1945. Parrington was never happy about his visits to the German 'holiday camps' and whilst there reminded the men that, as prisoners of war, it was their duty to escape. To compound matters, the Prisoner of War Directorate of the German High Command refused to release him, making his appointment academic.

During 1944 the SS intended to send selected British and American prisoners to their training school at Bad Tölz for fortnightly classes, but when the training staff were despatched to the front the plan had to be scrapped. The men of the Britische Freikorps initially wore their own uniforms with German insignia, but on 2 April 1944 they were issued with Waffen-SS uniforms with a Union Jack shield on the lower left arm and a cuff title embroidered Britische Freikorps below it, with three embroidered leopards on the right-hand collar patch. The unit's first commanding officer, SS-Hauptsturmführer Roggenfeld, was replaced by SS-Hauptsturmführer Roepke.

Recruits perhaps understandably were still not forthcoming and the exercise turned into a farce. New Zealander Regan and Corporal Peter Butcher, another ex-BUF member, occasionally accompanied by the American Tyndall, visited forty camps during March and April 1944. Regan, from a list of 270 mainly South African names, recruited just five men, while Butcher did no better, recruiting just one by the name of Frank MacCarthy. A few other recruits included a man named Wood, who had been in the SS before being transferred, and a Canadian comically called 'Buck Rogers'. The latter was a friend of South African Theo Martens.

Recruiting had completely dried up by June 1944 and Berger noted 'the method of recruiting hitherto used among British prisoners of war is not leading to the success we hoped for'. He suggested placing SS 'talent spotters' in the prisoner of war camps and that 'any adherents of the British Legion idea ... be transferred ... immediately so that the other inmates of the camp will no longer be able to exert any influence over them'. It seems that Berger's soft formula approach did work, for Hughes recalls MacLardy telling him that the 'Big Six' sent Hitler a pledge of loyalty. It stated, 'We, the true soldiers of Britain, wish to swear allegiance to the Führer and German Reich. We volunteer to fight side by side with the Germans and beat the enemies of Europe.' It was a hollow promise.

With imagination, much greater use might have been made of the Britische Freikorps. SS-Obersturmbannführer Otto Skorzeny could have found employment for them in Operation Greif, for example. This was the commando part of Operation Wacht am Rhein or Herbstnebel, better known as the Battle of the Bulge, fought in December 1944. In it Skorzeny led the 150th Brigade impersonating US troops to seize the Meuse bridges. In reality, even had Skorzeny obtained permission, it is likely that the Britische Freikorps would have refused to cooperate; marching round in German uniforms was one thing, but fighting American or British troops was a completely different matter. Skorzeny's operation proved a failure, with eighteen Germans caught in American uniforms shot as spies.

At the end of 1944 the pathetically small Britische Freikorps moved to Dresden and then Stettin. By January 1945 some of them had been armed, but not issued with any ammunition, and came under the 4th SS Polizei Panzergrenadier Division. The latter, after serving in the Balkans and Greece, where it committed atrocities, transferred from the collapsing Eastern Front to the Stettin and Danzig area. The division came under Steiner's 3rd (Germanische) SS Panzer Corps, part of General Hasso von Manteuffel's 3rd Panzer Army, which at one point included General

Andrei Vlassov's 600th and 605th Panzergrenadier Divisions of the rebel Russian Liberation Army. Whilst in Stettin the Britische Freikorps experienced its baptism of fire courtesy of nearby Soviet artillery.

On 22 March 1945 two units of the Britische Freikorps numbering twenty men were attached to Nordland, with one group dug in at Schönberg, north of Berlin, and the other near Angermunde. With the end now in sight, the Britische Freikorps' Berlin liaison office moved to Bremen. Its staff included SS-Sturmbannführer Vivian Stranders, SS-Hauptsturmführer Archie Webster, SS-Obersturmführer Kumcarre, and Butcher, who had been promoted to SS-Sturmscharführer. About ten able-bodied men remained in Berlin and they were also ordered to Bremen, although a few stayed behind for the assault on the city. Webster reported to Steiner, then ordered Butcher and his men to rejoin the main unit at Schönberg.

After Stargard, Steiner was ordered to move 50km northeast of Berlin to hold von Manteuffel's southern sector in the forests of Eberswalde. When Nordland moved to the Berlin area, the Britische Freikorps was excluded, apparently on Steiner's orders. He left its units at Schönberg and Angermunde. Perhaps one or two members died as volunteers in the desolation of the German capital. In the confusion the bulk of the 4th SS seems to have remained in the Stettin area, although some of them fought in Berlin and escaped westwards, surrendering to the Americans. When the Freikorps was alerted for active duty, most of the men, fearing the consequences of being taken by the Soviets, decided to get rid of their uniforms and head west in order to surrender to the Americans.

Holding the central area of the 9th Army, 56th Panzer Corps lay directly in the path of the main Soviet thrust on the German capital. As the Eastern Front collapsed under the sledgehammer blows of the Soviet blitzkrieg, the Britische Freikorps never fired a shot. Nordland, through lack of petrol, failed to get into line or counterattack at the Seelow Heights 45km from Berlin and withdrew on the city. The Freikorps at Schönberg retreated to Templin in Mecklenburg, though some went to Berlin. During the final battle most of them escaped the city, though Reginald Leslie Cornford was allegedly killed on 27 April 1945 resisting Soviet T-34 tanks and Corporal Turner was wounded.

Steiner in the meantime, at the headquarters of the 25th Panzergrenadier Division at Nassenheide, was ordered to attack across the line of the 1st Belorussian Front's assault. Steiner refused; he had hardly any artillery and only a few anti-tank guns and tanks – in his own words 'a completely mixed up heap' – and avoided Berlin, retreating through Brandenburg to prudently surrender to the Americans. Von Manteuffel also ordered an unauthorized withdrawal for which he was relieved of his command. The defenders of 'Fortress Stettin' had nothing with which to stop the Soviets; the 3rd Panzer Army, desperately short of artillery, had stripped the Stettin area of 600 anti-aircraft guns. It is likely the 4th SS Panzer had ceased to exist or had withdrawn south with Steiner.

The Germans received little help, except possibly from a handful of the Britische Freikorps, who were rapidly captured. It was not a very glorious end. Butcher and his group of about thirty men surrendered to the Americans in the Schwerin area. Thomas Cooper was captured by American paratroops near Schwerin and handed over to the British 2nd Army.

A few of the Freikorps escaped in the chaos but with the end of the war in May 1945 those captured were handed over to the British authorities. British Military Police then set about rounding up those collaborators still at large. There were to be no shaven heads or punishment beatings for those detained, a fate that befell many European collaborators, particularly the unfortunate women and girls who had consorted with German soldiers. The British media, though, had a field day screaming 'Traitor!' from every headline.

Amery managed to get as far as Milan with his girlfriend, whilst several others were found in France. John Beckwith of the SS Kurt Eggers Regiment of war correspondents was also captured in Milan. Frank Wood surrendered to the Americans after escaping from Berlin, whilst Regan and MacCarthy were captured in Brussels. Hughes was picked up in Leipzig. There was little question over Amery's fate. In late 1945, dressed in a brown overcoat and bright green and black-striped scarf, with sleek black hair curling over his coat collar, he walked into the dock at the Old Bailey in London facing treason charges. Only once did he turn and catch the eye of his brother Julian, the only family member present. It was reported that no recognition passed between them. The trial ended eight minutes later after he had pleaded guilty in a clear voice to eight charges.

His counsel, Mr G.O. Slade, KC, had tried to persuade him to change his plea but he refused and insisted on admitting his guilt. Mr Justice Humphreys said to the accused, 'I never accept a plea of guilty on a capital charge without assuring myself that the accused person thoroughly understands what he is doing and what the immediate results must be.' He requested an assurance from Slade, which was given; Amery himself had nothing to add. Aged just 33, he was sentenced to death and hanged on

19 December 1945. Cooper and Purdy were also convicted of treason but had their sentences commuted to life imprisonment.

Whilst waiting at Wandsworth Prison, it is alleged that Amery was sick and confined to the infirmary. His father was quick to squash rumours that he was in bed having lost the will to live. Amery senior also denied that his son had been visited by a Harley Street specialist to examine his lungs. Amery's plea of guilty, made perhaps to ease the suffering of his family, led some to conclude that he may not have been of sound mind. Shortly after his death questions about his mental state were asked in the House of Commons. The Home Secretary was pressed as to why he had refused to allow a consultation between the psychiatrist Lord Horder and the Home Office doctor Edward Glover. It mattered little; Amery had condemned himself both in and out of the court by his actions. The nation was not about to posthumously forgive him whatever his frame of mind – someone had to be punished for the creation of the British SS.

In order to save their necks, many of the accused claimed they had been acting as double agents. This was true in the case of Battery Quartermaster John Brown, who had done all he could to thwart the Britische Freikorps whilst a member. At Hughes's trial, he claimed that he and Eric Wilson had collected the names of all the Freikorps to help the Allies, and also that during raids on Berlin he and Carpenter had cut the wires on 243 German telephone kiosks. Hughes further alleged that the German Foreign Office had informed him that Collander had been shot by the Gestapo. Hughes was sentenced to five years and Wilson ten.

During the trials of Barker, Berry, Leister, Minchin and Rowlands, Captain R.S. Findlay Notman, a former prisoner of war in Bremen, stated that he had seen two of the five former prisoners in the dock walking around in German uniforms and that he had seen a photograph of three of them similarly clad. One of the few photos in existence indeed shows Berry and Minchin in Britische Freikorps uniforms, their arms crossed and grinning without a care in the world at the German propaganda photographer. It was clear that Himmler's British Waffen-SS had been a failure from start to finish.

Chapter Twenty-Three

Superheroes or Monsters?

Were the Waffen-SS superheroes or evil monsters? The easy answer is in some cases both. Field Marshal von Manstein rather naively wanted to believe that they were ideologically deluded. 'Without a doubt a large proportion of them,' he wrote, 'would have been only too glad to be withdrawn from the jurisdiction of a man like Himmler and incorporated into the army.' What he liked about them was that they 'always showed themselves courageous and reliable'. He was, though, of course referring to the Reichsdeutsche Waffen-SS divisions rather than the ill-disciplined foreign units that were tacked on to their order of battle.

General Heinz Guderian likewise held them in high regard:

> I fought with the SS-Leibstandarte Adolf Hitler and with the SS Division Das Reich: later, as Inspector-General of Armoured Troops, I visited numerous SS divisions. I can therefore assert that to my knowledge the SS divisions were always remarkable for a high standard of discipline, of esprit de corps, and of conduct in the face of the enemy.

Their combat reputation was largely thanks to their performance on the Eastern Front. In early 1943 they had helped save the day at Kharkov following the German defeat at Stalingrad. Although they failed to give Hitler victory at Kursk in the summer of 1943, they subsequently rescued large pockets of trapped German troops and helped halt the massive Soviet advance in the summer of 1944. On the Western Front they helped hold the Allies in Normandy for three long months. Guderian felt that General Paul Hausser was ultimately responsible for much of their success, stating, 'The Waffen-SS had every reason to feel gratitude towards this remarkable man.' In contrast he had little time for Himmler, remarking, 'He seemed like a man from some other Planet ... the impression he made was one of simplicity.' Field Marshal Kesselring likewise viewed Hausser as 'the most popular and ablest of the SS generals'.

After the 20 July 1944 bomb plot, Hitler increasingly put his faith in the Waffen-SS as he no longer trusted the regular armed forces. They finally fell from grace after they failed to give him victories in the Ardennes, Alsace and at Balaton in the winter of 1944/1945. 'The fact that in March 1945 he ordered them to surrender their armbands', said Guderian, 'is indicative of the degree of estrangement that by then existed between Hitler and the Waffen-SS.'

Field Marshal von Manstein felt that ultimately the Waffen-SS was a waste of manpower. He observed:

> Yet, bravely as the Waffen-SS divisions always fought, and fine though their achievements may have been, there is not the least doubt that it was an inexcusable mistake to set them up as a separate military organization. Hand-picked replacements who could have filled the posts of NCOs in the army were expended on a quite inadmissible scale in the Waffen-SS, which in general paid a toll of blood incommensurate with its actual gains.

Major General von Mellenthin agreed that the Waffen-SS ultimately dissipated the army's strength. 'Unfortunately,' he said, 'the German Supreme Command had adopted the faulty policy of continually forming new armoured units – chiefly in the Waffen-SS – and neglected the supply of men and equipment to the old panzer divisions.' Nor was the army able to get rid of the more unreliable and ill-disciplined SS units. 'We were also given a Russian division,' recalled von Mellenthin, while serving on the Western Front, 'the 30th SS Grenadier – but it was in a mutinous mood and we advised that it should be disbanded. The request was refused.' The result was that much of the division deserted to the French.

Albert Speer, Hitler's armaments minister, tried to warn the Führer that the Waffen-SS, the Labour Service and the Todt Organization as autonomous subdivisions of the armed forces were causing logistical problems, but he would not listen. 'Clothing, food, communications and intelligence, health, supplies, and transportation are all organized separately,' said Speer. 'The result, I stated, was a waste of manpower and material.'

It was the attempt on Hitler's life in July 1944 that firmly convinced him that he had done the right thing in expanding the Waffen-SS. 'Under one man, the Wehrmacht is a menace!' ranted Hitler afterwards. 'Do you still think it was chance that I had so many divisions of the Waffen-SS raised? ... that was all done to split up the army as much as possible.' This divide and rule policy inevitably caused bitter acrimony. Major Bernd

Freytag von Loringhoven, who served on Hitler's staff, noted, 'Although subject to the orders of the Army for their deployment, the Waffen-SS always did their utmost to short-circuit them. The private accusations brought by the SS against the Army commanders simply served to poison relations between the two groups and to do damage to overall cohesion.' General Guderian was of a different view, noting, 'But this favouritism was unimportant in comparison to the feelings of comradeship which existed on the battlefield between the Waffen-SS and army formations.'

Whilst the core SS divisions proved tough and often able fighters, they still committed war crimes on the battlefield and there is no hiding their links to the concentration camps and the Holocaust. One of the very first Waffen-SS atrocities occurred in Poland on 19 September 1939. A member of an SS-artillery regiment and an army policeman shot fifty Jews in cold blood in a synagogue. Although the SS soldier was court-martialled, his death sentence was quashed by a senior German judge on the grounds that he 'was in a state of irritation as a result of the many atrocities committed by the Poles against ethnic Germans. As an SS man he was also particularly sensitive to the sight of Jews and the hostile attitude of Jewry to Germans; and thus acted quite unpremeditatedly in a spirit of youthful enthusiasm.' So much for the rule of law in wartime.

The Totenkopf Division committed war crimes in France in May 1940 against British prisoners at the small village of Le Paradis. Totenkopf also committed war crimes on the Eastern Front, where it shot captured Russian partisans as a matter of course. It is worth noting that most of the atrocities carried out by the Waffen-SS were by units commanded by officers who had previously served with Eicke's Totenkopf. Pacification operations conducted on the Eastern Front by the SS also regularly resulted in civilians being executed. Despite Totenkopf's reputation for brutality, Field Marshal von Manstein thought highly of it, stating, 'I had it under my command on frequent occasions later on and I think it was probably the best Waffen-SS division I ever came across.' However, he also pointed out that the division's lack of training led to unnecessarily heavy casualties and missed opportunities.

The Leibstandarte Division executed British prisoners in France in 1940 at Wormhoudt. In contrast, when Leibstandarte captured British troops in Greece they conducted themselves properly. In Russia they showed no such restraint. Likewise, members of Leibstandarte conducted the infamous Malmedy massacre in the Ardennes in the winter of 1944. In 1941 the Florian Geyer Division, while conducting security operations in the Pripet Marshes in Russia, executed 6,500 civilians, while killing just 259 Soviet soldiers. This looked more like genocide than pacification. That same year Das Reich assisted in the massacre of Jews near Minsk. Das Reich also infamously committed war crimes in France in 1944 when it massacred French civilians at Oradour-sur-Glane. In contrast Frundsberg and Hohenstaufen treated the British paras captured at Arnhem with great civility.

Hitler undoubtedly bore full responsibility for the atrocities committed on the Eastern Front against both civilians and prisoners of war. In the summer of 1943, Albert Speer recalled, 'In the course of advances by SS units it had been established . . . that Soviet troops had killed their German prisoners. Hitler had then and there announced that a thousandfold retaliation in blood must be taken.' He prevailed on Hitler that it would be better to send Soviet prisoners to the German factories as slave labour. It mattered little as the Waffen-SS was already regularly executing prisoners. Elsewhere it was a similar story. In Greece the 4th SS Polizei Panzergrenadier Division went on the rampage in the village of Distomo. Likewise, the 16th SS Panzergrenadier Division Reichsführer-SS slaughtered civilians at Sant'Anna di Stazzema and Marzabotto in Italy. In all three instances the units involved claimed they were punishing partisans, but the victims were old men, women and children.

Guderian felt that the Allgemeine-SS, especially once its members were armed and used as police, brought the Waffen-SS into disrepute. 'The number of foreign formations was here also constantly on the increase,' he said, '[and] these were markedly worse than the units of the Waffen-SS.' However, in the closing days of the war the Waffen-SS committed atrocities against its own people. Kangaroo courts conducted by members of the Waffen-SS, SD and army field police summarily executed those suspected of desertion and helpless civilians caught without adequate papers. Wehrmacht figures show that some 14,500 people were shot or hanged by the roving security patrols. In other words, they massacred an entire division of Germans. At a time when Germany was losing the war, such senseless slaughter did little to bolster morale or the will to resist.

Trying to differentiate between the Allgemeine-SS, SS-police, Waffen-SS and units designated der SS is a largely pointless exercise, as they were all armed SS and therefore bear collective responsibility for the crimes they committed. This was especially the case with the Polizei and Totenkopf Divisions as they were clearly cross-over formations. Similarly apportioning blame among the Reichsdeutsche, Volksdeutsche and

(*Above*) Leibstandarte panzergrenadiers in Honsfeld examining equipment abandoned by the US 30th Infantry Division. (*Below left*) A Panther and a PaK 40 anti-tank gun lost in Stavelot on the Amblève river. (*Below right*) After Leibstandarte was driven back in the Ardennes, it was discovered that the division had murdered 362 American prisoners and 111 Belgian civilians in the Malmedy area.

Massacres took place in a dozen locations, including Honsfeld, Büllingen, Ligneuville, La Gleize and Stoumont.

Belgian civilians killed in cold blood by the SS. Dietrich, Peiper and other senior SS officers were put on trial for war crimes at the end of the war and found guilty.

Exhausted-looking youngsters from Hitlerjugend captured by the Americans. Such recruits showed that Himmler was running out of manpower for the Waffen-SS.

German assault gun with American insignia from the 150th Panzer Brigade in the Ardennes, which included SS units.

German panzer lost during the Battle of the Bulge crudely disguised to look like an American tank destroyer.

Frundsberg Panthers in Alsace. Himmler's attack in mid-January 1945 achieved limited success before losing momentum.

Sturmgeschütz III assault guns belonging to the Wiking Division on their way from Warsaw to Budapest to take part in Hitler's Hungarian offensive.

(*Above*) Leibstandarte half-tracks in Hungary during Hitler's ill-fated Operation Spring Awakening conducted in March 1945. (*Below left*) SS-Obersturmbannführer Otto Skorzeny commanded Himmler's SS commandos and gained a reputation for being Hitler's fixer. (*Below right*) Skorzeny was tried by the US Military Tribunal in Dachau in 1947 for ordering his men to wear American uniforms.

Members of the tiny ill-fated Britische Freikorps. The SS raised numerous foreign volunteer legions of extremely varying quality.

A number of Waffen-SS units fought to the last against the Red Army defending the central government district during the Battle for Berlin.

The final battles for the Waffen-SS were on the streets of Berlin and Prague.

Himmler with Reinhard Heydrich, who was a protégé of his and a key architect of the Holocaust. Heydrich was mortally wounded in Prague in 1942. At the end of the war Himmler also escaped justice by committing suicide on 23 May 1945.

Armour belonging to Das Reich lost in Normandy. Ultimately, even the tough fighting reputation of the premier Waffen-SS panzer divisions was tainted by atrocities and abhorrent Nazi ideology.

Many senior members of the Nazi Party and SS were put on trial for horrific war crimes, including officers and soldiers of the Waffen-SS.

non-Germanic divisions also seems a spurious pastime. They were essentially all part of the same organization and answered to the same master.

Many members of the Waffen-SS and other SS organizations were tried by the International Military Tribunal at Nuremberg and the Malmedy massacre trial at Dachau after the war ended. Arguments put forward by Paul Hausser and others that the Waffen-SS was purely a military organization were rightly not accepted. The Tribunal concluded that the Waffen-SS 'was in theory and practice as much an integral part of the SS organization as any other branch of the SS'.

Furthermore, and equally damning, it judged the Waffen-SS was 'directly involved in the killing of prisoners of war and the atrocities in the occupied countries. It supplied personnel for the Einsatzgruppen, and had command over the concentration camp guards after its absorption of the Totenkopf SS.' This meant that it had the blood of millions of innocent people on its hands. The tough fighters of the elite Reichsdeutsche Waffen-SS divisions, while perhaps not quite as bad as many of the other SS units, remain tainted by association and their inherent Nazi ideology and everything it so repugnantly represented.

The senior commanders of the Waffen-SS suffered varying fates. Himmler escaped justice by taking his own life on 23 May 1945 while in British custody. Theodor Eicke died in 1943 on the Eastern Front when his plane was shot down. Gottlob Berger was sentenced to twenty-five years in prison but only served six and a half. Sepp Dietrich served ten years for his involvement in the Malmedy massacre, while Jochen Peiper served twelve years for his role. Peiper eventually settled in France where he was murdered in 1976. No one was ever found responsible for his death. He was always held in high esteem by his former comrades who called him 'Der Peiper'. Hermann Priess, commander of Leibstandarte, was sentenced to death for Malmedy. This was later commuted and he was released from prison in 1956.

It was not just officers who were put on trial for Malmedy. SS-Oberscharführer Werner Kindler from Leibstandarte recalled, 'SS-Rottenführers Rudi Schwambach, Toni Motzheim, Axel Rodenburg and SS-Grenadier Günther Weiss were all sentenced to death by the American victors.' Many Waffen-SS veterans felt all those involved had been poorly treated by the Allies. 'Much has already been written about the "facts" offered as "evidence", said Kindler, 'and the methods of torture and mock executions staged by the Americans to extract statements.' Such allegations were always refuted.

Charges against Felix Steiner at Nuremberg were dropped and he was released in 1948. Wilhelm Bittrich was tried twice by the French for war crimes but on each occasion was eventually released. Otto Weidinger was investigated by the French authorities for any involvement in the Oradour and Tulle massacres, but was acquitted. Kurt 'Panzer' Meyer was put on trial by a Canadian court accused of the murder of Canadian soldiers in Normandy. He was found guilty and sentenced to death. This was subsequently reduced to life imprisonment.

SS-Obersturmführer Fritz Knöchlein, the officer responsible for the Le Paradis massacre, was tried after the war and hanged by the British in 1948. He was only caught after a villager from Le Paradis happened to recognize him in Hamburg.

Jurgen Stroop was executed in Warsaw in 1951 for crushing the Jewish Warsaw Ghetto uprising. Wilhelm Mohnke was investigated for the war crimes committed at Wormhoudt and Malmedy but was never charged. Leon Dégrelle, while living in Spain in the mid-1960s, openly flouted his immunity from extradition by proudly wearing his SS uniform to his daughter's wedding.

Mohnke acknowledged, 'Although, as a professional soldier, I believe most of the Waffen-SS fought bravely against the Russians, and that they as good soldiers respected that fact, still, many cold-blooded crimes had been committed.' Until his dying day in 1972, Paul Hausser championed the rehabilitation of the Waffen-SS. He argued that they were just soldiers like everyone else. He even wrote a book entitled *Soldiers Like Any Other*. Guderian, in support of Hausser, said 'so many untrue and unjust things have been said and written about them'. Kurt 'Panzer' Meyer contended that they 'did nothing more than fight for their country'. This author remains to be convinced by such spurious claims.

Epilogue

To the Last

Members of the SS defended Berlin to the very last against the Red Army. SS-Brigadeführer Wilhelm Mohnke, with a rag-tag force of some 2,000 men, found himself holding the central government district, including the old Reichstag and Reich Chancellery buildings, beyond which lay the Führer bunker. Hitler's immediate bodyguard, some thirty strong, came under SS-Sturmbannführer Franz Schädle. The SS Hermann von Salza Battalion, with a handful of Tiger tanks, took up position in the wooded Tiergarten in a desperate attempt to ward off Soviet tanks. This whole area was called the Citadel and its defence was dubbed Operation Clausewitz. Once Berlin's outer defences had been pierced, almost 10,000 men from a variety of army and SS units were squeezed back into the city centre and isolated in various pockets. These were shelled and rocketed into oblivion.

If Mohnke had time, he might have reflected on his past glory days fighting with the Leibstandarte and Hitlerjugend Divisions. Now he was witness to the final agonizing collapse of the Waffen-SS. His men were far from the original elite SS, but rather a collection of Waffen-SS units including Hitler's personal guard battalion from Leibstandarte, plus terrified Hitler Youth, despondent regular soldiers and Volkssturm home guard. He was ordered to fight to the death but only his few remaining hard-core German, Belgian, Danish, Dutch, French, Latvian, Spanish and Swedish Waffen-SS grenadiers heeded such a pointless act of self-sacrifice.

Members of the Charlemagne and Nordland Divisions, under SS-Brigadeführer Gustav Krukenberg and SS-Brigadeführer Joachim Ziegler respectively, rallied to the defence of Berlin. Also amongst the flotsam were several SS-companies of Spaniards under SS-Standartenführer Miguel Ezquerra, which were assigned to Nordland. When Krukenberg and a battalion of his men drove towards the city, Himmler haughtily passed by in a car without even acknowledging them, such was his total disregard for the loyal foreign volunteers of the Waffen-SS. Another battalion of Frenchmen belonging to Charlemagne remained behind at Neustrelitz to the north of Berlin. Rumours began to circulate that more divisions were on their way to relieve the beleaguered Nazi capital.

To the north of Berlin the 3rd (Germanische) SS Panzer Corps, previously part of SS-Obergruppenführer Felix Steiner's short-lived 11th SS Panzer Army, was supposed to fight its way to rescue the Führer. Before his death Hitler had signalled, 'Upon the successful conclusion of your mission depends the fate of the German capital.' However, in reality Steiner's command had the manpower of a single division and he refused to cooperate. 'The plan of attack was based on facts that had no basis in reality, but only in the fantasies of the Chancellery,' said Steiner dismissively. When pressed he explained, 'I just don't have the troops. I don't have the slightest chance of succeeding.' Instead Steiner ordered his men to withdraw towards the Elbe so they could surrender to the Americans and avoid Stalin's terrible Gulag. Hitler, in conference with his generals on 23 April 1945, stated, 'I have no use for these dull, undecided SS leaders. In no circumstances whatever do I want Steiner to be in command.' He ordered that Steiner be replaced. Once Hitler fully appreciated that neither Steiner's forces nor the exhausted German 9th and 12th Armies, trapped to the south of Berlin, were coming, he cried in rage, 'It's all finished, everything, everything.'

The once-impressive military might of the Waffen-SS did Himmler no good in the end either. Hitler declared him a traitor after he foolishly named himself successor. Stripped of his titles, he withdrew humiliated to Flensburg, protected by just 150 loyal guards. SS-Gruppenführer Hermann Fegelien, Himmler's SS representative at the Führer's headquarters, was arrested and shot for desertion. He had been caught fleeing in civilian clothing, every pocket stuffed with money. Hitler's ranting moved Goebbels to write, 'In general, the Führer is of the opinion that no high-class commander has emerged from the SS.' It seemed Hitler's ingratitude knew no bounds.

Mohnke gave his demented Führer one final tiny victory on 27 April 1945 when his men bravely managed to halt Soviet tanks crossing the Potsdamer Platz. 'Their tanks were highly unmanoeuvrable, blocked by rubble,' reported Mohnke, 'and were sitting ducks in this classic street fighting situation.' The Soviets simply withdrew and contented themselves with shelling the unfortunate defenders into submission. Krukenberg had established his headquarters at the Stadtmitte U-Bahn station, but he soon regretted it. 'On 27 April a Russian artillery shell had exploded right in our midst in the station,' he said, 'killing four and wounding fifteen.' The following day SS-Sturmbannführer Schädle was hit in the leg by shrapnel and his wound soon turned gangrenous, making it increasingly painful to walk.

Some of Krukenberg's 500 French volunteers were deployed as tank hunter squads, which proved particularly effective in the ultimately uneven struggle. Along with members of Ziegler's Nordland, they tried to block Soviet tanks coming up Friedrichstrasse and the Wilhelmstrasse by holding the buildings overlooking the Belle-Alliance-Platz for as long as possible. Men of Nordland also held the Air Ministry building south of the Chancellery. They were grateful for the presence of a solitary Hermann von Salza Tiger tank on the Potsdamer Platz, which prevented anything coming up the Saarlandstrasse on their right flank.

Such was the bravery of the Charlemagne men that two French soldiers, SS-Oberscharführer François Apollot and SS-Unterscharführer Eugène Vaulot were awarded Knight's Crosses for destroying fourteen enemy tanks. One of their German officers, SS-Obersturmführer Wilhelm Weber, also received one for knocking out eight tanks. Apollot and Vaulot were subsequently killed, while Weber managed to survive the war. Four other Frenchmen were awarded the Iron Cross for claiming another fifteen tanks. One of them, SS-Unterscharführer Roger Albert, was also killed before the battle ended.

By this stage the remaining Waffen-SS units had become completely mixed up. Krukenberg recalled:

> At least half my troops were non-Germans, either Scandinavians and Dutchmen from the Norland Division, or Frenchmen from my own battlegroup Charlemagne, ... I had also inherited a battalion of Latvian rifle men. By now I had the definite feeling that these Europeans had really been doing more of the fighting than Mohnke's own LAH troops in and about the Potsdamer Platz.

One of the reasons for the latter observation was that Mohnke, a dour and brutal character, seems to have inspired little camaraderie with his men.

Inevitably Mohnke's surviving SS forces were overwhelmed. The Red Army stormed into the Reichstag and bludgeoned its way to within just a few blocks from the Chancellery. The latter was held by 700 members of the Leibstandarte guard force. Just to the north the Soviets reached the

Hotel Adlon near the Wilhelmstrasse. Most of the Tiergarten had been lost and the German positions on the Postsdamer Platz were almost surrounded. Just seventeen French soldiers remained defending the Potsdamer railway station just south of the platz. Krukenberg found the Air Ministry was now unguarded, despite the close proximity of Soviet guns and mortars. To his surprise in the cellars he discovered a hundred airmen and an elderly Luftwaffe general sound asleep.

In the early hours of 30 April Mohnke received a phone call from SS-Unterscharführer Rochus Misch summoning him to see Hitler in the Führer bunker. 'Unterscharführer, as an old Leibstandarte hand,' said Mohnke, 'please tell me the unvarnished truth. What temper is the Führer in?' Misch responded 'Der Chef is now in a calm and relaxed mood ... Just a moment ago he said he wanted to have a talk with his old friend Mohnke.' As instructed, Mohnke reported to the Führer and laid out a map that showed what remained of the Third Reich. He explained solemnly:

> In the north the Russians have moved close to the Weidendammer Bridge. In the east they are at the Lustgarten. In the south, at Potsdamer Platz and the Aviation Ministry. In the west they are in the Tiergarten, somewhere between 170 and 250 feet from the Reich Chancellery.

Hitler nodded and asked how much longer the defence could last. 'I no longer can guarantee that my exhausted, battle-weary troops', replied Mohnke, 'can hold for more than one more day.' Despite this news, Hitler found it in his heart to finally compliment the performance of the Waffen-SS. 'Let me say that your troops have fought splendidly,' he said, 'and I have no complaints. Would that all the others had fought as tenaciously.'

A despairing Hitler took his own life that day. Mohnke, with a tear in his eye, told Krukenberg that 'A blazing comet is extinguished.' He then attempted to break out with his men only to be caught by the Soviets. Krukenberg was also eventually captured and Ziegler died of his wounds. Ezquerra was taken prisoner but escaped and returned to Spain. The critically wounded Schädle committed suicide. Just as the Berlin garrison was surrendering, SS engineers from Nordland carried out a final act by blowing up the tunnel under the Landwehr Canal. This was intended to stop Soviet troops from using the U-Bahn tunnels to get behind the

Chancellery. It was too late. The war for Nazi Germany, and indeed the Waffen-SS, was all but over.

By a quirk of fate Berlin was not actually the Waffen-SS's final battle. Although the garrison laid down their arms on 2 May, it would be another six days before Germany officially surrendered. In the meantime, elements of the Waffen-SS fought on, most notably Das Reich's two panzergrenadier regiments. On 30 April SS-Obersturmbannführer Otto Weidinger and his Der Führer Regiment were ordered to deploy to Prague on a desperate rescue mission. The city's inhabitants were on the verge of rising up against their occupiers because the Red Army and American forces were rapidly approaching. Field Marshal Ferdinand Schörner, trying to extricate his Army Group Centre from the enveloping grasp of the Soviets in Czechoslovakia, was really not in a position to help the German administrators and rear echelon units in the Czech capital.

The uprising commenced on 5 May and the German garrison was swiftly trapped. The Governor, SS-Obergruppenführer Karl Frank, with a force of SS and police units, held the Hradčany citadel. Frank, responsible for earlier massacres at Lidice and Ležáky, was understandably hated by the Czechs. In a pointless display of firepower, he now attempted to crush the insurgents using artillery and tanks, as had been done in Warsaw. In the closing days of the Second World War some 3,000 Czechs were needlessly slaughtered. To complicate matters, the Czechs were initially assisted by a division of troops belonging to the pro-Nazi Russian Liberation Army. These men had become turncoats in the vain hope of winning favour with the Allies. Ultimately they found themselves disowned by both sides and fought their way out of the city alongside the SS. Once the Red Army reached Prague, the mayhem escalated, with Germans and Czech collaborators butchered on the streets.

Weidinger's kampfgruppe reached the city on 6 May and was placed under the command of Field Marshal Schörner. Ordered to destroy the insurgents, Weidinger's men found the streets blocked and progress into the city centre was slow. Every time they stopped to dismantle a barricade they came under fire. A Czech officer tried to negotiate their withdrawal but Weidinger, determined to carry out his mission, would only agree to a temporary ceasefire. He warned the Czechs that if they attempted to interfere, he would use the full force of his kampfgruppe. Once in the city he found German wounded abandoned on a troop train left in a railway siding, along with military stragglers, unarmed female signals auxiliaries and civilian administrators.

Weidinger decided that organizing an evacuation was his first priority, regardless of what senior SS officers in the city might want. He gathered a convoy of a thousand vehicles to transport the wounded and civilians and escorted them out of Prague. Despite being under attack by the Czechs and the Soviets, the Der Führer Regiment successfully reached American lines at Rokiczany and surrendered. The Americans eventually handed Frank over to the Czechs to face justice and execution.

In some quarters it was feared that the more fanatical elements of the Waffen-SS might fight on, despite Germany's surrender. Field Marshal Kesselring, the German C-in-C West, said 'I had advised SS General Hausser as my special representative to see to it that the surrender of the SS troops proceeded in exact observance of my directives; that – in a nutshell – no follies, such as escape into the mountains, should be committed at the last moment.' For good measure Kesselring signalled Dietrich at 1400 hours on 9 May stressing 'the armistice terms are equally binding on the Waffen-SS'. Dietrich's headquarters' did not acknowledge this message until late in the evening.

Das Reich's Deutschland Panzergrenadiers remained defiant to the last, signalling on 9 May, 'Tomorrow the Regiment will march into captivity all heads held high. The Regiment which had the honour of bearing the name Deutschland is now signing off.' Just 30 per cent of its manpower and equipment had survived. Werner Kindler and the remnants of Leibstandarte fled to Ternberg on the Enns river in a bid to escape capture by the Red Army. They drove the last of their armoured personnel carriers into the river on 10 May 1945 before surrendering to the Americans.

Appendix I

Glossary

Allgemeine-SS – General SS
Einsatzgruppen – Task forces, SD/SS execution squads
Einsatzkommando – Einsatzgruppen sub-unit
Freiwilligen – Volunteer
Führer – Leader
Gebirgs – Mountain
Heeres – Army
Geheime Staatspolizei – Gestapo, Secret State Police
Jagdverbände – Hunting Group
Kampfgeschwader – Bomber Wing
Kavallerie – Cavalry
Kriegsberichter – War correspondent
Kriegsmarine – Navy
Kriminalpolizei – KRIPO, Criminal Police
Ordnungspolizei – Order Police (Orpo)
Panzergrenadier – Motorized/armoured infantry
Reichsarbeitsdienst – RAD, Reich Labour Service
Reichsdeutsche – Person born in Germany
Reichsführer-SS – Commander-in-Chief of the SS
Schutzpolizei – Protection Police (part of Orpo)
Schutzstaffel – Security or protection squad
Sicherheitsdienst – SD, Security and Intelligence Service
Sicherheitspolizei – SIPO, Security Police
SS-Hauptamt – SS Main Office, responsible for recruiting the Waffen-SS
Stabswache – Headquarters Guard
Standarte – Regiment equivalent
Sturm – Company equivalent

Sturmbann – Battalion equivalent
Totenkopfstandarte – Deathshead Regiment
Totenkopfverbände – Collective name for Death's Head Units
Verfügungsstruppe – Armed SS dispositional troops
Volksdeutsche – Person born outside Germany of German stock
Volkssturm – People's Storm Militia/Home Army
Waffen-SS – Armed SS
Wehrmacht – Armed Forces (army, navy, air force)

Equivalent SS Ranks

German Army	Waffen-SS	British Army	US Army
Feldmarschall	Reichsführer-SS	Field Marshal	General of the Army
Generaloberst	SS-Oberstgruppenführer	General	General
General der Panzer-truppen, etc.	SS-Obergruppenführer	Lieutenant General	Lieutenant General
Generalleutnant	SS-Gruppenführer	Major General	Major General
Generalmajor	SS-Brigadeführer	Brigadier	Brigadier General
Oberst	SS-Oberführer or SS-Standartenführer	Senior Colonel/ Colonel	Colonel
Oberstleutnant	SS-Obersturmbannführer	Lieutenant Colonel	Lieutenant Colonel
Major	SS-Sturmbannführer	Major	Major
Hauptmann	SS-Hauptsturmführer	Captain	Captain
Oberleutnant	SS-Obersturmführer	Lieutenant	1st Lieutenant
Leutnant	SS-Untersturmführer	2nd Lieutenant	2nd Lieutenant
Stabsfeldwebel	SS-Sturmscharführer	Regimental Sergeant Major	Sergeant Major
Hauptfeldwebel	SS-Hauptscharführer	Sergeant Major	Master Sergeant
–	SS-Oberscharführer	–	Technical Sergeant
Feldwebel	SS-Scharführer	Staff Sergeant	Staff Sergeant
Unteroffizier	SS-Unterscharführer	Sergeant	Sergeant
Stabsgefreiter	–	–	Staff Corporal
Obergefreiter	SS-Rottenführer	Corporal	Senior Corporal
Gefreiter	SS-Sturmmann	Lance Corporal	Corporal
Oberschütze	SS-Oberschütze	–	Private 1st Class
Schütze	SS-Schütze	Private	Private

Waffen-SS Divisions

Units that were of the SS but not fully part of it have the suffix 'der SS' after the divisional description/function, i.e. Waffen-Grenadier Division der SS, rather than the prefix 'SS', i.e. SS-Panzer Division. Note that for presentational ease the divisions here are only individually listed by number, name and SS status. Reichsdeutsche Waffen-SS wore the distinctive SS double lightning bolt runes on the right collar patch. The insignia worn on the left showed the wearer's rank. In contrast Volksdeutsche and the Freiwilligen, foreign volunteers without ethnic German origins, had special unit collar patches instead of the runes. All officers' caps featured the Totenkopf or death's head symbol. An embroidered version was also worn on field and side caps by all ranks.

Armoured Divisions
1st SS Leibstandarte-SS Adolf Hitler
2nd SS Das Reich
3rd SS Totenkopf
5th SS Wiking
9th SS Hohenstaufen
10th SS Frundsberg
12th SS Hitlerjugend

Panzergrenadier Divisions
4th SS Polizei
11th SS Nordland
16th SS Reichsführer-SS
17th SS Götz von Berlichingen
18th SS Horst Wessel
23rd SS Nederland (replaced Kama in late 1944)
28th SS Wallonien

Cavalry Divisions
8th SS Florian Geyer
22nd Maria Theresia der SS

33rd Ungarische Nr 3 der SS
37th SS Lützow

Grenadier Divisions

14th Galizische/Ukrainische Nr 1 der SS
15th Lettische Nr 1 der SS
19th Lettische Nr 2 der SS
20th Estnische Nr 1 der SS
25th Ungarische Nr 1 Hunyadi der SS
26th Ungarische Nr 2 Hungaria der SS
27th SS Flämische Nr 1 Langemarck
29th Russiche Nr 1 der SS
29th Italienische Nr 1 der SS
30th Russiche Nr 2 der SS
31st SS Böhmen-Mähren
32nd SS 30 Januar
33rd Französische Nr 1 Charlemagne der SS
34th Landstorm Nederland der SS
35th SS Polizei
36th Dirlewanger der SS
38th SS Nibelungen

Mountain Divisions

6th SS Nord
7th SS Prinz Eugen
13th Kroatische Nr 1 Handschar der SS
21st Albanische Nr 1 Skanderbeg der SS
23rd Kroatische Nr 2 Kama der SS
24th Karstjäger der SS

Appendix IV

Waffen-SS Divisional Organization

The following lists the main combat units of each division. Some of these regiments were retitled or replaced, and in the case of the later divisions their component units were often little more than paper formations based on wishful thinking. On at least three occasions a division was disbanded and its number reallocated to a replacement unit that had nothing to do with its predecessor.

1st SS Leibstandarte SS Adolf Hitler
  1st SS-Panzer Regiment
  1st SS-Panzergrenadier Regiment
  2nd SS-Panzergrenadier Regiment
  1st SS-Panzer Artillery Regiment

2nd SS Das Reich
  2nd SS-Panzer Regiment
  3rd SS-Panzergrenadier Regiment Deutschland
  4th SS-Panzergrenadier Regiment Der Führer
  2nd SS-Panzer Artillery Regiment

3rd SS Totenkopf
  3rd SS-Panzer Regiment
  5th SS-Panzergrenadier Regiment Thule
  6th SS-Panzergrenadier Regiment Theodor Eicke
  3rd SS-Panzer Artillery Regiment

4th SS Polizei
  1st Polizei Schützen Regiment (renamed 1st SS-Grenadier Regiment)
  2nd Polizei Schützen Regiment (renamed 2nd SS-Grenadier Regiment)
  3rd Artillery Regiment
  Then:
  7th SS-Panzergrenadier Regiment
  8th SS-Panzergrenadier Regiment
  4th SS-Artillery Regiment
  4th SS-Assault Gun Battalion

5th SS Wiking
  5th SS-Panzer Regiment
  9th SS-Panzergrenadier Regiment Germania
  10th SS-Panzergrenadier Regiment Westland
  5th SS-Panzer Artillery Regiment

6th SS Nord
  11th SS-Gebirgsjäger Regiment Reinhard Heydrich
  12th SS Gebirgsjäger Regiment Michael Gaissmair
  6th SS-Gebirgs Artillery Regiment
  6th SS-Assault Gun Battery

7th SS Prinz Eugen
  13th SS-Freiwilligen Gebirgsjäger Regiment Artur Phleps
  14th SS-Freiwilligen Gebirgsjäger Regiment Skanderbeg
  7th SS-Freiwilligen Gebirgs Artillery Regiment
  7th SS-Assault Gun Battalion

8th SS Florian Geyer
  15th SS-Kavallerie Regiment
  16th SS-Kavallerie Regiment
  18th SS-Kavallerie Regiment
  8th SS-Artillery Regiment (motorized)
  8th SS-Panzerjäger Battalion

9th SS Hohenstaufen
  9th SS-Panzer Regiment
  19th SS-Panzergrenadier Regiment
  20th SS-Panzergrenadier Regiment
  9th SS-Panzer Artillery Regiment

10th SS Frundsberg
  10th SS-Panzer Regiment
  21st SS-Panzergrenadier Regiment
  22nd SS-Panzergrenadier Regiment
  10th SS-Panzer Artillery Regiment

11th SS Nordland
  11th SS-Panzer Battalion Hermann von Salza
  23rd SS-Panzergrenadier Regiment Norge
  24th SS-Panzergrenadier Regiment Danmark
  11th SS-Panzer Artillery Regiment

12th SS Hitlerjugend

12th SS-Panzer Regiment
25th SS-Panzergrenadier Regiment
26th SS-Panzergrenadier Regiment
12th SS-Panzer Artillery Regiment

13th Kroatische Nr 1 Handschar der SS

27th SS-Waffen Gebirgsjäger Regiment
28th SS-Waffen Gebirgsjäger Regiment
13th SS-Waffen Artillery Regiment
13th SS-Panzerjäger Battalion

14th Ukrainische Nr 1 der SS

29th Waffen-Grenadier Regiment der SS
30th Waffen-Grenadier Regiment der SS
31st Waffen-Grenadier Regiment der SS
14th Waffen-Artillery Regiment der SS

15th Lettische Nr 1 der SS

32nd Waffen-Grenadier Regiment der SS
33rd Waffen-Grenadier Regiment der SS
34th Waffen-Grenadier Regiment der SS
15th Waffen-Artillery Regiment der SS

16th SS Reichsführer-SS

16th SS-Panzer Battalion
35th SS-Panzergrenadier Regiment
36th SS-Panzergrenadier Regiment
16th SS-Panzer Artillery Battalion

17th SS Götz von Berlichingen

37th SS-Panzergrenadier Regiment
38th SS-Panzergrenadier Regiment
17th SS-Panzer Artillery Regiment
17th SS-Panzerjäger Battalion

18th SS Horst Wessel

39th SS-Panzergrenadier Regiment
40th SS-Panzergrenadier Regiment
18th SS-Artillery Regiment
18th SS-Panzerjäger Battalion

19th Lettisches Nr 2 der SS
42nd Waffen-Grenadier Regiment der SS Voldemars Veiss
43rd Waffen-Grenadier Regiment der SS Heinrich Schuldt
44th Waffen-Grenadier Regiment der SS
19th Waffen-Artillery Regiment

20th Estnische Nr 1 der SS
45th Waffen-Grenadier Regiment der SS
46th Waffen-Grenadier Regiment der SS
47th Waffen-Grenadier Regiment der SS
20th Waffen-Artillery Regiment

21st Albanische Nr 1 Skanderbeg der SS
50th Waffen-Gebirgs Regiment der SS
51st Waffen-Gebirgs Regiment der SS
21st Waffen-Gebirgs Artillery Regiment

22nd Maria Theresia der SS
52nd Freiwilligen-Kavallerie Regiment der SS
53rd Freiwilligen-Kavallerie Regiment der SS
54th Freiwilligen-Kavallerie Regiment der SS
55th Freiwilligen-Kavallerie Regiment der SS

23rd Kama der SS
56th Waffen-Gebirgsjäger Regiment der SS
57th Waffen-Gebirgsjäger Regiment der SS
58th Waffen-Gebirgsjäger Regiment der SS
23rd Waffen-Gebirgs Artillery Regiment der SS

23rd SS Nederland (replaced above)
48th SS-Freiwilligen Panzergrenadier Regiment General Seyffardt
49th SS-Freiwilligen Panzergrenadier Regiment De Ruiter

24th Karstjäger der SS
59th Waffen-Gebirgsjäger Regiment der SS
60th Waffen-Gebirgsjäger Regiment der SS
24th Waffen-Gebirgs Artillery Regiment

25th Ungarishche Nr 1 Hunyadi der SS
61st Waffen-Grenadier Regiment der SS
62nd Waffen-Grenadier Regiment der SS
63rd Waffen-Grenadier Regiment der SS
25th Waffen-Artillery Regiment der SS

26th Ungarische Nr 2 Hungaria der SS
64th Waffen-Grenadier Regiment der SS
65th Waffen-Grenadier Regiment der SS
66th Waffen-Grenadier Regiment der SS
26th SS-Panzer Battalion

27th SS Flämische Nr 1 Langemarck
67th SS-Freiwilligen Grenadier Regiment
68th SS-Freiwilligen Grenadier Regiment
Only ever reached regimental strength

28th SS Wallonien
69th SS-Freiwilligen Grenadier Regiment
70th SS-Freiwilligen Grenadier Regiment
71st SS-Freiwilligen Grenadier Regiment
Only ever reached regimental strength

29th Russiche Nr 1 der SS
Formed from the Kaminski Brigade and absorbed into the Russian Liberation Army. Never reached full divisional strength.

29th Italienische Nr 1 der SS
Replaced the above, only ever reached regimental strength.

30th Russiche Nr 2 der SS
75th Waffen-Grenadier Regiment der SS
76th Waffen-Grenadier Regiment der SS
77th Waffen Grenadier Regiment der SS
30th Waffen-Artillery regiment der SS

31st SS Böhmen-Mähren
78th SS-Freiwilligen Grenadier Regiment
79th SS-Freiwilligen Grenadier Regiment
80th SS-Freiwilligen Grenadier Regiment

32nd SS 30 Januar
86th SS-Freiwilligen Grenadier Regiment
87th SS-Freiwilligen Grenadier Regiment
88th SS-Freiwilligen Grenadier Regiment
Only ever reached regimental strength.

33rd Ungarische Nr 3 der SS
Strength unknown, possibly a cavalry regiment.

33rd Fränzösische Nr 1 Charlemagne der SS (replaced above)
57th Waffen-Grenadier Regiment der SS
58th Waffen-Grenadier Regiment der SS
57th SS-Artillery Battalion
57th SS-Panzerjäger Battalion
SS-Field Replacement Battalion
SS-Training and Replacement Battalion Greifenberg

34th Landstorm Nederland der SS
83rd SS-Freiwilligen Grenadier Regiment
84th SS-Freiwilligen Grenadier Regiment
SS-Panzerjäger Battalion Nordwest
SS-Flak Battery Clingendaal

35th SS Polizei
14th Polizei Regiment (renamed 91st Polizei Grenadier Regiment)
29th Polizei Regiment (renamed 89th Polizei Grenadier Regiment)
30th Polizei Regiment (renamed 90th Polizei Grenadier Regiment)
Never reached full divisional strength.

36th Dirlewanger der SS
Formed from the Dirlewanger Brigade. Never reached full divisional strength.

37th SS Lützow
92nd SS-Kavallerie Regiment
93rd SS-Kavallerie Regiment
Never reached full divisional strength

38th SS Nibelungen
Formed using staff and cadets from the SS-Junkerschule at Bad Tölz. Only ever reached regimental strength.

* * *

The following 'divisions' seem to have been purely paper formations. Only Wallenstein seems to have come into very brief existence operating as a series of ad hoc kampfgruppen led by SS instructors in Prague at the end of the war:

39th Gebirgs Division der SS Andreas Höfer
40th SS-Freiwilligen Panzergrenadier Division Feldherrnhalle
41st Waffen-Grenadier Division der SS Finnische Nr 1 Kalevala

42nd SS Division Niederschsen
43rd SS Division Reichsmarschall
44th SS Panzergreandier Division Wallenstein
45th SS Division Warager

Independent SS Heavy Panzer Battalions
101st (redesignated 501st in 1944, part of 1st SS Panzer Corps)
102nd (redesignated 502nd in 1944, part of 2nd SS Panzer Corps)
103rd (redesignated 503 in 1944, part of 3rd SS Panzer Corps)

Appendix V

Foreign Volunteer Units

Most of these units were short-lived, with their recruits absorbed into the SS divisions. Some were initially formed by the army before being taken over by the Waffen-SS.

SS-Freikorps Danmark
SS-Freiwilligen Brigade Estnische
SS-Freiwilligen Legion Flandern
SS-Freiwilligen Legion Lettische
SS-Freiwilligen Legion Niederlande
SS-Freiwilligen Legion Norwegen
SS-Freiwilligen Regiment Galizisches (Nos 4–8)
SS-Freiwilligen Sturmbrigade Französisches
SS-Freiwilligen Sturmbrigade Langemarck
SS-Freiwilligen Sturmbrigade Wallonie
Britische Freikorps
Finnische-Freiwilligen Batallion der Waffen-SS
Freiwilligen Sturmbrigade Italienische der SS
Indische Freiwilligen Legion der Waffen-SS
Kaukaischer Waffenverband der SS
Spanische-Freiwilligen Kompanie der SS (101 and 102; some sources say there were three companies)
Osttürkische Waffenverband der SS

Allgemeine-SS
The Allgemeine-SS set up a number of national branches in the occupied territories and Germany, which often acted as recruiters for the foreign Waffen-SS units:

Germaansche-SS en Nederland
Germanske-SS Norge
Germaansche-SS in Vlaanderen
Schalburg Korpset Danmark
Germanische Sturmbanne (recruited from foreign workers to serve in Germany)

Principal SS Corps Campaigns

Kharkov, March 1943
  Army Group South
  SS Panzer Corps (later 2nd Panzer Corps)
    1st SS Panzergrenadier Division Liebstandarte Adolf Hitler
    2nd SS Panzergrenadier Division Das Reich
    3rd SS Panzergrenadier Division Totenkopf

Kursk, July 1943
  Army Group South
  2nd SS Panzer Corps
    1st SS Panzergrenadier Division Liebstandarte Adolf Hitler
    2nd SS Panzergrenadier Division Das Reich
    3rd SS Panzergrenadier Division Totenkopf
    5th SS Panzergrenadier Division Wiking (Reserve)

Kamenets-Podolskiy, March 1944
  2nd SS Panzer Corps
    9th SS Panzer Division Hohenstaufen
    10th SS Panzer Division Frundsberg

Normandy, June 1944
  Army Group B
  1st SS Panzer Corps
    1st SS Panzer Division Liebstandarte Adolf Hitler
    12th SS Panzer Division Hitlerjugend
    17th SS Panzergrenadier Division Götz von Berlichingen
    Panzer Lehr Division

Normandy, July–August 1944
  Army Group B
  1st SS Panzer Corps
    1st SS Panzer Division Liebstandarte Adolf Hitler
    12th SS Panzer Division Hitlerjugend
    716th Infantry Division

2nd SS Panzer Corps
  9th SS Panzer Division Hohenstaufen
  10th SS Panzer Division Frundsberg
  277th Infantry Division

Narva, June 1944
Army Group North
3rd (Germanische) SS Panzer Corps
  11th SS Panzergrenadier Division Nordland
  20th SS Grenadier Division Estnisches Nr 1
  4th SS Volunteer Panzergrenadier Brigade Netherlands

Arnhem, September 1944
Army Group B
2nd SS Panzer Corps
  9th SS Panzer Division Hohenstaufen
  10th SS Panzer Division Frundsberg

Ardennes, December 1944
Army Group B
1st SS Panzer Corps
  1st SS Panzer Division Liebstandarte Adolf Hitler
  12th SS Panzer Division Hitlerjugend
  501st SS Heavy Panzer Battalion (attached)
  3rd Parachute Division
  12th Volksgrenadier Division
  277th Volksgrenadier Division
  150th Panzer Brigade
2nd SS Panzer Corps
  2nd SS Panzer Division Das Reich
  9th SS Panzer Division Hohenstaufen

Hungary, January 1945
Army Group South
4th SS Panzer Corps
  3rd SS Panzer Division Totenkopf
  5th SS Panzer Division Wiking

Arnswalde, February 1945
Army Group Vistula
3rd (Germanische) SS Panzer Corps
  11th SS Panzergrenadier Division Nordland

23rd SS Panzergrenadier Division Nederland
27th SS Grenadier Division Langemarck
281st Infantry Division

Hungary, March 1945
Army Group South
1st SS Panzer Corps
    1st SS Panzer Division Liebstandarte Adolf Hitler
    12th SS Panzer Division Hitlerjugend
2nd SS Panzer Corps
    2nd SS Panzer Division Das Reich
    9th SS Panzer Division Hohenstaufen

Drava, March 1945
Army Group E
15th SS Cossack Cavalry Corps
    1st Cossack Division
    2nd Cossack Division

Berlin, April 1945
Berlin Defence Area
Elements of:
    1st SS Panzer Division Leibstandarte Adolf Hitler
    11th SS Panzergrenadier Division Nordland
    33rd Waffen-Grenadier Division der SS Charlemagne
    Spanische-Frewilligen Kompanie der SS Unit Ezquerra
    Both the French and Spanish forces were attached to Nordland

Commanders of the Premier Waffen-SS Armoured Divisions

1st SS Leibstandarte Adolf Hitler

SS-Brigadeführer Theodor Wisch	7 Apr 1943–20 Aug 1944
SS-Brigadeführer Wilhelm Mohnke	20 Aug 1944–6 Feb 1945
SS-Brigadeführer Otto Kumm	6 Feb–8 May 1945

2nd SS Das Reich

SS-Gruppenführer Heinz Lammerding	23 Oct 1943–24 July 1944
SS-Standartenführer Christian Tychsen	24 July–28 July 1944
SS-Brigadeführer Otto Baum	28 July–23 Oct 1944
SS-Gruppenführer Heinz Lammerding	23 Oct 1944–20 Jan 1945
SS-Standartenführer Karl Kreutz	20 Jan–29 Jan 1945
SS-Gruppenführer Werner Ostnedorff	29 Jan–9 Mar 1945
SS-Standartenführer Rudolf Lehmann	9 Mar–13 Apr 1945
SS-Standartenführer Karl Kreutz	13 Apr–8 May 1945

3rd SS Totenkopf

SS-Gruppenführer Theodor Eicke	1 Nov 1939–7 July 1941
SS-Oberführer Matthias Kleinheisterkamp	7 July–18 July 1941
SS-Brigadeführer Georg Keppler	18 July–19 Sep 1941
SS-Obergruppenführer Theodor Eicke	19 Sep 1941–26 Feb 1943
SS-Gruppenführer Hermann Priess	26 Feb–27 Apr 1943
SS-Gruppenführer Heinz Lammerding	27 Apr–1 May 1943
SS-Gruppenführer Hermann Priess	1 May 1943–20 June 1944
SS-Standartenführer Karl Ullrich	20 June–13 July 1944
SS-Brigadeführer Hellmuth Becker	13 July 1944–8 May 1945

5th SS Wiking

SS-Gruppenführer Felix Steiner	1 Dec 1940–1 May 1943
SS-Gruppenführer Herbert Gille	1 May 1943–6 Aug 1944
SS-Standartenführer Eduard Deisenhofer	6 Aug–12 Aug 1944

SS-Standartenführer Johannes-Rudolf Mülenkamp
                                          12 Aug–9 Oct 1944
SS-Oberführer Karl Ullrich   9 Oct 1944–5 May 1945

9th SS Hohenstaufen

SS-Obergruppenführer Willi Bittrich   15 Feb 1943–29 June 1944
SS-Oberführer Thomas Müller   29 June–10 July 1944
SS-Brigadeführer Sylvester Stadler   10 July–31 July 1944
SS-Oberführer Friedrich-Wilhelm Bock   31 July–29 Aug 1944
SS-Standartenführer Walter Harzer   29 Aug–10 Oct 1944
SS-Brigadeführer Sylvester Stadler   10 Oct 1944–8 May 1945

10th SS Frundsberg

SS-Gruppenführer Karl Fischer von Treuenfeld
                                         15 Nov 1943–27 Apr 1944
SS-Gruppenführer Heinz Harmel   27 Apr 1944–27 Apr 1945
SS-Obersturmbannführer Franz Roestel 27 Apr–8 May 1945

12th SS Hitlerjugend

SS-Brigadeführer Fritz Witt   24 June 1943–14 June 1944
SS-Brigadeführer Kurt Meyer   14 June–6 Sep 1944
SS-Obersturmbannführer Hubert Meyer 6 Sep–24 Oct 1944
SS-Brigadeführer Fritz Kraemer   24 Oct–13 Nov 1944
SS-Brigadeführer Hugo Kraas   13 Nov 1944–8 May 1945

17th SS Götz von Berlichingen

SS-Gruppenführer Werner Ostendorff   30 Oct 1943–15 June 1944
SS-Standartenführer Otto Binge   17 June–20 June 1944
SS-Brigadeführer Otto Baum   20 June–1 Aug 1944
SS-Standartenführer Otto Binge   1 Aug–29 Aug 1944
SS-Oberführer Dr Eduard Deisenhofer 30 Aug–Sep 1944
SS-Oberführer Thomas Müller   Sep 1944
SS-Standartenführer Gustav Mertsch   Sep–Oct 1944
SS-Gruppenführer Werner Ostendorff   21 Oct–Nov 1944
SS-Standartenführer Hans Linger   Nov 1944–Jan 1945
Oberst Gerhard Lindner   15 Jan–21 Jan 1945
SS-Oberführer Fritz Klingenberg   21 Jan–22 Mar 1945
SS-Oberführer Georg Bochmann   Mar–8 May 1945

Organization of an SS Panzer Division in 1944

At full strength a division could number up to 15,000 fighting men plus 6,000 support troops. The latter comprised administrative staff, clerks, drivers, field post office, medical personnel, military police and quartermasters. Typically, a panzer division comprised one tank regiment, two armoured infantry regiments and one artillery regiment plus supporting heavy weapons and logistical units.

A panzer regiment normally comprised two battalions, each of four companies, numbering up to 2,000 men with 120 panzers. A panzergrenadier regiment usually comprised three battalions, each with five companies equipped with half-tracks. At full establishment they could number about 4,000 men. The panzer artillery regiment was organized into twelve batteries in four battalions, with one battery in each battalion equipped with self-propelled guns; the rest were towed. Manpower stood at about 2,000 men. The reconnaissance and pioneer battalions also amounted to almost 1,000 men. From September 1944 Nebelwerfer (smoke mortar) battalions were added to the strength of the panzer divisions for firing high explosives.

No two Waffen-SS panzer divisions were ever the same. The following, based on the organization of Hitlerjugend, gives a general impression of their structure.

Divisional Staff

Divisional Commander	Divisional Quartermaster
Staff Officers	Mechanics
Cartographers	Staff Doctor
Signallers	Staff Dentist
Divisional Escort	Mechanics
Military Police	Weapons Platoon

Panzer Regiment

1st Battalion	2nd Battalion
Four Tank Companies (1–4)	Four Tank Companies (5–8)
Workshop Company	Workshop Company

Panzerjäger (tank destroyer) Battalion
Three Companies of Self-propelled Guns

1st Panzergrenadier (armoured infantry) Regiment
1st Battalion
Four Panzergrenadier Companies (1–4)
2nd Battalion
Four Panzergrenadier Companies (5–8)
3rd Battalion
Four Panzergrenadier Companies (9–12)

Support Units

Heavy Gun Company (13)	Recce Company (15)
Flak Company (14)	Pioneer Company (16)

2nd Panzergrenadier Regiment
Organization as above.

Panzer Reconnaissance Battalion

Two Companies of Armoured Cars	Two Recce Companies
	One Heavy Company

Panzer Artillery Regiment

1st Battalion	Werfer Battalion (mortars)
Three Batteries	Four Batteries
2nd Battalion	Flak Battalion (anti-aircraft)
Three Batteries	Five Batteries
3rd Battalion	
Three Batteries	

Panzer Pioneer (engineers) Battalion

One Armoured Company	One Bridging Company
Three Pioneer Companies	

Panzer Signals Battalion

One Telephone Company	One Radio Company

Divisional Supply Troop

Six Companies of Lorries	One Supply Company

Armoured Maintenance Battalion

Three Workshop Companies One Spares Company
One Weapons Company

Housekeeping Battalion

Bakery Company Cooks
Butchery Company Field Post Office

Appendix IX

Knight's Cross Awards to Waffen-SS Divisions

Members of the Waffen-SS won a total of 638 Knight's Crosses. They also gained 27 Oakleaves, 24 Oakleaves with Swords and 2 Oakleaves with Swords and Diamonds. If gallantry awards are used as a measure of a unit's combat performance the following distribution of Knight's Crosses by division is quite instructive:

1st SS Leibstandarte Adolf Hitler	58
2nd SS Das Reich	69
3rd SS Totenkopf	47
4th SS Polizei	25
5th SS Wiking	55
6th SS Nord	4
7th SS Prinz Eugen	6
8th SS Florian Geyer	22
9th SS Hohenstaufen	12
10th SS Frundsberg	13
11th SS Nordland	25
12th SS Hitlerjugend	14
13th Handschar-Kroatische der SS	4
14th Galizische Nr 1 der SS	1
15th Lettische Nr 1 der SS	3
16th SS Reichsführer-SS	1
17th SS Götz von Berlichingen	4
18th SS Horst Wessel	2
19th Lettische Nr 2 der SS	12
20th Estnische Nr 1 der SS	5

21st Skanderbeg-Albanische Nr 1 der SS 0

22nd Maria Theresia der SS 6

23rd Kama-Kroatische Nr 2 der SS 0

23rd SS Nederland 19

24th Karstjäger der SS 0

25th Hunyadi-Ungarische Nr 1 der SS 0

26th Ungarische Nr 2 der SS 0

27th SS Langemarck 1

28th SS Wallonien 3

29th Russiche Nr 1 der SS 0

29th Italienische Nr 1 der SS 0

30th Russiche Nr 2 der SS 0

31st SS Böhmen-Mähren 0

32nd SS 30 Januar 0

33rd Charlemagne-Französische Nr 1 der SS 3

33rd Ungarische Nr 3 der SS 0

34th Landstorm Nederland der SS 3

35th SS Polizei 0

36th Dirlewanger der SS 1

37th SS Lützow 0

38th SS Nibelungen 0

Bibliography

Abbott, Peter and Pinak, Eugene. *Ukrainian Armies 1914–55* (Oxford: Osprey, 2004).

Baxter, Ian. *SS Totenkopf at War: A History of the Division* (Barnsley: Pen & Sword, 2017).

Baxter, Ian. *SS Polizei at War 1940–1945: A History of the Division* (Barnsley: Pen & Sword, 2018).

Baxter, Ian. *5th SS Wiking at War 1941–1945: A History of the Division* (Barnsley: Pen & Sword, 2018).

Baxter, Ian. *6th SS Mountain Division Nord at War 1941–1945* (Barnsley: Pen & Sword, 2019).

Beevor, Antony. *Berlin: The Downfall 1945* (London: Viking, 2002).

Bishop, Chris and McNab, Chris. *Campaigns of World War II Day by Day* (London: Amber, 2009).

Bormann, Martin. *Hitler's Table-Talk* (Oxford: Oxford University Press, 1988).

Bruce, George. *The Warsaw Uprising* (London: Pan, 1974).

Burleigh, Michael. *The Third Reich: A New History* (London: Pan, 2001).

Butler, Rupert. *Curse of the Death's Head: The Story of the SS-Totenkopf Division* (London: Arrow, 1989).

Butler, Rupert. *Hitler's Jackals* (Barnsley: Leo Cooper, 1998).

Butler, Rupert. *Legions of Death: The Nazi Enslavement of Europe* (Barnsley: Pen & Sword, 2004).

Butler, Rupert. *The Black Angels: The Story of the Waffen-SS* (Barnsley: Pen & Sword, 2005).

Chant, Christopher (ed). *Hitler's Generals and their Battles* (London: Salamander, 1976).

Cimino, Al. *The Story of the SS: Hitler's Infamous Legions of Death* (London: Arcturus, 2019).

Dargie, Richard. *The Plots to Kill Hitler: The Men and Women who tried to change History* (London: Arcturus, 2020).

Davies, Norman. *Rising '44: The Battle for Warsaw* (London: Macmillan, 2003).

Fest, Joachim. *Inside Hitler's Bunker: The Last Days of the Third Reich* (London: Pan, 2005).

Fey, Will. *Armor Battles of the Waffen-SS 1943–45* (Mechanicsburg, PA: Stackpole, 2003).

Guderian, General Heinz. *Panzer Leader* (London: Futura, 1974).

Hargreaves, Richard. *The Germans in Normandy* (Barnsley: Pen & Sword, 2006).

Hastings, Max. *Das Reich: Resistance and the march of the 2nd SS Panzer Division through France, June 1944* (London: Michael Joseph, 1981).

Heiden, Konrad. *Der Führer: Hitler's Rise to Power* (London: Victor Gollanz, 1944).

Hook, Patrick. *Hohenstaufen: 9th SS Panzer Division* (Hersham: Ian Allan, 2005).

Humble, Richard. *Hitler's Generals* (St Albans: Panther, 1976).

Jones, Michael. *After Hitler: The Last Days of the Second World War in Europe* (London: John Murray, 2015).

Kinder, Werner. *Obedient unto Death: A Panzer Grenadier of the Leibstandarte-SS Adolf Hitler Reports* (Barnsley: Frontline, 2019).

Le Tissier, Tony. *SS-Charlemagne: the 33rd Waffen-Grenadier Division of the SS* (Barnsley: Pen & Sword, 2019).

Loringhoven, Bernd Freytag von. *In the Bunker with Hitler* (London: Weidenfeld & Nicolson, 2006).

Lucas, James. *War on the Eastern Front 1941–1945* (London: Jane's, 1980).

Lucas, James. *Last days of the Third Reich: The Collapse of Nazi Germany, May 1945* (London: Cassell, 2000).

McNab, Chris (Ed). *Hitler's Elite: The SS 1939–45* (Oxford: Osprey, 2013).

Manstein, Field Marshal Erich von. *Lost Victories* (Elstree: Greenhill, 1987).

Mazower, Mark. *Hitler's Empire: Nazi Rule in Occupied Europe* (London: Penguin, 2009).

Mellenthin, Major General F.W. von. *Panzer Battles* (London: Futura, 1977).

Messenger, Charles. *Hitler's Gladiator. The Life and Times of Oberstgruppenführer and Panzergeneral-Oberst der Waffen-SS Sepp Dietrich* (London: Brassey's, 1988).

Mollo, Andrew. *The Armed Forces of World War II: Uniforms, insignia and organization* (London: Black Cat, 1987).

Mollo, Andrew and Smith, Digby. *World Army Uniforms Since 1939* (Poole: New Orchard, 1986).

Mūnoz, Antonio. *Iron Fist: A Combat History of the 17th SS Panzergrenadier Division Götz von Berlichingen 1943–1945* (Axis Europa Books, 1999).

O'Donnell, James P. *The Berlin Bunker* (London: J.M. Dent & Sons, 1979).

Pallud, Jean-Paul. *Ardennes 1944: Peiper and Skorzeny* (London: Osprey, 1987).

Quarrie, Bruce. *Hitler's Samurai: the Waffen-SS in Action* (Cambridge: Patrick Stephens, 1986).

Quarrie, Bruce. *Hitler's Teutonic Knights: SS Panzers in Action* (Cambridge: Patrick Stephens, 1986).

Quarrie, Bruce. *Weapons of the Waffen-SS: From Small Arms to Tanks* (Cambridge: Patrick Stephens, 1988).

Reitlinger, Gerald. *The SS: Alibi of a Nation 1922–1945* (London: Arms & Armour Press, 1981).

Reynolds, Michael. *The Devil's Adjutant: Jochen Peiper, Panzer Leader* (Barnsley: Pen & Sword, 2016).

Reynolds, Michael. *Men of Steel: I SS Panzer Corps, The Ardennes and Eastern Front 1944–45* (Barnsley: Pen & Sword, 2016).

Reynolds, Michael. *Sons of the Reich: II SS Panzer Corps Normandy, Arnhem, the Ardennes and on the Eastern Front* (Barnsley: Pen & Sword, 2017).

Rikmenspoel, Marc. *Knight's Cross Winners of the Waffen-SS* (Barnsley: Pen & Sword, 2020).

Ripley, Tim. *Steel Storm: Waffen-SS Panzer Battles on the Eastern Front 1943–1945* (Stroud: Sutton, 2000).

Ripley, Tim. *Steel Rain: Waffen-SS Panzer Battles in the West 1944–1945* (London: Brown Partworks, 2001).

Ripley, Tim. *Elite Units of the Third Reich: German Special Forces in World War II* (Miami: Lewis International, 2002).

Bibliography

Roland, Paul. *The Nuremberg Trials: The Nazis and their Crimes Against Humanity* (London: Arcturus 2012).

Roland, Paul. *Life in the Third Reich: Daily Life in Nazi Germany 1933–1945* (London: Arcturus, 2019).

Roland, Paul. *The Secret Lives of the Nazis* (London: Arcturus, 2017).

Ronald, Seth. *Jackals of the Reich* (London: New English Library, 1972).

Rutherford, Ward. *Hitler's Propaganda Machine* (London: Bison, 1987).

Ryan, Cornelius. *The Last Battle* (London: Collins, 1966).

Sagarra, Eda. *An Introduction to Nineteenth Century Germany* (Harlow: Longman, 1980).

Saunders, Tim. *Hill 112: Battles of the Odon* (Barnsley: Leo Cooper, 2001).

Scurr, John. *Germany's Spanish Volunteers 1941–45* (London: Osprey, 1980).

Sharpe, Michael and Davis, Brian L. *Leibstandarte: Hitler's Elite Bodyguard* (Hersham: Ian Allan, 2002).

Sharpe, Michael and Davis, Brian L. *Das Reich: Waffen-SS Armoured Elite* (Hersham: Ian Allan, 2003).

Simms, Brendan. *Hitler: Only the World Was Enough* (London: Allen Lane, 2019).

Skorzeny, Otto. *Skorzeny's Special Missions: the Memoirs of Hitler's Most Daring Commando* (Barnsley: Frontline 2011).

Speer, Albert. *Inside the Third Reich* (London: Phoenix, 1995).

Trevor-Roper, H.R. *The Last Days of Hitler* (London: Pan, 1965).

Trevor-Roper, H.R. (ed). *Hitler's War Directives 1939–1945* (London: Pan, 1966).

Tucker-Jones, Anthony. *Falaise The Flawed Victory: The destruction of Panzergruppe West, August 1944* (Barnsley: Pen & Sword, 2008).

Tucker-Jones, Anthony. *Tiger I & Tiger II* (Barnsley: Pen & Sword, 2012).

Tucker-Jones, Anthony. *Armoured Warfare and the Waffen-SS, 1944–1945* (Barnsley: Pen & Sword, 2017).

Tucker-Jones, Anthony. *Slaughter on the Eastern Front: Hitler and Stalin's War 1941–1945* (Stroud: The History Press, 2017).

Tucker-Jones, Anthony. *Kursk 1943: Hitler's Bitter Harvest* (Stroud: The History Press, 2018).

Tucker-Jones, Anthony. *D-Day 1944: The Making of Victory* (Stroud: The History Press, 2019).

Tucker-Jones, Anthony. *The Devil's Bridge: The German Victory at Arnhem, 1944* (Oxford: Osprey, 2020).

Tucker-Jones, Anthony. *Hitler's Panzers: The Complete History 1933–1945* (Barnsley: Pen & Sword, 2020).

Tucker-Jones, Anthony. *The Battle for the Mediterranean: Allied and Axis Campaigns from North Africa to the Italian Peninsula, 1940–45* (London: Arcturus, 2021).

Tucker-Jones, Anthony. *Hitler's Winter: The German Battle of the Bulge* (Oxford: Osprey 2022).

Ungváry, Krisztián. *Battle for Budapest: One Hundred Days in World War II* (London: I.B. Tauris, 2003).

Vickers, Philip. *Das Reich: 2nd SS Panzer Division Das Reich – Drive to Normandy, June 1944* (Barnsley: Leo Cooper, 2000).

Weal, Adrian. *Renegades: Hitler's Englishmen* (London: Pimlico, 2002).

Whiting, Charles. *Massacre at Malmedy: The Story of Jochen Peiper's Battle Group Ardennes, December 1944* (London: Leo Cooper, 1971).

Williamson, Gordon. *German Military Police Units 1939–45* (Oxford: Osprey, 1989).

Williamson, Gordon. *The SS: Hitler's Instrument of Terror* (London: Sidgwick & Jackson, 2002).

Williamson, Gordon. *Waffen-SS Handbook 1939–1945* (Stroud: Sutton. 2003).

Windrow, Martin. *Waffen SS* (London: Osprey, 1971).

Index

Waffen-SS units